The Miracle of Man

The Miracle of Man

Evidence for God from Human Nature

Jim Howard

RESOURCE *Publications* • Eugene, Oregon

THE MIRACLE OF MAN
Evidence for God from Human Nature

Copyright © 2016 Jim Howard. All rights reserved. Except for brief quotations in critical publications or reviews, no part of this book may be reproduced in any manner without prior written permission from the publisher. Write: Permissions, Wipf and Stock Publishers, 199 W. 8th Ave., Suite 3, Eugene, OR 97401.

Resource Publications
An Imprint of Wipf and Stock Publishers
199 W. 8th Ave., Suite 3
Eugene, OR 97401

www.wipfandstock.com

PAPERBACK ISBN: 978-1-4982-0612-9
HARDCOVER ISBN: 978-1-4982-0614-3
EBOOK ISBN: 978-1-4982-0613-6

Manufactured in the U.S.A.   JANUARY 4, 2017

Excerpts from The Collected Poems—Five Sonnets, by C. S. Lewis are reprinted by permission of The C. S. Lewis Company.

Excerpts from "Sweet Beulah Land," by Squire Parsons are reprinted by permission of Capitol CMG Publishing.

In Loving Memory of
Thomas Howard Bishop
December 2, 1990—June 14, 2008

Contents

Introduction | 1

1. "Men Are Different" | 7
2. "I Yam What I Yam" | 16
3. "Elementary, My Dear Watson" | 24
4. "When You Come to a Fork in the Road, Take It!" | 34
5. "If There Is No God, Everything Is Lawful" | 43
6. "We Have Met the Enemy and He Is Us!" | 57
7. "I Can't Get No Satisfaction" | 71
8. "The Most Urgent Wish of Mankind" | 83
9. "The Good, the True, and the Beautiful" | 91
10. Nothing Comes from Nothing | 102
11. The Miracle of Life | 115
12. "A Creator as well as a Creature" | 129
13. "A Cosmos rather than a Chaos" | 143
14. Why, Lord? | 157
15. Old Answers to an Old Question | 165
16. Don't All Roads Lead to God? | 179
17. "How Should We Then Live?" | 193
18. Cross Examination | 205

Bibliography | 221
Name and Subject Index | 237
Scripture Index | 243

Introduction

"[A]lways be ready to give a defense to everyone who asks you a reason for the hope that is in you, with meekness and fear."

—I PETER 3:15[1]

THERE IS NOTHING ORIGINAL in this book. Every original idea I ever had was stolen! But I am old-fashioned enough to believe that truth is more important than originality. So borrowing from many authors, I have attempted to write an easy-to-read summary of one aspect of what is called "Christian apologetics," arguments for the truth of Christianity. I want to look at evidence for the existence of God, and especially that evidence which can be found in human nature and experience.

I am not a philosopher, a theologian, or even a preacher. I am a trial lawyer and a former judge. What business does a lawyer have writing a book about God? That is a good question, but I would suggest two reasons why a lawyer might be a good candidate to write a book such as this. First, attorneys are trained to evaluate the strengths and weaknesses of both evidence and arguments, and we do so all the time. Second, as trial lawyers, we present expert testimony from scientists, doctors, engineers, and so forth, much of it quite complicated, and then try to explain to a jury in ordinary language what those experts have said. That is my effort here. The real philosophers and theologians have written many books on apologetics, and I have read quite a few of them. If I can express the thoughts of those wise men in plain, twenty-first-century language, I believe that would be worthwhile.

1. All Scriptural quotations are from the *New King James Version* (NKJV), except where otherwise indicated. The Greek word translated in this verse as "defense" is *apologia*, from which we get our word, "apologetics."

Why should you read a book of Christian apologetics? *Because truth matters, and Christianity claims to be true.* Some say that religion is only a matter of faith, but faith is of no value if what we believe is not real. It may make us feel better for a while, but it will be of no help when we really need it.

In the classic movie, "Miracle on 34th Street," Maureen O'Hara's character tells her daughter, "Faith is believing what your common sense tells you isn't true."[2] They are talking about Santa Claus. But Christian faith must be honest, believing what our reason and common sense tell us is true. Believing a falsehood is not a virtue. Christians believe that God gave us our ability to reason—it is one of the primary characteristics which distinguish us from other animals—and He expects us to use it. C. S. Lewis wrote, "God is no fonder of intellectual slackers than of any other slackers."[3]

Of course, merely believing that God exists is not what Christians mean by faith. The Apostle James pointed out that demons believe that![4] Christian faith involves a commitment of our lives, not just an opinion about God. So we cannot intellectually "convince" anyone to become a Christian. But to use an old analogy, if those making intellectual arguments for God neither sow the seeds nor harvest the crops, they may be useful in clearing the field of rocks and thistles, by answering honest questions which prevent someone from believing in Christ. They may also help other Christians grow in their faith, and be better able to share that faith with their family and friends.

Some say that we should not ask questions such as those we will consider, but should simply accept the revelation which God has given us in the Bible. Christianity teaches that God has revealed Himself to us through His Son, Jesus Christ,[5] through Scripture,[6] and through nature.[7] I believe in all these, and I accept the Bible as God's divinely-inspired Word. But if we are speaking with nonbelievers, who are not convinced either that Jesus was

---

2. "Miracle on 34th Street," Twentieth Century Fox, 1947.
3. Lewis, *Mere Christianity*, 61.
4. James 2:19.
5. In John 14:9, Jesus said, *"He who has seen me has seen the Father."* Hebrews 1:1–2 says, *"God, who at various times and in various ways spoke in time past to the fathers by the prophets, has in these last days spoken to us by His Son."*
6. II Timothy 3:16 says, *"All scripture is given by inspiration of God, and is profitable for doctrine, for reproof, for correction, for instruction in righteousness."*
7. In Romans 1:19-20, the Apostle Paul wrote, *"[W]hat may be known of God is manifest in them [unbelievers], for God has shown it to them. For since the creation of the world His invisible attributes are clearly seen, being understood by the things that are made."*

God's Son nor that the Bible is His Word, surely it is appropriate to argue the evidence from nature, including human nature.[8]

We can never get to know God on our own. "Man's search for God" inevitably ends in failure. C. S. Lewis wrote, "[I]f Shakespeare and Hamlet could ever meet, it must be Shakespeare's doing."[9] This is why, according to Christians, God took the initiative and revealed Himself to us. But that revelation includes His creation. So it is appropriate to look at what we know about ourselves and the universe, and see how these facts fit, either with Christianity or any other world-view. This is what we will attempt to do.

"Questions Without Answers"

"'Is the universe designed?' is not a scientific question . . . we will learn the answer neither by looking for items trademarked 'Heavenly Construction Company' nor by coming upon objects stamped 'Blind Chance Rules.'"

—OWEN GINGERICH[10]

I would like to make three other points before we begin. First, there is a popular idea that a statement is trustworthy only if it can be proven scientifically, if it can be observed, measured, or repeated, as in a test-tube experiment.[11] But we very reasonably hold many beliefs which cannot be proven in this way, including everything we believe about our family and friends, about history, or about philosophy or religion. For me to demand scientific proof to believe that my wife is an honest person, that George Washington was our first President, or that there either is or is not a God, would not show my wisdom, but my foolishness. Even the statement, "We can only rely on something which can be proven by the scientific method," cannot be proven by the scientific method.

---

8. Quaker theologian Elton Trueblood wrote, "Revelation must be tested by reason for the simple reason that there are false claims to revelation." Trueblood, *Philosophy of Religion*, 32. Furthermore, if we are attempting to determine whether the Scriptures are true and whether the God about whom they teach is real, I do not see how we can use them as proof for themselves. Such an argument seems to me to be circular.

9. Lewis, *Surprised by Joy*, 227.

10. Gingerich, *God's Universe*, 70.

11. This idea was proposed by the eighteenth-century Scottish philosopher, David Hume. Hume wrote that we can speak meaningfully only about abstract matters which are true by definition, such as mathematics, or about matters which can be empirically verified (scientifically proven). Hume, *An Enquiry Concerning Human Understanding*, 211. But this argument refutes itself—it is neither true by definition nor empirically verifiable.

The study of questions such as the existence of God or the meaning of life is sometimes called "metaphysics," meaning after or beyond the physical. It is said that the word came about because the ancient Greek philosopher Aristotle's writings on this subject were found following his death, untitled and placed *after* his treatise on physics![12] Since the word physics was originally used for all sciences, "metaphysical" is generally used to mean beyond science. The point is that there are things beyond science. Science is important—it is the study of nature and natural laws—but it is not the study of everything.

Notre Dame philosopher Alvin Plantinga wrote, "Science can't tell us whether slavery is wrong."[13] In fact, science can't tell us anything about right or wrong, meaning or purpose, love or beauty. But man, from his earliest beginnings, has believed in all these things. You can say that all mankind has been wrong about these beliefs (it seems to me you are being rather presumptuous), but you cannot answer these questions based on science alone.

Francis Collins is one of the leading geneticists in the world. He was head of the Human Genome Project, which first sequenced the human genome, is now Director of the National Institutes of Health, and is a devout Christian. In a recent interview with *Newsweek* magazine, he said:

> "[S]cience is the way to uncover valid, trustworthy information about how nature works, about things about the natural world. But if you limit yourself to the kinds of questions that science can ask, you're leaving out some other things that I think are also pretty important, like why are we here and what is the meaning of life and is there a God? Those are not scientific questions."[14]

Owen Gingerich, long-time professor of astronomy at Harvard, suggested, perhaps tongue-in-cheek, that science succeeds because it chooses to answer the questions which have answers, and leaves for philosophy the "questions without answers," such as why anything exists or whether the universe has a purpose.[15] Science explains how the universe works, but not why. In this book, we will look at the questions without scientific answers. We will consider the scientific evidence, but no one can prove by that evidence that God either does or does not exist.

---

12. Davies, *The Mind of God*, 31.
13. Plantinga, *Where the Conflict Really Lies*, 167.
14. Begley, "Francis Collins Talks about Science and Faith," 62.
15. Gingerich, *God's Universe*, 84.

The Missing Piece of the Puzzle

> "No one has ever seen three feet of love or two pounds of justice, but one would be foolish indeed to deny their reality."
>
> —PAUL LITTLE[16]

This brings us to our second point. If science cannot answer the question, how do we determine if there is a God? In my profession, we use scientific evidence, such as DNA, but we never require anything to be *proven* scientifically. Instead, facts are proven, to such an extent that we may imprison a man for life, primarily by testimony about things which witnesses have seen or heard, things which happened in the past and can never be repeated. Neither does the law require absolute certainty. To convict a man of the most serious crimes, we only require proof beyond a "reasonable doubt." In most civil (non-criminal) cases, the standard is a "preponderance of the evidence," meaning more likely than not.

In any question of philosophy or religion, I would suggest that this is the proper standard. To use any other standard is to "rig" the question by requiring one side to prove more than the other. If we are intellectually honest, we should believe whatever appears to us most likely to be true. So our question is, looking at all the evidence, what is the most likely explanation for the universe or for man? What system of belief best explains the facts we know, and illuminates those areas where we cannot see?

We will consider several different characteristics of what we call "human nature." Why do we start with human nature? Because we are human. We have "inside information"[17] about ourselves that we do not have about anything else in the universe. We know something of the drives, thoughts, and emotions that make up a human being.

I do not claim that any one of these characteristics proves the existence of God by itself. But taking them all together, I find the evidence to be quite compelling, far beyond a mere preponderance. I will argue that the traditional teachings of Christianity explain more of the facts than any other alternative, that they are the missing piece of the puzzle that makes sense of everything else. As British theologian Alister McGrath wrote, "Once the world has been seen through a Christian set of spectacles, the relative inadequacy of other perspectives becomes clear."[18] So let me set out the evidence as I understand it, and see if you find it as persuasive as I do.

16. Little, *Know Why You Believe*, 21.
17. Lewis, *Mere Christianity*, 19.
18. McGrath, *Mere Apologetics*, 71.

Your Philosophy

"There are some people . . . and I am one of them, who think that the most practical and important thing about a man is . . . his view of the universe."

—G. K. CHESTERTON[19]

Third, please do not be afraid of the word, "philosophy." Literally, the word means the "love of truth." It is frequently defined as the search for truth. We will use the word most often in the sense of "your philosophy" or "my philosophy." Used this way, we mean the beliefs we hold concerning the big questions of life—Is there a God? What is the meaning of life? Where did we come from? Where are we going? Your beliefs regarding these questions are sometimes called your "world-view."

Thanks

Finally, I must express my thanks to a great many people. The greatest influences on my life have undoubtedly been my parents, Ivan and Martha Howard. My father was a theologian and my mother an educator, but more importantly, I believe they were the two most morally and ethically incorruptible people I have ever known. Dennis Kinlaw, who was President of Asbury College when I was a student there, has greatly impressed me by his preaching, his writing, and his life.

I owe a great debt to many whom I have known only through their books. My daughter says that I cannot speak or write on any subject without quoting C. S. Lewis. This book proves that statement! I have also been greatly influenced by the writings of Peter Kreeft, G. K. Chesterton, Francis Schaeffer, Charles Colson, Ravi Zacharias, and many others.

I am also much indebted to John Neihof and Gary Cockerill of Wesley Biblical Seminary for their advice and assistance with the manuscript and in finding a publisher. Most of all, I must thank my wife Sharon and my daughter Ellen for their encouragement, proof-reading, and patience, and the many other friends and family, "in-laws and outlaws," who have read and commented on various sections. I could not have completed this project without their help.

---

19. Chesterton, *Heretics*, 3.

Chapter 1

"Men Are Different"
Eight Things I Know About You

"Men are different. They propound mathematical theorems in beleaguered cities, conduct metaphysical arguments in condemned cells, make jokes on scaffolds, discuss the last new poem while advancing to the walls of Quebec, and comb their hair at Thermopylae. This is not *panache*; it is our nature."

—C. S. LEWIS[1]

You and I are human beings, men and women. But what is a man?[2] On the biological level, we are animals—*homo sapiens*. We share with other animals all our basic biological systems, including our brains and nervous systems, hearts and circulatory systems, skeletons, digestive systems, and sexual function. Even our cells and DNA have the same basic structure. But *men are different*. From consciousness and reason to free will and notions of morality, from symbolic language to romantic love, from science and technology to art or music, the differences between man and the other animals are at least as great as the similarities.

What makes us different? Our twenty-first century culture says that the difference is only one of degree—our brains are just more developed than those of other animals. Traditional Western culture taught that we are different in our very nature—we are made in the image of God. Which view

---

1. Lewis, "Learning in War-Time," 50.
2. Throughout this book I will use the word "man" in the older sense, meaning all humans of both sexes. I do not wish to offend anyone or to be thought sexist, but I do wish to be economical with words.

is correct? Are we just physical beings—"trousered apes"[3] or "grown-up germs"[4]—or are we also spiritual beings? Are we the accidental products of nature, or were we created by God for a purpose? Are you a child of The King or just a child of King Kong?[5]

What is a man? The modern answer was stated by the atheist philosopher, Jean-Paul Sartre: "You are your life and nothing else."[6] In other words, all you have is yourself and you will last no longer than the uncertain span of your earthly life. This conclusion is unavoidable if you are only a product of nature. But some 2800 years ago, the Psalmist asked the same question and got a very different answer:

> "What is man, that You are mindful of him,
> And the son of man, that You visit him?
> For You have made him a little lower than the angels,
> And You have crowned him with glory and honor."[7]

I want to look at human beings and see what we can observe about ourselves, and then ask what conclusions we can draw from these characteristics about the big questions of life—especially, is there a God and if so, what is He like? In the end, I am going to argue that we cannot explain human nature without God. I am going to propose something which is quite radical in our culture, that *men are miracles*. We are not only natural beings, related horizontally to the rest of nature. We are also supernatural beings, related vertically to a Creator God.

Self-Evident Truths

I do not know you, but I believe I know at least eight things about you. If you are reading this book, you are human, and these eight facts are true of all human beings. They are part of human nature. In fact, I believe they are "self-evident." By this I mean that they are obvious to anyone who takes the time to think about them, and we can safely assume them to be true, without requiring proof. Thomas Jefferson wrote, in the American Declaration of Independence:

---

3. Kreeft, *Christianity for Modern Pagans*, 62.
4. Colson and Pearcey, *How Now Shall We Live?* 115.
5. Kreeft, *Because God Is Real*, 8.
6. Sartre, "No Exit," 45.
7. Psalm 8:4–5; quoted in Hebrews 2:6–7, as referring to Jesus.

"We hold these truths to be self-evident: that all men are created equal, that they are endowed by their Creator with certain inalienable rights, among these are life, liberty and the pursuit of happiness."

In believing in self-evident truth, Jefferson represented the mainstream of human thought, going back at least as far as the Greek philosopher, Aristotle, in the fourth century, BC. Aristotle taught that we must accept some truths as self-evident if we are going to think at all,[8] and he was right. You cannot reason your way to any conclusion if you do not start from some assumption.

I will suggest that we can reasonably accept as starting points for our thinking several self-evident truths about human beings, because these truths have been obvious to most all men throughout history. They are part of the general understanding of reality that we sometimes call "common sense," and that I will call "universal human experience."[9]

I am not very interested in any belief system which requires me to say that our universal human experience is an illusion, whether that belief system is secular or religious. The "Christian Scientist" movement, so far as I can understand it, teaches that human sickness is not a physical reality, but is only in the mind. I would suggest that the appropriate response to this idea is the joke about the Christian Scientist who met a friend and asked, "How is your father?" The friend answered, "Not well. He has cancer." The Christian Scientist responded, "He's not really sick. He just thinks he is." A few weeks later, they met again. The Christian Scientist again asked, "How is your father?" The friend replied, "Not well. Now he thinks he's dead."[10] Please forgive me if I am being flippant, or if I misunderstand the Christian Scientists. But the idea that physical illness is only in the mind violates our universal human experience. Therefore, it is very unlikely to be true.

The ancient Greek philosopher, Socrates, said, "Know thyself." That sounds good to us—our motto is "be yourself." But by "know thyself," Socrates seems to have meant know what it means to be human, what you

---

8. Reynolds, *When Athens Met Jerusalem*, 188–189.

9. I use the term "universal human experience" to mean the common experience of most all men throughout history. There could, of course, be an occasional person who does not share one or more of these experiences. As C. S. Lewis wrote about the basics of the moral law, "[Y]ou might . . . find an odd individual here and there who did not know it, just as you find a few people who are color-blind or have no ear for a tune. But taking the race as a whole, [our ancestors] thought that the human idea of decent behavior was obvious to everyone. And I believe they were right." Lewis, *Mere Christianity*, 4.

10. Colson and Pearcey, *How Now Shall We Live?* 203.

have in common with all men.[11] This is the question I want to explore. So here is my list of eight characteristics which you and I have in common, but which distinguish us from all other creatures:

1. You are a conscious self, aware of your own existence. You are the sort of being that says, "I am."

2. You can think rationally. You can reason from one point to another, about abstract things like mathematics, or about physical realities beyond what you can perceive with your senses, and you can get true answers.

3. You have what we commonly call "free will." You make real choices, in a real world, with real consequences.

4. You have an innate sense of morality, basic notions that certain conduct is right and other conduct is wrong.

5. You have these moral notions, but you fail to live up to them. Am I wrong? Are you always as loving, truthful, kind, and fair to others as you expect them to be to you?

6. You are never satisfied. You have, deep in your heart, a secret longing which you cannot name, but which always leaves you wanting something more.

7. You want to live forever, and naturally believe you should live forever. But you know that you will die.

8. You believe in certain things—that life has meaning, that men have dignity and equality and rights, such as freedom, that love and beauty are real, and your life would be miserable without these beliefs.

We will discuss each of these characteristics, one at a time, in the chapters that follow, and argue that each of them points to the existence of a Creator. We will then look briefly at other evidence for God by asking the questions, why does anything exist, why does life exist, why does intelligent life exist, and why is there order in the universe rather than chaos? We will attempt to answer some of the objections frequently raised against the belief in God, such as the question of suffering, why the theistic religions believe theirs is the only way to God, and the evil that has been done in the name of these religions. Finally, we will conclude with the practical question, if the God of Scripture is real, how should we live?

---

11. Kreeft, *Philosophy 101 by Socrates*, 16. This advice was inscribed over the oracle's temple at Delphi and was often quoted by Socrates. Ibid.

The God Question

"Is ultimate reality God or the cosmos? Is there a supernatural realm or is nature all that exists? Has God spoken and revealed His truth to us, or is truth something we have to find, even invent, for ourselves? Is there a purpose to our lives, or are we cosmic accidents emerging from the slime?"

—CHARLES COLSON AND NANCY PEARCEY[12]

Human beings are naturally religious. The Bible does not even argue against atheism, only against idolatry, the worship of false gods.[13] If atheism is true, most all men throughout history have been wrong about the belief which mattered to them most.[14] This does not prove there is a god, much less that He is the God of Scripture, but it is an important piece of evidence to notice as we begin. If there is no God, why have we evolved so as to believe in something which does not exist?[15]

There are three basic answers to "the God question."[16] The first is *atheism*, which says that there is no God and nature is all there is. Everything which exists is the result of an uninterrupted chain of natural causes. And since, naturally speaking, something never comes from nothing, that chain of natural causes must go back forever. As the popular scientist Carl Sagan said, "The Cosmos is all that is, or ever was, or ever will be."[17]

We will also refer to this view as "naturalism" (the belief that only nature exists) or "materialism" (the belief that only matter and energy exist). While some naturalists or materialists consider themselves agnostics (one who does not know if there is a god), rather than atheists, these philosophies agree with atheism that everything is explainable by natural causes—any god who might exist has no effect on our everyday lives. So we will use these terms interchangeably.

The second answer is *pantheism*, common to most of the Eastern religions such as Hinduism or Buddhism.[18] George Lucas' "Star Wars," with

---

12. Colson and Pearcey, *How Now Shall We Live?* 20.
13. Ibid., 54.
14. Lewis, *Mere Christianity*, 29.
15. D'Souza, *What's So Great about Christianity?* 15.
16. Moreland, *The God Question*.
17. Sagan, *Cosmos*, 4.
18. Scholars identify two main branches of Hinduism, the more philosophical pantheistic branch which we will discuss, which believes in one impersonal deity coextensive with nature, and a polytheistic branch, popular with the common folk, which includes the worship of many gods. Jeyachandran, "Tough Questions about Hinduism

"The Force" as a deity, is a modern, Western example of such a belief.[19] "Pan" means all or everything, so pantheism is the belief that god is everything and everything is god, the good and the bad, the beautiful and the ugly. I am god and so are you. A star is god and so is a pebble. Where an atheist says nature is all that exists, a pantheist can say god is all that exists. But this god is not a person; it is just a name for everything. A pantheistic god is not *super*natural. God and nature are never separate or distinct, and one did not create the other.

The third answer is *theism*, or monotheism, which says that there is one God and He is eternal, self-existent, and all-powerful. He is not part of the physical universe and it is not part of Him, but He created the entire natural order—matter and energy, space and time, even scientific laws—out of nothing. He is infinite (limitless), personal (conscious, rational, purposeful, and relational), and good (both just and loving). This is a very old view, but it was introduced as we know it by the Israelites at the time of Moses, about 3500 years ago.[20]

By this definition, Jews, Christians, and Muslims are all theists. All believe in one God, and that He is the God of Abraham, as described in the Old Testament. However, I am not qualified to write about Jewish or Muslim theology. And from my limited understanding, it seems that Muslims have somewhat different beliefs about the character of God and the character of man. So we will discuss traditional Christian beliefs. But we should recognize that almost all these beliefs are shared by traditional Judaism, and many by Islam as well.

---

and Transcendental Meditation," 158–163. Buddhists are considered pantheists, but generally do not believe in a god at all. As strange as it sounds to Western ears, Buddhism is "a religion without God." Zacharias, *The Lotus and the Cross*, 91.

19. "Star Wars," Twentieth Century Fox, Lucasfilm, 1977. Lucas is a follower of the "New Age" movement, a modern Western version of pantheism, with particular influences from Hinduism. Noebel, *Understanding the Times*, 74–75.

20. The popular theory is that the first religions were animistic (worshipping natural objects), then polytheistic (worshipping many gods), and that pantheism and monotheism developed later. But recent archeological evidence indicates that monotheism is the oldest form of religion. Geisler, *Baker Encyclopedia of Apologetics*, 497–498.

The Man Question

"Four hundred years ago there was a collection of molecules named Shakespeare which produced *Hamlet*."

—GEORGE WALD, NOBEL PRIZE-WINNING PHYSIOLOGIST[21]

"[W]e are composite creatures, rational animals, akin on one side to the angels, on the other to tom-cats."

—C. S. LEWIS[22]

The answer to the God question holds the key to "the man question"—what are we? If nature is all there is, we are nothing more than our natural bodies. I am just "a collection of molecules named Howard." We have no meaning or purpose other than what we can make for ourselves, and no destiny other than death and disintegration.

If pantheism is true, we can say that we are a part of "god." But this god is merely an impersonal force. The "self" is an illusion, and our ultimate destiny is *nirvana*, which means extinction, being absorbed into the vast, impersonal everything.

If the God of the Old Testament is real and made us in His image, we are what Lewis called "composite creatures." Genesis says that God *"formed man of the dust of the ground,"* and *"breathed into his nostrils the breath of life."*[23] So we are both physical and spiritual, both body and soul. We have a purpose, God's purpose for creating us. And because He has an eternal plan for us, we have hope for the future.

But these are reasons to want to believe in God, not evidence that He exists. So we will approach the question from the other direction. We will look first at man, and see what we can conclude from human nature about God.

---

21. From a speech given at a conference in Acapulco, Mexico; quoted Schaeffer, *How Should We then Live?* 180.

22. Lewis, *The Four Loves*, 100.

23. Genesis 2:7.

"Chronological Snobbery"

> "We are dwarves standing on the shoulders of giants. We see farther than the ancients not because we are taller than they, but because we have their shoulders to stand on."
>
> —SIR ISAAC NEWTON[24]

In looking at such questions, we should be humble. A friend of Socrates once asked the Oracle of Delphi, "Who is the wisest man in Athens? She answered, "Socrates." When told of this, he objected that he did not know anything! But the Oracle was supposed to be infallible. After much thought, Socrates told his followers that he accepted her verdict. He explained this by comparing himself to another supposedly wise man: "[A]lthough I do not suppose that either of us knows anything really beautiful and good, I am better off than he is, for he knows nothing, and thinks that he knows; I neither know nor think that I know."[25]

As a young lawyer I worked for a senior partner who had once studied philosophy. One day, after receiving a strongly-worded court order rejecting his legal argument, he remarked, "I should have stayed with philosophy. Then I'd never know when I was wrong!"

But it is not only philosophers who need to be humble. Martin Luther, who led the Protestant Reformation in the sixteenth century, said that all humanity is like a drunk who, after falling off his horse on the right side, the next time falls off it on the left.[26] C. S. Lewis said that the devil sends errors into the world in pairs of opposites, and uses our fear of one to lead us into the other.[27]

To what errors are we most prone? I believe that we suffer from what Lewis called "chronological snobbery."[28] Because of our technological advances, we think that we are more advanced than previous generations in wisdom, as well. But as Jesus said, *"[W]isdom is justified by her children"*[29]— by what it produces. Can anyone look at the hatred, violence, corruption, and poverty in our twenty-first-century world and think we are wise?

G. K. Chesterton, a British writer in the early twentieth century, wrote, "Tradition means giving votes to the most obscure of all classes, our

---

24. Quoted Kreeft, *Making Sense Out of Suffering*, 20.
25. Plato, "The Apology of Socrates," 7.
26. Luther, *Table Talk*; quoted Lewis, "The World's Last Night," 84.
27. Lewis, *Mere Christianity*, 145.
28. Lewis, *Surprised by Joy*, 206.
29. Matthew 11:19.

ancestors. It is the democracy of the dead."[30] I believe that in matters of religion and philosophy, like in old Chicago, the dead should be given a vote! I am not Tevye, from "The Fiddler on the Roof,"[31] calling out for "Tradition!" just because it is tradition. But neither do I think we should reject ideas just because they are old. Do we tell truth by a calendar?[32]

It is a great irony that the twentieth century, which killed more men, women, and children in its wars and genocides than were killed in all the previous centuries of human history combined,[33] was also the century which decided it was so morally wise that it could disregard the wisdom of those previous centuries. So let us put aside questions of whether an idea is old or new, and simply ask which best explains this world, the naturalist or super-naturalist world-view? Which best explains you and me?

Socrates insisted, "We must follow the argument wherever it leads."[34] This is what we will attempt to do. When we do, I believe we will find that traditional Christian teachings explain the facts and fit with our universal human experience better than any other system of belief, whether ancient or modern, secular or religious. I will suggest that this is where the argument—and the evidence—leads. Alister McGrath wrote, "Faith . . . doesn't just make sense to me; it makes sense of me as well."[35]

---

30. Chesterton, *Orthodoxy*, 39.

31. Harnick, Sheldon and Bock, Jerry, "Fiddler on the Roof," Musical Theatre, 1964.

32. *Kreeft, Because God Is Real*, 62.

33. Elford, "Christianity and War," 172; Kreeft, *C. S. Lewis for the Third Millennium*, 19.

34. Quoted Flew, *There Is a God*, 22.

35. McGrath, *Mere Apologetics*, 122.

Chapter 2

"I Yam What I Yam"

Evidence from Human Consciousness

> "Like apes, we breed, sleep and die. Yet like God we say, 'I am.'"
> —PETER KREEFT[1]

DO YOU REMEMBER POPEYE's famous line? "I yam what I yam." This proves that Popeye is human—or at least that his creators were! The first thing I know about you is that you are a conscious self, aware of your own existence.

I refer to myself as "I." I say, "I am." *I am* a man, a husband and a father. *I am* an American, a lawyer, and a University of Kentucky Wildcats fan. *I am* conscious—even of being conscious, of reasoning, and of making choices. This sense of self is part of our human nature, but so far as we know, it is not shared by any other creature in the universe. Certainly the universe itself is not conscious. The seventeenth-century French philosopher and scientist Blaise Pascal wrote:

> "Man is only a reed, the most feeble thing in nature; but he is a thinking reed. The entire universe need not arm itself to crush him. A vapor, a drop of water suffices to kill him. But, if the universe were to crush him, man would still be more noble than that which killed him, because he knows that he dies and the advantage which the universe has over him; the universe knows nothing of this."[2]

---

1. Kreeft, *Jesus Shock*, 47.
2. Pascal, *Pensees*, #347, 97.

Peter Kreeft and Ronald Tacelli wrote, "As great as the forces of nature are, they do not know themselves. Yet we know them and ourselves."[3] *We are conscious creatures in an unconscious world.*

The First Artists

One aspect of our consciousness is what we call "perspective," being aware of both the relationship and the distinction between ourselves and other persons, creatures, or things. I am not you, my wife, or my daughter. I am not a dog, a tree, or a rock. I can distinguish all these things and distinguish myself from them.

Without perspective, we could not represent ourselves or anything else artistically. Yet the only thing we really know about the earliest cave-dwelling humans is that they were artists. We are all familiar with the common myth of the caveman as an ignorant brute, dragging his club with one hand and his woman with the other. But the findings in his cave support none of this. What have been found are his paintings, which show a clear sense of self and an incredible sophistication of perspective, distance, and movement. G. K. Chesterton said of the first archeologist who discovered these cave paintings, "[H]e had dug very deep and found the place where a man had drawn the picture of a reindeer. But he would dig a good deal deeper before he found a place where a reindeer had drawn a picture of a man."[4] C. S. Lewis wrote:

> "[T]he very first picture of all did not 'evolve' itself [from something lesser]; it came from something overwhelmingly greater than itself, from the mind of that man who by seeing for the first time that marks on a flat surface could be made to look like animals and men, proved himself to excel in sheer blinding genius any of the artists who have succeeded him."[5]

The fact that the earliest cave-dwellers were artists shows that they were human. The fact that human beings are artists shows that we are something absolutely unique in nature.

---

3. Kreeft and Tacelli, *Handbook of Christian Apologetics*, 66.
4. Chesterton, *The Everlasting Man*, 27–30, 33.
5. Lewis, "The Funeral of a Great Myth," 90.

The Real You

"There is no location in the brain where the 'I' is located."

—ROY ABRAHAM VARGHESE[6]

Traditionally, men have referred to our consciousness, reason, and will as the "soul." You may use that word or not, but our experience is that we are conscious, we are rational, and we make choices. We also believe that we are more than just our physical bodies. "When the scientist closes his laboratory and goes home and kisses his wife, he does not believe that there is nothing there but hormones and neurons and molecules."[7]

How many young lovers have said, "I want him (or her) to love me for who I really am?" Your soul is the "real you." The cells in your body keep changing—the majority are replaced every seven years[8]—but you remain, the same person you were ten, twenty, even eighty or ninety years ago. My mother lived to be ninety-five, and still vividly remembered her childhood, and herself as a child. *Apparently, there is more to our selves than our cells.*

Christianity teaches that we are both bodies and souls. It takes both to make a man. This is why we regard either corpses or ghosts as wrong—they are meant to be together.[9] The seventeenth-century poet John Donne wrote of the unity of body and soul as "the subtle knot which makes us men."[10]

What is the soul or self? There are only three possibilities—it is an illusion, it is an accidental product of nature, or it is a gift from God.

"How Do I Know I Exist?"

Many Pantheists deny the existence of the self. Buddha taught that both the self and material reality are "*maya*," illusions.[11] The ninth-century Hindu philosopher Shankara said much the same thing.[12] Pantheism also teaches that this illusion will disappear when we reach our ultimate destiny, the state of "*nirvana*," or non-existence. Could the pantheist be right that the self is an illusion? The story is told of a student who asked her professor, "How do

---

6. Varghese, *The Wonder of the World*, 303.
7. Kreeft and Tacelli, *Handbook of Christian Apologetics*, 264.
8. Moreland, *Scaling the Secular City*, 88.
9. Kreeft, *Everything You Always Wanted to Know about Heaven*, 93.
10. Quoted Lewis, *The Discarded Image*, 167.
11. Varghese, *The Wonder of the World*, 350.
12. Ibid., 91.

I know I exist?" He answered with another question: "Who is asking?"[13] The only answer is, "I am."

"The Ghost in the Machine"

"If we begin with less than personality, we must finally reduce personality to the impersonal ... plus complexity."

—FRANCIS SCHAEFFER[14]

Materialists necessarily argue that human consciousness is just the result of natural processes in the brain. But natural processes are not conscious. Can consciousness come from the unconscious, or personhood from the impersonal? Can water rise above its source?

Secular scientists have tried very hard to discover a physical cause for our sense of self. They have learned much about the human brain. But no one can explain how the matter in our brains could produce consciousness. Harvard psychologist Stephen Pinker is one of the world's leading experts on the brain. He wrote a book titled, *How the Mind Works*. But regarding human consciousness, he could only say, "Consciousness . . . is still a riddle wrapped in a mystery inside an enigma."[15]

Richard Dawkins is an evolutionary biologist at Oxford University and has been called "the world's best-known atheist." But in a debate with Dr. Pinker, he said:

> "Neither Steve Pinker nor I can explain human subjective consciousness . . . Steve elegantly sets out the problem . . . and asks where it comes from and what's the explanation. Then he's honest enough to say, 'Beats the heck out of me.' That is an honest thing to say and I echo it. We don't know. We don't understand it."[16]

Sam Harris is a philosopher and neuroscientist who, along with Dawkins and others, is one of the "new atheists," a group of writers aggressively promoting atheism. But he wrote:

> "The idea that the brain *produces* consciousness is little more than an article of faith among scientists at present . . .

---

13. Ibid., 59.
14. Schaeffer, *He Is There and He Is Not Silent*, 286.
15. Pinker, *How the Mind Works*, 60.
16. Dawkins and Pinker, "Is Science Killing the Soul?"

The problem . . . is that nothing about a brain, when surveyed as a physical system, declares it to be a bearer of that peculiar, interior dimension that each one of us experiences as consciousness in his own case."[17] (emphasis in original)

Canadian surgeon Wilder Penfield has been called the "father of modern neurosurgery." He was one of the first to map the anatomy of the human brain, identifying the functions of various regions. During the mid-twentieth century, he sometimes performed brain surgery on conscious patients, so that he could talk to them during the surgery. He reported that he could electrically stimulate various parts of the brain and cause the patient to move his arms or legs, turn his head or eyes, or swallow. Invariably the patient would say, "I didn't do that, you did." But Penfield also performed experiments where he would ask the patient to resist, to hold his left hand with his right, for instance, while he stimulated the brain to move the left hand. Thus, one hand was under the control of an electrical current, but the other was under the voluntary, conscious control of the patient—his soul or spirit. Penfield concluded, "What a thrill it is . . . to discover that the scientist, too, can legitimately believe in the existence of the spirit."[18]

Materialists believe that nothing, including man, exists outside of the blind, impersonal system of natural causes. But they find in themselves something they cannot explain naturally, a conscious, free, rational self. So they are left with a mystery. This is why some have referred to man as "the ghost in the machine."[19] You are nothing but a machine, your body. Your "self" is just an electro-chemical phenomenon, a ghost, produced by your physical brain. Nobel Prize-winning biologist Francis Crick wrote:

> "You, your joys and your sorrows, your memories and your ambitions, your sense of personal identity and free will, are in fact no more than the behavior of a vast assembly of nerve cells and their associated molecules."[20]

This is the logical conclusion of materialism. But Crick's fellow Nobel Prize winner, neurophysiologist John Eccles, disagreed:

> "[T]he only certainty we have is that we exist as unique, self-conscious beings . . . The evolutionary process gives rise to my body

---

17. Harris, *The End of Faith*, 208.
18. Penfield, *The Mystery of the Mind*, 76–77, 85.
19. Ryle, *The Concept of Mind*, 15–16. Ryle coined this term to represent the views of Rene Descartes, the seventeenth-century French philosopher, and other theists. But it seems to me to better represent the materialist's view of a human being.
20. Crick, *The Astonishing Hypothesis*, 3.

and my brain . . . But the conscious self is not in the Darwinian evolutionary process at all. I think it is a divine creation."[21]

If you are only your cells, and most of your cells are replaced every seven years, are your childhood pictures really of you? How can we hold a man in prison for something he did thirty years ago, if he is a different person now?[22]

As we consider various pieces of evidence, I will suggest certain conclusions, which I will facetiously call *"Howard's Laws."* So here is Howard's Law #1: *If your philosophy cannot say that your baby pictures are really you, your philosophy is probably wrong.*

But if materialism is true, there is no real you. You are just the ever-changing cells which make up your body. Put the other way around, if there is a real you or real me, we must be more than our bodies, more than just products of nature. We must be, in some sense, *super*natural.

Another aspect of the self is that we are purposeful. Every day we make our plans and attempt to carry them out. Materialism says that nature has no purposes. Everything is the result of chance or natural laws. But as philanthropist John Templeton asked, "Would it not be strange if a universe without purpose accidentally created humans who are so obsessed with purpose?"[23] Philosopher Alfred North Whitehead suggested that it would be interesting to do a psychological study of those "animated by the purpose of proving that they are purposeless."[24]

Our sense of self is why we feel shame. Only humans wear clothing. Mark Twain said, "Man is the only animal that blushes. Or needs to."[25] This is also an aspect of our consciousness which is unique to humans.

Our consciousness of self and our perspective are inborn, not learned. Young children draw pictures of themselves and their families, even arranging each family member by height. The prehistoric caveman, the ancient philosopher, the modern scientist, and every child share this sense of self and perspective.

---

21. Eccles, "A Divine Design: Some Questions on Origins," 163–164.
22. Moreland, *Scaling the Secular City*, 88.
23. Templeton, *The Humble Approach: Scientists Discover God*, 19.
24. Whitehead, *The Function of Reason*, 16.
25. Twain, "Pudd'nhead Wilson's New Calendar," quoted Benardete, *Mark Twain's Wit and Wisecracks*, 7.

God of the Gaps?

Might scientists someday find a physical explanation for consciousness? It would not destroy my faith. Many have cautioned against "God of the gaps" arguments, resorting to the supernatural to explain things which science cannot yet explain, but might be able to in the future. It has happened in the past that events for which Christians have proposed supernatural explanations have turned out to have natural causes.

But scientists also commonly rely on what is called the "inference to the best explanation."[26] This means that of competing theories, the one which best explains the facts is the one most likely to be true. For example, Charles Darwin argued that his theory of the origin of species better explained the biological facts than any other theory. I would submit that for human consciousness and many of the other characteristics we will consider, the belief in a supernatural Creator best explains the facts, and therefore is the explanation most likely to be true.

Neither a Christian nor a materialist can give a *natural* explanation for human consciousness. This is a problem for the materialist, who says everything must have a natural cause. So he asks us to "take it by faith" that scientists will someday find one. But "an explanation yet to come is no explanation at all."[27] Is "science of the gaps"[28] any more reasonable than God of the gaps?

Furthermore, it is difficult to imagine how human consciousness could ever be explained naturally. Sir Nevill Mott, Nobel Prize-winning physicist at Cambridge, after warning against God of the gaps arguments, wrote, "I believe there is one 'gap' for which there will never be a scientific explanation, and that is man's consciousness."[29]

"I Am Who I Am"

Christianity has no problem explaining human consciousness. We are conscious selves because God is a conscious self and made us in His image. We are persons because God is a personal God. We are more than "ghosts in the machine" because the machine (the natural order) is not all that exists. *Rather, there is both a natural world and a supernatural world, and man belongs to both.*

26. Meyer, *Signature in the Cell*, 154–155.
27. D'Sousa, *What's So Great about Christianity*, 248.
28. Gleiser, *A Tear at the Edge of Creation*, 123.
29. Mott, "Science Will Never Give Us the Answers to All Our Questions," 66.

In Exodus chapter 3, God appeared in a burning bush and told Moses that He was sending him to rescue the Israelites from their slavery in Egypt. Moses asked, *"Who am I that I should go to Pharaoh?"* God said, *"I will ... be with you."* Then Moses asked, who are you? God answered with His personal name: *"I AM WHO I AM ... This you shall say to the children of Israel, I AM has sent me to you."*[30] Eternal existence, consciousness, reason, and will are among the most basic characteristics of the God of Scripture. I am a little "I am," because He is the great "I AM," who made me in His image.

A problem arises when I place my "I am" against God's "I AM." This is what the Bible calls sin, rebellion against God. According to Scripture, God intended that mankind rule, as stewards, over His entire creation. Instead, in the persons of Adam and Eve, we chose autonomy, self-rule, making our own decisions. By this standard, Popeye was not only human, he was also a sinner! His full line was, "I yam what I yam, and that's all that I yam," or as we might say, "I've got to be myself." But when we make ourselves autonomous, we lose the only explanation for our existence. Because modern man does not know that he is made in the image of God, he cannot explain himself.

So our first piece of evidence is consciousness, the human self. I do not claim that our consciousness, by itself, proves there is a God. But it is a strong piece of evidence, because it is a phenomenon which Christianity can explain, and which either atheism (which can only say it is a mystery) or pantheism (which says it is an illusion) cannot. Only creation by a personal God can explain human personhood.

---

30. Exodus 3:11–12, 14.

Chapter 3

"Elementary, My Dear Watson"
Evidence from Human Reason

"All men, by nature, desire understanding."
—ARISTOTLE[1]

"The most incomprehensible thing about the universe is that it is comprehensible."
—ALBERT EINSTEIN[2]

SIR ARTHUR CONAN DOYLE's famous detective, Sherlock Holmes, is noted for his skills in deduction.[3] In the short story, "The Sign of Four," his friend, Dr. Watson, hands Holmes a watch and asks what he can tell from examining it. After only a few minutes, Holmes tells him that it originally belonged to Watson's father, then to his older brother, before being acquired by Watson himself; that his brother was an "untidy and careless" man, who "was left with good prospects, but . . . threw away his chances, lived for some time in poverty with occasional short intervals of prosperity, and finally, taking to drink, he died."[4] All this is true, figured out by Holmes just from looking at the watch.

---

1. Aristotle, *Metaphysics*, 12.
2. Quoted Rees, *Just Six Numbers*, 11.
3. For the philosophy students—I know. What Holmes did was *induction*, not *deduction*. I am using the word in the ordinary, layman's sense. In my defense, Holmes called what he did deduction, as well! See Doyle, "A Study in Scarlet," 18–20.
4. Doyle, "The Sign of Four," 103.

The second thing I know about you is that you can think rationally. When the seventeenth-century French philosopher Rene Descartes famously said, "I think, therefore I am,"[5] his self-evident starting point was, "I think." Sherlock Holmes was fictional, but Arthur Conan Doyle was not. We all share, to a greater or lesser degree, the ability to be detectives, to reason and reach true conclusions. *The universe is not only comprehensible; it is comprehensible to us.*

We perceive truth first by our senses, by what we can see, hear, touch, taste, or smell. But we also do so by the process called "inference," by reasoning from what we already know to other, previously unknown facts. The most obvious example of this is in mathematics. If we have forgotten that four times five equals twenty, we can figure it out, assuming we have all our fingers and toes! But we can also reason our way to truth about physical realities, even those beyond our senses. C. S. Lewis wrote, "[W]e infer the existence of our own brains from what we find inside the skulls of other creatures like ourselves in the dissecting room."[6]

We use this ability every day. Every scientific experiment assumes the reliability of human reasoning, and it works. It works so well that we can send a spacecraft millions of miles, hit the exact spot we are aiming for, and receive back detailed photographs.[7] *The success of science proves the validity of human reasoning.* In my profession, every jury is asked to use this kind of thinking. We rely on our ability to reason both to send a man to the moon and to send a man to prison!

Our reasoning is limited. We make mistakes, as in doing our multiplication tables. We are sometimes dishonest with ourselves, even without realizing it, so as to come to the conclusions we want to reach. "Truth is objective, but people usually aren't."[8] But we can comprehend truth about the universe, in a way that no other creature can. As Francis Collins observed, "No other organism has sequenced its own genome."[9]

Dogs and Meaning

We can understand not only facts but also meaning. C. S. Lewis gave the perfect illustration of the difference between the two:

5. Descartes, *Discourse on Method*, Part 4, 25.
6. Lewis, *Miracles*, 21.
7. Michael Behe uses this as an illustration of how well we know the laws of physics. Behe, *Darwin's Black Box*, ix.
8. Kreeft and Tacelli, *Handbook of Christian Apologetics*, 16.
9. Collins, *The Language of God*, 125.

"You will have noticed that most dogs cannot understand pointing. You point to a bit of food on the floor; the dog, instead of looking at the floor, sniffs at your finger. A finger is a finger to him, and that is all. His world is all fact and no meaning."[10]

But we are more than animals. And as physician Geoffrey Simmons points out, we are also more than machines:

"A computer might identify the presence of chocolate, but it cannot enjoy the taste. A program might identify a laugh, but it cannot enjoy a joke ... A machine might be able to recite the Lord's Prayer, but when will it pray?"[11]

Are Our Thoughts Trustworthy?

"[W]ith me the horrid doubt always arises whether the convictions of man's mind, which has been developed from the mind of the lower animals, are of any value or at all trustworthy."

—CHARLES DARWIN[12]

We all believe that we have this ability, to understand both facts and meaning. Materialism, in particular, claims to be based on "reason, not faith." But reasoning is an act of faith—we trust that our thoughts are reliable.[13] And yet materialism cannot explain why they should be reliable. If nature is all there is, everything, including your thoughts and mine, must be the result of natural causes, "merely the last link of a causal chain in which all the previous links were irrational."[14] Can non-rational causes produce rational thoughts? Would you trust a computer to give the right answers if it was not programmed by an intelligent programmer, but came together as the result of random forces?

In everyday life, we recognize that if our thoughts are influenced by drugs or lack of sleep, they are not trustworthy. The same is true if they are caused by our genetic makeup or by some event which happened in our childhood. We say, "You only think that because you were raised to think

---

10. Lewis, "Transposition," 114.
11. Simmons, *What Darwin Didn't Know*, 94.
12. Darwin, letter to William Graham, July 3, 1881; *Life and Letters of Charles Darwin*, Vol. 1, 285.
13. Chesterton, *Orthodoxy*, 25.
14. Lewis, "Religion Without Dogma?" 136.

that way," or "because that medicine makes you paranoid." To the extent that non-rational, natural causes influence our thoughts, they are unreliable. But materialism says that all our thoughts result solely from non-rational, natural causes. *If materialism is true, we have no reason to trust the thoughts which led us to conclude that materialism is true.*

Many materialistic thinkers recognize this problem. University of Calgary philosopher Thomas Nagle wrote, "Evolutionary naturalism provides an account of our capacities that undermines their reliability, and in doing so undermines itself."[15] MIT philosopher and linguist Noam Chomsky wrote that science depends on our ability to accurately perceive truth about the world, but in the next sentence he added that this ability is "just blind luck."[16]

Matter That Thinks?

"Either there is no philosophy, no philosophers, no thinkers, no thought, no anything; or else there is a real bridge between the mind and reality."

—G. K. CHESTERTON[17]

To put this argument another way, my reasoning is reliable only if my thoughts represent a true understanding of reality. If I calculate the answer to four times five, do my thoughts represent a real insight into mathematics or are they just the product of electrical currents inside my brain? If I say, "The Mississippi River flows south into the Gulf of Mexico," am I expressing a true understanding of geography or just experiencing a chemical reaction? Do my thoughts have rational reasons or only non-rational causes? If my thoughts are not true insights, why do I usually get the right answers? Why do we all usually get the same answers? It appears that there is a real connection between our thoughts and external reality.

Human reasoning works. A friend once said to the eighteenth-century philosopher, Immanuel Kant, "Astronomically speaking, man is utterly insignificant." Kant replied, "You are forgetting that astronomically speaking, man is the astronomer."[18] *We are rational creatures in a non-rational world.*

15. Nagle, *Mind and Cosmos*, 27.
16. Chomsky, *Language and the Problems of Knowledge*, 157–158.
17. Chesterton, *Saint Thomas Aquinas*, 137.
18. Quoted Kreeft, *Socrates Meets Kant*, 106. Blaise Pascal wrote, a century earlier, "It is not from space that I must seek my dignity, but from the government of my thought . . . By space the universe encompasses and swallows me up like an atom; by thought I comprehend the world." Pascal, *Pensees* #348, 97.

Scientists have spent much time studying the brain and can tell us in considerable detail which parts are used for reasoning. But even if they could identify the exact cell in which every thought occurred, the question would still remain: "Why should what goes on in our heads have any rational connection with what goes on in the world?"[19] Lewis wrote:

> "We are compelled to admit between the thoughts of a terrestrial astronomer and the behavior of matter several light-years away that particular relation which we call truth. But this relation has no meaning at all if we try to make it exist between the matter of the star and the [matter of the] astronomer's brain . . . to talk of one bit of matter as being true about another bit of matter seems to me to be nonsense."[20]

Materialism says we are just matter that thinks. University of California philosopher John Searle called the brain, "cognitive [thinking] meat."[21] But how can meat think? How can matter perceive truth or develop complicated theories? Would pen and paper, by themselves, ever sequence the human genome? Of course not. Such achievements require conscious, purposeful, human reasoning. A Christian can explain this ability. He can say that there is a connection between the mind and external reality, because there is a connection between our minds and the ultimate, eternal mind which created that reality. Therefore, our ability to perceive truth is not "just blind luck."

Howard's Law #2 is: If your philosophy says that meat can think, your philosophy is probably wrong.

Our senses provide a good illustration of this connection between the mind and reality. The nerve impulses from our eyes or ears or fingers are of limited use until they are transformed into the conscious state which we call "understanding." But science can only tell us how the senses communicate impulses to the brain, not how we understand what is being communicated. These are not the same thing. If my eyes see written words, whether I understand the meaning depends on whether I know the language in which they are written. If they are in Chinese, my eyes and nerves may work just fine, but I will not *see* anything but marks on paper.[22]

In a real sense, our eyes do not see any more than a camera does. Our ears do not hear any more than a tape recorder does. *We* use our eyes to see and our ears to hear. But the brain is also just a physical organ. Materialists say that the mind is nothing but a natural phenomenon produced by the

---

19. Dembski, *The End of Christianity*, 104.
20. Lewis, "De Futilitate," 63–64.
21. Quoted Oakes, "Pascal: The First Modern Christian," 83.
22. Varghese, *The Wonder of the World*, 164.

brain. But our shared experience tells us—and many scholars agree[23]—that the real you and real me *use* our brains to understand what our eyes see and our ears hear. If the brain is damaged, we may not think clearly, just as when our eyes are damaged, we cannot see clearly. In either case, we need good instruments. But a brain in a vat cannot think at all. Thinking requires a living, conscious person, using that brain. Once again, there appears to be a "real me" which is more than just my body (my brain). *Apparently our minds are more than matter.*

Is Anything Really True?

"Truth is discovered, not invented ... Gravity existed prior to Newton."
—NORMAN GEISLER AND FRANK TUREK[24]

"Today non-Christians do not object to Christianity because they doubt its claims are true; they object to Christianity because it claims to be true."
—CHARLES COLSON[25]

Believing that we can comprehend truth requires believing there is real truth. This may be the greatest single dividing line between traditional theism and modern materialism. Most of our culture believes, or thinks it believes, that truth is "relative."[26] The "truths" we think we know are really just statements of the way we look at things. There is no real truth, only "my

---

23. The "mind-body problem" has generated much debate. Nobel Prize-winning neurophysiologist John Eccles referred to the mind as "an entity distinct from the brain," and said, "The brain is in the material world and the mind is in the world of subjective experience ... One has to have the idea that thoughts exist ... Thoughts, of course, do eventually find expression in language ... So that part of the story is fairly clear; that we do have mental events before they are converted into brain events." Eccles, "Modern Biology and the Turn to Belief in God," 48–49. Yale physicist Henry Margenau wrote, "[T]he mind cannot be treated as a body; it is a unique entity which affects and regulates the human body." Margenau, "The Laws of Nature are Created by God," 61.

24. Geisler and Turek, *I Don't have Enough Faith to Be an Atheist*, 37.

25. Colson, "The Common Cultural Task: The Culture War from a Protestant Perspective," 19.

26. To a great extent, this idea originated with the eighteenth-century German philosopher, Immanuel Kant. Kant was a Christian, but he held that we can only know what external things are to us, not what they are in themselves. Kant, *The Critique of Pure Reason*, 22. The problem with this idea is that if all I know are my own thoughts, rather than truth about external reality, I cannot say for sure that there is any external reality—it may be "all in my mind." But this conclusion contradicts our universal human experience.

truth" and "your truth." The atheist Friedrich Nietzsche wrote, "There are many kinds of eyes. Even the Sphinx has eyes—and consequently there are many kinds of 'truths,' and consequently there is no truth."[27]

This is materialism thought through to its logical conclusion. Our thoughts are only chemical reactions, and chemical reactions are neither true nor false, so our thoughts are neither true nor false. But the idea of relative truth only comes from a materialistic philosophy, never from human experience. In our everyday lives, everything we do and say shows that we believe in real truth, and that we have the ability to perceive it.

It has been said that some ideas are so ridiculous, only highly-educated people (like attorneys!) could believe them—anyone with common sense knows better. I would suggest that relative truth is one of those ideas, because in everyday life, we all know better. We never apply the idea of relative truth to taking medicine, or driving a car, or paying our taxes. Would you tell the IRS, "Your claim that I owe $5000 in back taxes is true for you, but not for me?" How far do you think that would get you?

Howard's Law #3 is: If you cannot file your taxes according to your philosophy, your philosophy is probably wrong.

If I am charged with assault and the complaining witness testifies that I punched him in the face and bloodied his nose, I may swear that he has me confused with someone else. But if I take the witness stand and say, "Well, that is your truth; my truth is different. What is truth, anyway?" I can tell you one thing that will be true—that jury is going to find me guilty and send me to jail! This is because every juror knows that there is such a thing as real truth, and it is his job to find it, to the best of his ability. If there is only my truth and your truth, what is the jury attempting to find? Our entire legal system is based on the understanding that there is real truth.

Western civilization was built on this belief. If Thomas Jefferson and the American founding fathers had believed that truth was relative, they could never have written, "We hold these truths to be self-evident." They could only have written, "We hold these opinions to be our own."[28]

"What is truth?"[29] This is the question Pontius Pilate asked Jesus, although it is doubtful that he was really looking for an answer. The best definition I have found is from the Greek philosopher, Aristotle: "[T]o say of what is that it is, and of what is not that it is not, is true."[30] *Truth is what corresponds to reality.* And reality is what we run into when we are wrong about truth![31]

27. Nietzsche, *The Will to Power*, 291.
28. Geisler and Turek, *I Don't Have Enough Faith to Be an Atheist*, 176.
29. John 18:38.
30. Aristotle, *Metaphysics*, §1011b, 1597.
31. Willard, *A Place for Truth*, 16.

Self-Defeating Arguments

Both the argument that there is no absolute truth and the argument that we cannot know truth are self-defeating. Is it absolutely true that there is no absolute truth? If we cannot know anything, how can we know that we cannot know anything? It is told that Albert Einstein, in his later years teaching at Princeton, used to walk the halls, whistling and disturbing other classes. As he walked by a philosophy class one day, he heard the professor say, "We can't be certain of anything." Einstein stuck his head in the door and asked, "Professor, are you certain?" and then walked on down the hall, whistling loudly.

Our ability to comprehend truth about the universe requires not only that we must be able to reason, but that the universe must operate by rational laws—and it does, both scientific laws and the laws of logic. One of the laws of logic is the law of non-contradiction, which says that if A is true and B contradicts A, then B cannot also be true. Young children understand this law—opposites cannot both be true. In fact, we have to assume the law of non-contradiction to argue against it. To argue that opposites can both be true, we must assume that the opposite of *that* statement is false. The eleventh-century Muslim philosopher Avicenna provided a humorous illustration of this point:

> "Those who deny a first principle [referring to the law of non-contradiction] should be beaten and exposed to fire until they concede that to burn and not to burn, or to be beaten and not to be beaten, are not identical."[32]

Hopefully, he was joking! But the laws of logic are self-evident truths, and any attempt to deny them disproves itself.

Elephants and Reality

> "Those who deny rationality in the world deploy rational arguments to prove their point . . . Those who say that scientific theories are merely transient paradigms or tentative research projects don't mind flying in planes that assume the truth of aerodynamic laws."
>
> —ROY ABRAHAM VARGHESE[33]

---

32. Quoted Scotus, *Philosophical Writings*, 9.
33. Varghese, *The Wonder of the World*, 324.

Some modern thinkers have suggested that the universe is not rational, but random. Again, this is a logical conclusion of materialism, but it is unlivable. Christian philosopher Ravi Zacharias tells of an incident when he was a guest at Ohio State University, and was proudly shown the new Wexler Center for the Performing Arts. This building was designed to illustrate the supposed randomness of nature. It includes pillars which hang from the ceiling but do not touch the floor, stairways that go nowhere, pods of grass in random places, and so forth. Zacharias viewed all this and then asked, "Are the foundations built on the same principle?"[34] Of course they were not, because we know that if a building is going to be safe to work in, a bridge to drive over, or an airplane to fly in, it must be built according to the rational, uniform laws of nature.

John Cage was an orchestra conductor and composer in the mid-twentieth century, who decided to write music to illustrate his belief that reality is random. He developed an elaborate system of tossing coins to randomly choose each note. But when his orchestra played this "music" for a live audience, the crowd booed.[35]

As Cage grew older, he became a lover of mushrooms. But he explained that he did not apply his theory of randomness to picking mushrooms: "I became aware that if I approached mushrooms in the spirit of my chance operations, I would die shortly . . . So I decided that I would not approach them in this way."[36] I do not doubt that Cage was sincere in his belief, but he could not live by it.

Some pantheists deny material reality altogether—the things we think we see and hear and touch are not real, but illusions. Zacharias tells a story about Shankara, the great Indian philosopher of the ninth century. One day while he was lecturing the king about his belief that material things are not real, an elephant went on a rampage, and Shankara climbed a tree to save his life. After he came down, the king asked him why he fled, if the elephant was not real. Shankara replied, "What the king saw was a non-real me climbing a non-real tree!"[37] The story may be a fable, but it illustrates the fact that such philosophies break down, not over some deep point of theory, but over universally-observed reality.

---

34. Zacharias, *Can Man Live Without God?* 21.
35. Schaeffer, *The God Who Is There*, 78.
36. Ibid., 79.
37. Zacharias, *Jesus Among Other Gods*, 119.

God Is Truth

"Only Mind can beget mind . . . I think; therefore God exists."
—ROY ABRAHAM VARGHESE[38]

Christians have no trouble explaining truth, nor our ability to perceive it. Two of the greatest Christian philosophers, St Augustine in the fifth century and St. Thomas Aquinas in the thirteenth century, both said that our ability to reason is the primary way we are made in God's image.[39] For a Christian, there is such a thing as truth because God is truth. The universe is ordered because He ordered it. We can understand truth about the universe because God gave us a bit of His divine reason. This belief, shared by Galileo, Copernicus, Newton, and many others, was the basis for modern science. Human reason is our second piece of evidence, because only one who believes in a divine Creator can explain why the universe is comprehensible to us. *Only a theist can say that mind comes from mind.*

---

38. Varghese, *The Wonder of the World*, 60.

39. Augustine wrote, "We are quite right, therefore, to take the words, 'Let us make man in our image and likeness,' as . . . referring to the mind. It is this element, after all, which holds the leading place in human nature, which separates it from that of the brute beasts." Augustine, "Unfinished Literal Commentary on Genesis," 149. Aquinas wrote, "While in all creatures there is some kind of likeness to God, in the rational creature [man] alone we find a likeness of image . . . this image of God is not found even in the rational creature except in the mind . . . [Men] imitate God, not only in being and life, but also in intelligence." Aquinas, *Summa Theologica*, Vol. 1, part 1, q93, 473.

Chapter 4

"When You Come to a Fork in the Road, Take It!"

Evidence from Human Freedom

"[W]e have all been dealt a particular set of cards, and the cards will eventually be revealed. But how we play the hand is up to us."

—FRANCIS COLLINS[1]

IN THE MOVIE, "INDIANA Jones and the Last Crusade," one of the villains had to choose a goblet he thought was the Holy Grail and drink from it. If he chose correctly, he would receive its life-giving power. But as soon as he took the first drink, he began to age rapidly and within minutes died a painful death. The old knight who was watching the scene dead-panned, "He chose poorly."[2]

The next thing I would point out about human beings is that we all make conscious choices. Among modern intellectuals, the idea of free will is controversial. Many believe that our actions are all determined by natural causes. But there is a problem with this idea—we all experience life as if we were making free choices. *If that experience is not reality, our lives are one huge illusion, and that illusion has been shared by every human being who ever lived.*

We have no choice but to choose. If I got up one morning and said, "I am not going to make any choices today," that would be a choice. The philosopher Jean Paul Sartre wrote, "I am condemned to be free."[3] He was right.

1. Collins, *The Language of God*, 263.
2. "Indiana Jones and the Last Crusade," LucasFilms, 1989.
3. Sartre, *Being and Nothingness*, 439.

We have no option but to follow the advice of that other great philosopher, Yogi Berra: "When you come to a fork in the road, take it!"[4]

Real Choices in a Real World with Real Consequences

Our experience also tells us that our choices have consequences. "Other roads lead to other places."[5] One of the first words my daughter learned was the word "hot." She learned that if we told her something was hot, she should be careful about touching it or putting it in her mouth.

Our choices have consequences not only for us, but for others. Years ago when I was a young lawyer, I represented a man who was charged with murder, arising out of a drunk-driving accident. I did the best job I could for him. The jury found him guilty of a reduced charge of manslaughter. A few weeks after the trial, his wife came into my office and brought their ten-year-old daughter with her. She was a lovely little girl with beautiful long hair. I said something to her about how pretty her hair was, and her mother replied, "She says she's never going to cut it 'til her daddy comes home. He's always cut it for her."

I thought, of all the people who this man would never have wanted to hurt, his little girl had to be at the top of the list. But she would grow up throughout her teenage years without her daddy. There were also three other children whose mommy would never come home because of the choices he made. We make real choices in a real world with real consequences, for ourselves and for others.

"The Only Wild Animal"

"A history of cows in twelve volumes would not be very lively reading!"

—G. K. CHESTERTON[6]

So far as we know, we are the only animals who make conscious choices. Sometimes it seems that our pets may choose whether to chase a rabbit, for instance, or take a nap. (My old dog usually goes for the nap!) But we are "projecting" our decision-making process onto them, imagining them to be like us. Scientists do not believe that such animals consciously make choices. Rather, they just follow their instincts.

---

4. Berra, *When You Come to a Fork in the Road, Take It*.
5. Kreeft and Tacelli, *Handbook of Christian Apologetics*, 334.
6. Chesterton, *The Everlasting Man*, 137.

Are we just following our instincts when we appear to make choices? If we examine our experience closely, I believe we will see that we are not. Of course we have instincts, but many times we choose not to follow them, or we choose between competing instincts. If someone else is in danger, I have to choose between the instinct to help that person, sometimes called the "herd instinct," and the instinct for self-preservation. I am conscious of my options, the risks and rewards of each, and of making a choice. Peter Kreeft gives a great illustration of the difference between instinct and choice:

> "When you see something flying through the air at your face, you close your eyes instinctively, just as an animal does. But when you see something you think you shouldn't see, like the answers on the test paper of the classmate in front of you, you close your eyes deliberately and by free choice. Or else you look deliberately. You can choose to look or not to look, to cheat or not to cheat."[7]

Often, it is not clear what we will choose. This is what makes human history interesting. Harry Truman said, "Men make history and not the other way around."[8] But if we are truly free, we are absolutely unique in nature. G. K. Chesterton wrote, "We talk of wild animals; but man is the only wild animal. It is man that has broken out. All other animals are tame animals; following the rugged respectability of the tribe or type."[9] *We are free creatures in an unfree world.*

We are the only animals who can consciously control our instincts or passions. Some of us do this better than others, and we all do it better sometimes than at other times, but we all have this ability. For example, we have sexual instincts like other animals. But humans can do one thing which no other animal can do with regard to sex—we can say no. We can say no to the other person or to ourselves, in resisting temptation. And resisting temptation, controlling our passions, is an important part of being human. C. S. Lewis wrote, "To be a complete man means to have the passions obedient to the will, and the will offered to God."[10] In contrast, our culture chooses slavery to our animal passions, and calls it freedom.

---

7. Kreeft, *Because God Is Real*, 220.
8. Pine, *Wit and Wisdom of the American Presidents*, 55.
9. Chesterton, *Orthodoxy*, 136.
10. Lewis, *The Problem of Pain*, 128.

"How Like a Dog!"

Materialists, to be consistent, must believe that nothing exists except the system of natural causes, the machine, and neither God nor a truly free man ever intervenes in that system. If we think we are making real choices, we are only fooling ourselves, for we are also part of the machine. Harvard biologist E. O. Wilson wrote that we have only "the illusion of free will."[11]

The logic is inescapable—if everything is the result of natural causes, so are my actions. How can my "choice" to eat chicken tonight rather than steak, or to put a donation in the Salvation Army kettle rather than walk on by, be the result of purely natural causes and also my free choice? It cannot. If my apparent choices are the inevitable result either of my genetic code or of psychological conditioning, they are not my free choices at all. They are determined by a chain of natural causes going back to the beginning of time.

Cambridge physicist Stephen Hawking is recognized as one of the most brilliant men in the world. But in a speech titled, "Is Man Determined or Free?" Hawking concluded this way: "Is man determined? Yes. But since we do not know what is determined, he may as well not be."[12] In other words, we are not really free, but we think and act as if we were. Hawking is also widely and rightly admired for his courage in his decades-long battle with Lou Gehrig's disease. But if he is correct in his belief that our actions are all determined, there is nothing to admire. He has no choice.

B. F. Skinner was one of the most influential psychologists of the twentieth century. He taught that all human behavior is determined either by our genetic makeup (our DNA) or by psychological conditioning. He believed human behavior could be programmed, like Pavlov's dog. In contrast to Shakespeare's famous line from Hamlet, "How like a god,"[13] Skinner wrote that we should say about man, "How like a dog!"[14]

But Skinner's experiments and others after his time have failed to explain human behavior without free will. Most psychologists today acknowledge that we make conscious choices, even if they cannot explain how. University of Washington psychologist David Barash called this experience a "conundrum," and illustrated what he meant by writing:

> "Thus, to my mind (and I believe I write this of my own free will!), there can be no such thing as free will for the committed scientist . . .

---

11. Wilson, *Consilience: The Unity of Knowledge*, 119.
12. Quoted Zacharias, *Can Man Live Without God?* 170.
13. Shakespeare, *The Tragedy of Hamlet, Prince of Denmark*, Act II, scene 2, 65.
14. Skinner, *Beyond Freedom and Dignity*, 201.

> [T]he most hard-headed materialists live with an unspoken hypocrisy: even as we assume determinism in our intellectual pursuits and professional lives, we actually experience our subjective lives as though free will reigns supreme."[15]

The idea that our actions are all genetically or psychologically programmed is known as "determinism." But none of us live as if we believe our actions, or those of others, were determined. If your spouse were unfaithful, would you be angry with him or her? *If so, you believe in free will.* If he had no choice, you could not logically blame him or be angry.

Do you teach your child not to lie, cheat, or steal? Do you hold her responsible when she disobeys? *If so, you believe in free will.* And notice that when we teach our children these things, we do not believe that we are just programming machines or training performing animals. We believe that we are teaching free, rational beings to make good choices.

Howard's Law #4 is: If you cannot raise your children by your philosophy, your philosophy is probably wrong.

We are very good at using the little bit of psychology we have learned to make excuses for ourselves. We are a lot like the boy who brought home a bad report card, handed it to his father and asked, "Dad, which is it, heredity or environment?" We are like Adam, when God asked him in the garden, *"Have you eaten from the tree of which I commanded you that you should not eat?"* Adam answered, *"The woman whom You gave to be with me—she gave me of the tree, and I ate."*[16] Men have been blaming women (and women have been blaming men) ever since! But our universal human experience tells us that we make real choices, and we know that if we do, we are responsible for those choices.

The Dead-End of Determinism

> "The whole fabric of society would collapse if we acted as if determinism were true... determinism can only be preached, not practiced."
> —ROY ABRAHAM VARGHESE[17]

We make choices in every area of our lives. Science would be impossible without free will. Do you think Francis Collins' team of geneticists could

---

15. Barash, "Dennett and the Darwinizing of Free Will," 222.
16. Genesis 3:12.
17. Varghese, *The Wonder of the World*, 309.

have sequenced the human genome without consciously choosing which experiments to conduct?

Without human freedom, our laws make no sense. Why write a law to tell people not to do something, if they have no choice in what they do? *Every culture which ever existed and every code of laws ever written have assumed that men exercise real free will.*

Our politics assume free will. In President Obama's 2010 speech about the BP oil spill, he said, "[W]hat has defined us as a nation since our founding is the capacity to shape our destiny—our determination to fight for the America we want for our children."[18] If determinism is true, we have no "capacity to shape our destiny," or to "fight" for anything. We are just helpless objects in the current of a meaningless history, like oil in the Gulf of Mexico. But can you imagine a politician making a speech based on the idea that all the actions—or votes—of his listeners were determined?

Howard's Law #5 is: If you cannot base a politician's speech on your philosophy, your philosophy is probably wrong.

We cannot write a fictional story without the characters making free choices. There would be no drama. In Charles Dickens' *A Tale of Two Cities*, the famous last line is, "It is a far, far better thing that I do, than I have ever done; it is a far, far better rest that I go to, than I have ever known."[19] This line is uttered by Sidney Carton as he voluntarily goes to the guillotine, for the happiness of the woman he loves. *There is no story in all of literature which does not contain free creatures making real choices.*[20]

Our games require choice. I am not very good at chess, but I will challenge anyone to a game if I can choose my moves, and yours are predetermined! Every video game is based on the player making choices and the consequences of those choices. Otherwise, there would be no point to the game.

The determinist says that all human actions and beliefs result from heredity or environment. But if that is true, his belief in determinism must result from his heredity or environment, and his argument is not really an argument at all, only a programmed response! But he will try to convince us that he is right, as if we had the choice whether or not to agree. Free will is real, and in real life we know it. Determinism is a dead-end, and it dead-ends at the point where it runs into the reality of universal human experience.

---

18. Obama, "Remarks by the President to the Nation on the BP Oil Spill."
19. Dickens, *A Tale of Two Cities*, 304.
20. Kreeft, *The Philosophy of Tolkien*, 63.

Was Hitler Responsible for His Actions?

> "The determinists ... insult us infinitely more than any preacher who shouts sin and damnation at us. It is a great compliment to call a man a sinner. Only a free man can be a sinner."
>
> —PETER KREEFT[21]

Christians believe in a natural order of cause and effect, but we do not believe that this natural order is all that exists. *We believe in human freedom that is limited, but real.* Our genes and our environment both influence our actions. Each of us has certain tendencies and temptations. We should not judge one another, because we do not know what battles the other person is fighting. But tendency is not destiny. Rather, "Heredity plus environment plus free will equals the human act."[22]

Francis Collins, one of the world's leading geneticists, stated the only conclusion which is consistent with our experience, in the quote with which we introduced this chapter: "[W]e have all been dealt a particular set of cards, and the cards will eventually be revealed. But how we play the hand is up to us."[23]

Without free will, everything we hold meaningful in life disappears. If my wife has no choice but to love me, if it is just the inevitable result of a biochemical reaction (undoubtedly due to my extreme good looks!), her "love" for me means nothing.

This was perfectly illustrated in an old *Star Trek* episode. The crew of the *Enterprise* lands on a planet where a brilliant criminal scientist has been exiled all by himself. They are shocked to find him surrounded by dozens of beautiful young women, waiting on his every desire. But they discover that these young women are only robots he has made and programmed. He eventually falls on his knees, weeping, and begs the crew not to leave him because he is so lonely.[24] If love is not freely given, it does not satisfy us. But if materialism is true, all those whom we love or who love us are just machines, like those robots.

Likewise, if we do not make real choices, all our talk about morals or personal responsibility is meaningless. Without free will, we cannot logically praise a hero who gives his life for others or condemn a murderer. Without

---

21. Kreeft, *Three Philosophies of Life*, 29.
22. Kreeft and Tacelli, *Handbook of Christian Apologetics*, 137.
23. Collins, *The Language of God*, 263.
24. *Star Trek*, Season 2, Episode 8, "I, Mudd," CBS/Paramount, 1967.

free will, Hitler and the Nazis were not responsible for the Holocaust. They just "danced to a DNA that we do not like."[25]

In the 1924 murder case of Nathan Leopold and Richard Loeb, famed criminal defense lawyer Clarence Darrow was hired to represent the defendants, two rich college students with genius-level IQ's, who kidnapped and murdered a fourteen-year-old boy just to see if they could commit the "perfect crime." They couldn't—they were caught because Leopold dropped his glasses at the scene where they disposed of the body. Eventually, both confessed. Without much to go on, Darrow persuaded them to plead guilty and then argued at their sentencing that they were not responsible; their actions were determined by their heredity and environment:

> "Nature is strong and she is pitiless. She works in her own mysterious way, and we are her victims. We have not much to do with it ourselves. Nature takes this job in hand, and we play our parts . . . What had this boy to do with it? He was not his own father; he was not his own mother . . . And yet he is to be compelled to pay."[26]

The judge may or may not have bought this argument—he gave both defendants life in prison instead of possible death sentences. I believe Darrow was wrong in his determinism. But he was absolutely right that if our actions are due to natural causes, we are not responsible for those actions. *Without free will, I am no more responsible for throwing a rock at you than the rock is.*

Real Freedom in God's Image

"Man as created in God's image is therefore a significant man in a significant history, who can choose to obey the commandments of God and love Him, or revolt against Him."

—FRANCIS SCHAEFFER[27]

Scripture teaches that we are free because God is free and made us in His image. It also teaches that God is sovereign. We may go our own way for a little while, but in the end His purposes will prevail. All the characteristics in us which demonstrate God's image are reflections of His divine character,

---

25. Zacharias, "Existential Challenges of Evil and Suffering," 193.
26. Quoted Dembski and Witt, *Intelligent Design Uncensored*, 99–100.
27. Schaeffer, *The God Who Is There*, 113.

but only reflections. However, as St. Thomas Aquinas wrote, only if an all-powerful God made man in His image is real human freedom possible.[28]

Blaise Pascal wrote that God established prayer "to lend to His creatures the dignity of causality."[29] C. S. Lewis commented, "[W]henever we act at all, He lends us that dignity."[30] Of all the gifts which God has given us, this freedom may be the most remarkable. The God who created the universe has given us the ability to make real things happen! Francis Schaeffer called Adam an "unprogrammed man."[31] You and I are unprogrammed men as well. Our freedom is limited—thank God—but it is real.

In fact, while this is only one of our eight arguments from human nature for the existence of God, free will may provide the clearest test case for the two basic world-views. Let us admit that if free will is an illusion, Christianity is false. The Christian world-view requires free will, in order to explain a real right and wrong, personal responsibility, sin, suffering, or the need for salvation. *On the other hand, if free will is real, materialism is false.* This is not a God of the gaps argument, where science cannot yet explain something. Real freedom is fundamentally incompatible with a materialistic world-view, where the first principle is that everything must have a natural cause. This is why so many materialists feel compelled to deny free will, despite their own experience.

On which side is the greater evidence? Surely it is on the side of real human freedom. The experience of every man who has ever lived is that he makes free choices. A materialist cannot live by his own philosophy, because he too must practice free will. So human freedom is our third piece of evidence—I believe the strongest evidence so far. To explain free will, you must start with a free, personal Creator who made man in His image.

---

28. Aquinas, *Summa Theologica*; Vol 1, part 1, q93, 418; and Vol. 1, part 1, q105, 518.
29. Pascal, *Pensees*, §513; as quoted by Lewis, "The Efficacy of Prayer," 9.
30. C. S. Lewis, "The Efficacy of Prayer," 9.
31. Schaeffer, *Escape from Reason*, 220.

Chapter 5

"If There Is No God, Everything Is Lawful"

Evidence from Human Moral Understanding

"I refuse to believe the notion that man is mere flotsam and jetsam in the river of life . . . unable to respond to the eternal oughtness that forever confronts him."

—MARTIN LUTHER KING, JR.[1]

IN MARK TWAIN'S *TOM Sawyer*, Tom, Huck Finn, and Joe Harper run away from home and declare themselves to be pirates. They spend many hours planning their life of crime. But their first night under the stars, the boys cannot sleep. They have guilty consciences over a ham and bacon they have stolen. Finally, they "resolved that so long as they remained in the business, their piracies should never again be sullied with the crime of stealing."[2]

Let me begin this chapter by asking two questions. First, would you want to live in a world where there were no moral rules? Where everything was permitted, including murder, child abuse, or slavery? Second, can you imagine a morality that was really *different*? In which the moral laws read, "Thou shalt kill, thou shalt steal?" We may allow different exceptions, but we all recognize certain basic moral principles—that we should love and not hate, tell the truth and not lie, keep promises and not break them, look out for others and not only for ourselves. The next thing I know about you and

---

1. King, Martin Luther, Jr., in his speech accepting the 1964 Nobel Peace Prize; quoted Zacharias, *Can Man Live Without God?* 85.
2. Twain, *The Adventures of Tom Sawyer*, 87.

me is that we all share with Tom, Huck, and Joe basic notions that certain conduct is right and other conduct is wrong—to use Dr. King's word, notions of "oughtness."

These moral notions have remained remarkably similar throughout history. C. S. Lewis compiled an excellent, short collection of the moral codes from many different cultures in the Appendix to his book, *The Abolition of Man*. He showed that from the ancient Babylonians and Egyptians to the Greeks and Romans, from Hindus in India to Confucians in China, from the Old Norse to Native Americans to Australian Aborigines, all have recognized these same moral principles.[3] By the way, this is one of Lewis' greatest and most important books. If you have not read it, put this one down, go get it, and correct that flaw in your education immediately!

History provides many examples of how strongly we believe in right and wrong. Nikita Khrushchev was the leader of the Soviet Union, the most powerful atheist nation in history. Supposedly, he did not believe in moral absolutes. But when he became angry while at the United Nations, he took off his shoe, pounded it on the table, and screamed, "It's wrong! It's wrong!"[4]

The Marquis de Sade was a philosopher and writer in sixteenth-century France. He believed that human conduct is chemically determined, and he took this determinism to its logical conclusion—there is no such thing as right or wrong. He wrote, "What is, is right." De Sade applied this philosophy to relationships between the sexes: "As nature has made us [man] the strongest, we can do with her [woman] whatever we please."[5] Late in his life he was jailed for beating up a prostitute. It is from his name that we get our word, "sadism."[6] De Sade said, "What is, is right," but after he was put in prison, it is reported that he spent his last days complaining that he was being mistreated by his jailers.[7]

We come by these moral notions naturally. Just listen to a group of children on a playground: "It's not fair!" "He's cheating!" "I had it first!" British theologian N. T. Wright says, "We don't have to teach people that there is such a thing as justice."[8]

We are very good at rationalizing our own behavior. Columnist George Will once quipped that a certain politician had "wrestled with his conscience and won." We are all like that politician at times. Some of our excuses may be

---

3. Lewis, *The Abolition of Man*, 95–118.
4. Schaeffer, *Death in the City*, 269–270.
5. de Sade, *La Nouvelle Justine*; quoted Schaeffer, *How Should We then Live?* 177.
6. Schaeffer, *Escape from Reason*, 231–232.
7. Schaeffer, *Death in the City*, 269.
8. Wright, *Simply Christian*, 242.

legitimate—I may have a very good explanation of why it was right for me to lie in a particular situation—but my excuses only show how much I believe in the general principle that I should not lie. It is only my bad conduct I try to explain. "No one makes excuses for acting like Mother Teresa."[9]

The Natural Law

Our ancestors explained this agreement about moral principles by saying that there is a real law of right and wrong which men naturally recognize. They called this the "natural law" because they believed that it was built into human nature, much like the law of gravity is built into the physical universe. The difference, of course, is that we can choose whether or not to obey the moral natural law. We cannot choose whether to obey the law of gravity.[10] *But our ancestors did not believe we could choose whether or not the moral law was true.*

Thomas Jefferson wrote, "I believe that justice is . . . innate, that the moral sense is as much a part of our constitution as that of feeling, seeing or hearing."[11]

Mahatma Ghandi said that a good Hindu should study the law and "reject it if it is an excrescence [something abnormal], and . . . foster it and restore it to its pristine purity, if it represents a universal law."[12]

Martin Luther King, Jr., in his famous "Letter from a Birmingham Jail," wrote:

> "One has not only a legal but a moral responsibility to obey just laws. Conversely, one has a moral responsibility to disobey unjust laws . . .
> A just law is a man made code that squares with the moral law or the law of God . . . An unjust law is a human law that is not rooted in eternal law and natural law."[13]

The whole idea of civil disobedience is based on the belief in a higher moral law.

After World War II, when the Nazi leaders were put on trial at Nuremberg for war crimes, there was little established international law on which to base the prosecutions, and the Nazis had passed laws in Germany authorizing

---

9. Geisler and Turek, *I Don't Have Enough Faith to Be an Atheist*, 181.
10. Lewis, *Mere Christianity*, 3–7.
11. Quoted Pine, *Wit and Wisdom of the American Presidents*, 7.
12. Ghandi, "Introduction to Varnavyavastha," 216.
13. King, "Letter From a Birmingham Jail."

most everything they did. So the judges conducting the trials relied on what they called "the basic principles of jurisprudence, which are the assumptions of civilization."[14] *In other words, they relied on a natural moral law.*

Many people today do not believe in such a law. But we all possess this "moral sense." Where does it come from? There are only three possibilities—it comes from nature, it comes from society, or it comes from God.

The Law of the Jungle

Some have suggested that our moral notions are the results of evolution, instincts preserved by natural selection because they are useful to the survival of the species. This view was stated by philosopher Michael Ruse and biologist E. O. Wilson:

> "Morality, or more strictly, our belief in morality, is merely an adaptation put in place to further our reproductive ends . . . In an important sense, ethics as we understand it is an illusion fobbed off on us by our genes to get us to cooperate."[15]

But while our moral notions and our instincts sometimes agree, such as in telling us to care for our young or to bond socially, at other times our moral notions tell us to disobey one or more of our instincts or to choose between them, as we discussed in the last chapter. Furthermore, while all animals have instincts, these moral notions are unique to humans. Charles Darwin wrote, "[O]f all the differences between man and the lower animals, the moral sense or conscience is by far the most important."[16] Frans de Waal of Emory University is one of the world's leading primatologists and has emphasized the similarities between man and the apes. But he wrote:

> "It is hard to believe that animals weigh their own interests against the rights of others, that they develop a vision of the greater good of society, or that they feel life-long guilt about something that they should not have done."[17]

There is no right or wrong in the animal kingdom. When the lion has its teeth around the neck of the zebra, what moral standard can she appeal to? The only law is "the law of the jungle," the survival of the fittest. When

---

14. Montgomery, "Why Human Rights Are Impossible without Religion," 264–266.
15. Ruse and Wilson, "The Evolution of Ethics," 310.
16. Darwin, *The Descent of Man*, 134.
17. de Waal, *Good Natured: The Origins of Right and Wrong in Humans and other Animals*, 209.

my family and I were at Disney World a few years ago, the tour guide on one of the rides said, "Always remember the first rule of the jungle—don't be the zebra!" In the words of the nineteenth-century English poet, Alfred Lord Tennyson, nature is "red in tooth and claw."[18] Or as Brown University ethicist Richard Taylor put it:

> "A hawk that seizes a fish from the sea *kills* it, but does not *murder* it; and another hawk that seizes the fish from the talons of the first *takes* it, but does not *steal* it—for none of these things are forbidden [for the hawk]."[19] (emphasis in original)

There is no sexual morality in the animal kingdom. Even something as horrible as rape, universally condemned in human cultures, goes on all the time (the physical act) among animals. But we do not call it that, because we understand that to speak meaningfully of rape, we must have the idea of consent or lack of consent. One rabbit cannot "rape" another. Rabbits just mate, without free will and therefore without morals.

"A Behavior Not Supported by Natural Selection"

"If our standards are derived from this meaningless universe, they must be as meaningless as it."

—C. S. LEWIS[20]

Furthermore, while natural selection—the survival of the fittest—might explain some of our moral notions, it cannot explain the most important one, why you should *"love your neighbor as yourself."*[21] Natural selection is inherently selfish, rewarding behavior which helps the organism survive. But our moral notions often tell us to act against our self-interest. Where is the survival value in altruism (selfless concern for others)? Darwin wrote, "Natural selection will never produce in a being anything injurious to

---

18. Tennyson, "In Memoriam," Canto 56, 105.

19. Taylor, *Ethics, Faith and Reason*, 14. Taylor believes that we also are just animals and therefore: "[S]uch actions [if performed by men], though injurious to their victims, are no more unlawful, unjust or immoral than they would be if done by one animal to another." Ibid. This is the logical conclusion of his atheism: "The concept of moral obligation [is] unintelligible apart from the idea of God. The words remain but their meaning is gone." Ibid., 84.

20. C. S. Lewis, "On Living in an Atomic Age," 77.

21. Leviticus 19:18; quoted by Jesus in Mark 12:31.

itself."[22] Harvard evolutionary biologist Ernst Mayr wrote, "Altruism toward strangers is a behavior not supported by natural selection."[23]

Stephen Hawking argues that natural selection rewards aggression, making human beings naturally violent. So he fears for the survival of our species. His best hope is:

> "If we can keep from destroying each other for the next one hundred years, sufficient technology will have been developed to distribute humanity to various planets, and then no one tragedy or atrocity will eradicate us all at the same time."[24]

How sad if the last, best hope for mankind is that we can move far enough away from one another that our ability to kill will be limited by the need for long-distance space travel! But notice Hawking's point—natural selection rewards selfishness, even violence. If the survival of the fittest is the ultimate law of human nature, where does altruism come from?

Similarly, where is the survival value in truth? Is treachery or deception not more likely to be beneficial? *Materialistic evolution can provide no basis for true morals.*[25] Richard Dawkins acknowledged this in a recent interview with British journalist Justin Brierly. Dawkins first stated that he believed his "value judgments" may have "come from my evolutionary past."

Brierly: "So therefore it's just as random in a sense as any product of evolution."

Dawkins: "Well, you could say that. But it doesn't in any case—nothing about it makes it more probable that there is anything supernatural."

Brierly: "Okay, but ultimately, your belief that rape is wrong is as arbitrary as the fact that we've evolved five fingers rather than six."

Dawkins: "You could say that, yeah."[26]

---

22. Darwin, *On the Origin of Species*, 223.
23. Mayr, *What Evolution Is*, 259.
24. Quoted Zacharias, *Can Man Live Without God?* 170.
25. Francis Collins wrote, "Agape, or selfless altruism, presents a major challenge for the evolutionist. It is quite frankly a scandal to reductionist reasoning. It cannot be accounted for by the drive of individual selfish genes to perpetuate themselves." Collins, *The Language of God*, 27. Thomas Nagle, an atheist, wrote that natural selection cannot explain any "mind-independent moral . . . truth," because "the ability to detect such truth, unlike the ability to detect mind-independent truth about the physical world, would make no contribution to reproductive fitness." Nagle, *Mind and Cosmos*, 107.
26. Quoted McGrath, *Mere Apologetics*, 104–105.

Michael Ruse, who said that our moral notions are only "illusions fobbed off on us by our genes," also wrote an essay speculating about the possibility of an intelligent species on another planet which evolved differently, and for whom rape would not be forbidden.[27]

Howard's Law #6 is: If your philosophy cannot say that rape is absolutely wrong—on any planet—your philosophy is probably wrong.

In Charles Dickens' *A Christmas Carol*, when Ebenezer Scrooge was asked to give to the poor, he said let them die, it will "decrease the surplus population."[28] If the survival of the fittest is the ultimate law of human behavior, Scrooge had it right. You cannot get *"Love your neighbor"* or any meaningful moral code from the survival of the fittest. Yet our human natures demand morals. Benjamin Franklin said, "There is no man so bad but [that] he secretly respects the good."[29]

We are "moral creatures . . . in an amoral world."[30] How could our moral notions have come from this world?

Even the most committed materialist believes in right and wrong. Richard Dawkins wrote that the universe shows "[n]othing but blind, pitiless indifference"[31] toward life, including human life. But he also suggested that humans have now evolved far enough that:

> "We can even discuss ways of deliberately cultivating and nurturing pure, disinterested altruism—*something that has no place in nature*, something that has never existed before in the whole history of the world."[32] (emphasis added)

The obvious question is, where does Dawkins get his idea of altruism, if it "has no place in nature," and nature is all there is? In 1976, Dawkins wrote *The Selfish Gene*, arguing that evolution, even at the genetic level, is entirely "selfish," looking out only for the organism's own interests. But in 2006, he described himself as "mortified" that convicted Enron executive Jeffrey Skilling called this his favorite book, justifying business practices which almost everyone, including Dawkins, regarded as unethical.[33] The irony is that Skilling was only practicing the selfishness which Dawkins taught was the natural engine of evolution.

27. Ruse, "Is Rape Wrong on Andromeda?" 43.
28. Dickens, *A Christmas Carol*, 19.
29. Franklin, *Poor Richard's Almanac*, 47.
30. Dillard, *Pilgrim at Tinker Creek*, 177.
31. Dawkins, *River Out of Eden*, 133.
32. Dawkins, *The Selfish Gene*, 215n.
33. Dawkins, *The God Delusion*, 215.

We cannot get true morals from nature. If killing is not wrong for the hawk or the tiger, and we are only animals, why is it wrong for us?

If We Made the Rules, We Can Change Them

> "The fundamental question of ethics is, who makes the rules? God or Men? The theistic answer is that God makes them. The humanistic answer is that men make them. This distinction between theism and humanism is the fundamental division in moral theory."
>
> —MAX HOCUTT, SELF-PROFESSED "HUMANIST,"[34]

Many materialists say that our moral notions come from society, from us. And if we made the rules, we can change them. The idea that right and wrong are not absolute, but may change from time to time, place to place, or culture to culture, is called "moral relativism," and it is the dominant view in our society. It is a logical conclusion of materialism. *If there is no God, moral laws are not truths about the universe. They are just rules which men made up, reflecting society's judgment about what works best for the most people—or the most powerful.* They are social conventions, like whether we drive on the right side of the road or the left. We can see the change in our thinking in the language we use. We have substituted the word "values" for "virtues." The word virtues implies something objective or fixed. Values are subjective—yours may be different from mine.[35]

This idea of subjective values fits our individualistic culture very well. We want to make our own rules. Pastor and author Timothy Keller writes that we have "a deep belief that individual rights operate not only in the political sphere but also in the moral."[36] But Keller also points out that moral relativists are often very interested in social justice. As a youth, he was attracted to this combination of ideas: "[W]hat young person wouldn't be? Liberate the oppressed and sleep with who you wanted! But I kept asking the question, if morality is relative, why isn't social justice as well?"[37]

Most of the time, we want morality to be relative, so that we can make our own rules, in only one area, sex. In other areas of traditional morality—"*Thou shalt not kill, thou shalt not steal, thou shalt not bear false*

---

34. Hocutt, "Toward an Ethic of Mutual Accommodation," 137.

35. Mills, "To See through a Glass Darkly: C.S. Lewis, George Orwell and the Corruption of Language," 111.

36. Keller, *The Reason for God*, xviii

37. Ibid., xii.

witness."[38]—we generally like the old rules. But moral relativism says that there are *no* absolute rules. So it has no answer for the Marquis de Sade, or Jeffrey Skilling, or anyone who says, "I don't care about your morality. I don't care about anyone else. I only care about what I want." If there is no absolute moral law, such a person is not wrong. We just do not like his views.

In Fyodor Dostoevsky's classic novel, *The Brothers Karamazov*, Ivan, the atheist brother, argues that if God does not exist, "nothing then would be immoral, everything would be lawful."[39] Joy Davidman wrote, "[Y]ou can't get a moral law out of materialism. There is no logical reason why a materialist shouldn't poison his nagging wife, if he can get away with it."[40]

But are all questions of morality merely matters of opinion? Is a murderer just a minority? Is slavery only a different social custom? Are cannibals merely carnivores with unusual tastes? We can only say that such things are truly wrong if we believe in real moral truth.

"Says Who?"

> "It would take gods to give men laws."
> —JEAN-JACQUES ROUSSEAU[41]

> "[B]y denying the existence of any higher authority, atheism has the . . . potential to free humans completely from any responsibility not to oppress one another."
> —FRANCIS COLLINS[42]

When I was a boy, my friends and I often played Monopoly, and we sometimes got into arguments. One boy would do something new or different, and another would say, "You can't do that." The first boy would respond, "Says who?" Unless we could find it in the rule sheet, that response usually prevailed. This is the relevant question here—*do you believe murder or torture or racism is wrong? If there is no God, "says who?"* If there is no "rule sheet," why should one religion, if it has the power, not outlaw other religions? Why should one race not oppress another? Timothy Keller wrote:

38. Exodus 20:13, 15, 16 (King James Version).
39. Dostoevsky, *The Brothers Karamazov*, 60, 244, 599.
40. Davidman, *Smoke on the Mountain*, 79.
41. Rousseau, *The Social Contract*, 37–38.
42. Collins, *The Language of God*, 42.

"You may say, 'the majority has the right to make the law,' but do you mean that . . . the majority has the right to vote to exterminate a minority? If you say, 'No, that is wrong,' then you are back to square one. Who sez . . . ?"[43]

Thomas Jefferson wrote that all men are "endowed by their creator with certain inalienable rights." Near the end of his life, Jefferson wrote to a friend of "the palpable truth, that the mass of mankind has not been born with saddles on their backs, nor a favored few booted and spurred, ready to ride them."[44] Abraham Lincoln, speaking of slavery, wrote of the:

> ". . . evident truth—made so plain by our good Father in heaven, that all feel and understand it . . . although volume upon volume is written to prove slavery a very good thing, we never hear of the man who wishes to take the good of it, by being a slave himself."[45]

Jefferson and Lincoln believed in "palpable" or "evident" moral truth because they believed in a Creator who was the source of that truth. If there is no God there is no moral truth, and we cannot logically condemn slavery or oppression.

Different Strokes for Different Folks?

"If at least one thing is really morally wrong—like it's wrong to torture babies, or it's wrong to intentionally fly planes into buildings with innocent people in them—then God exists."

—NORMAN GEISLER AND FRANK TUREK[46]

Another problem with moral relativism is that no one can live by it. The story is told of a philosophy student who wrote a paper arguing that there are no moral absolutes. It was well-researched and well-written. He even placed it in an attractive blue cover. But when he got the paper back, the professor had written a large "F" on it with a note, "I don't like blue covers." The student stormed into the professor's office: "An F? That's not fair!" The

---

43. Keller, *The Reason for God*, 159.

44. Letter to Roger Weightman, June 24, 1826; quoted Kristol, William, *The Weekly Standard*, August 2. 2010, 7.

45. From Lincoln's hand-written notes for an 1858 speech; Basker, *Abraham Lincoln in His Own Words*, 9.

46. Geisler and Turek, *I Don't Have Enough Faith to Be an Atheist*, 192.

professor replied, "Wasn't your paper the one that argued there is no such thing as fairness or justice? That it's just a matter of taste, like your preference for chocolate or vanilla ice cream? My taste is that I don't like blue covers." A "light bulb" went on for the student as he realized that he really did believe in some moral absolutes, at least in the rule of justice.[47] We all believe in moral absolutes when we are the ones treated wrongly.

There is a currently-popular idea known as "multi-culturalism." It says that all cultures are morally equal, and we should not hold ours to be better than any other. But is a society in which all people are treated equally no better than one which practices racism? Abraham Lincoln referred to the Supreme Court decision in the *Dred Scott* case, approving of slavery, as "blowing out the moral lights,"[48] and we all agree. *Moral relativists do not just prefer a more tolerant society, they believe that such a society is morally better.* Absolutists agree, and we have a basis for such a belief. If a moral relativist were consistent, he could only say, "Different strokes for different folks."

There have been two major social developments in America in my lifetime, the civil rights movement and the sexual revolution. I regard the civil rights movement as a textbook example of moral progress and the sexual revolution as an unmitigated moral tragedy. You can argue with me, but only if you believe in real moral truth. For a relativist, there is no right or wrong answer and therefore nothing for us to argue about.

We talk about moral "progress." But this assumes that one society (that which we are trying to achieve) is better than another (that which we have now). G. K. Chesterton wrote:

> "Nobody has any business to use the word 'progress' until he has a definite creed and a cast-iron code of morals... Never perhaps since the beginning of the world has there been an age that had less right to use the word 'progress' than we."[49]

Mahatma Ghandi, Martin Luther King, Jr., and all the moral reformers throughout history have criticized their cultures by holding them up to a *higher* moral standard.

Howard's Law #7 is: If your philosophy disagrees with Thomas Jefferson, Abraham Lincoln, Mahatma Ghandi, and Martin Luther King, Jr. about the moral law, your philosophy is probably wrong.

Moral relativism says that men make the rules, but materialism also says that all our actions and thoughts are determined by natural causes. If

---

47. Ibid., 173–174.
48. Galesburg, IL debate with Stephen Douglas, October 7, 1858; quoted Wilson, *Lincoln Before Washington*, 158.
49. Chesterton, *Heretics*, 14–15.

this is true, we do not make the rules after all—nature does. Moral relativists logically must agree with those who say that our moral notions are just the accidental products of nature, "as arbitrary as the fact that we've evolved five fingers rather than six."

Only if we have an absolute standard can we make meaningful moral judgments. But that standard cannot come from nature—you cannot get morality from matter. And it cannot come from us—nothing man-made can be absolute.

The Supernatural Law

"I know more certainly that torturing babies is wrong than I know that carbon atoms exist."

—J. P. MORELAND[50]

Only a theist can say that our moral notions are *objectively* true, that the moral law does not depend on our opinions, but is true whether we believe it or not. Christian philosopher William Lane Craig illustrates what it means to say that something is objectively right or wrong:

> "[T]o say that the holocaust was objectively wrong is to say it was wrong even though the Nazis who carried it out thought that it was right, and it would still have been wrong even if the Nazis had won World War II and succeeded in exterminating or brainwashing everyone who disagreed with them so that it was universally believed that the holocaust was right."[51]

Was the holocaust really wrong, or is that just a matter of opinion? If we all agreed the Nazis were right, would that make it so?

The Apostle Paul asked, what about those who have never heard the Old Testament law? He answered that they will be judged by the law that is *"written on their hearts."*[52] Our ancestors called this the natural law, but perhaps they should have called it the supernatural law. Christians believe that it comes from the character of God. It is right to love because God is Love. It is right to tell the truth because God is Truth. In C. S. Lewis' phrase,

---

50. Moreland, *Scaling the Secular City*, 119.
51. Craig, *Reasonable Faith*, 173.
52. Romans 2:15.

He is "a God who takes sides, who loves love and hates hatred."[53] We reflect His image in that the basics of His law are *"written on [our] hearts."*

The philosopher Immanuel Kant wrote his own epitaph, which read, "Two things fill my mind with ever new and increasing wonder and awe, the more often and persistently I reflect upon them: the starry heavens above me and the Moral Law within me."[54]

If I had to state only one reason why I believe there is a God, it would be that I am absolutely convinced there is a real right and wrong, and I cannot find any explanation for that fact other than a God who is righteous and who gave us the moral law.

Don't Impose Your Values on Me!

Let me add three brief concluding thoughts. First, if there are no moral absolutes, every society is going to determine for itself what is acceptable, because we must have rules in order to survive. This means that those in power (hopefully representing the majority, but often not) will make the laws for everyone else. Thus, moral relativism inevitably results in one group of people "imposing their values on others," exactly what Christians are accused of.

Second, if someone says, "I don't care about other people, I only care about what I want," a society based on moral relativism cannot say that he is wrong; he just has a different opinion. But if he violates the laws of that society, they will lock him up in prison, not because the laws are right or just—those words have no meaning—but simply because they can. *When a society does not believe in an absolute moral law, all that is left is force.*

Finally, moral absolutists are often accused of being arrogant: "What right do you have to tell me how to live?" But I would suggest that the absolutists are really the humble ones. We acknowledge that the moral law comes from God, so we have no right to argue with it or try to change it. Is the arrogant position not the one that says, "I am so wise I can determine for myself what is right or wrong?"

So these notions of right and wrong, what Thomas Jefferson called the "moral sense," Abraham Lincoln, "moral lights," and Martin Luther King, Jr., "the eternal oughtness that forever confronts [us]," are our next piece of evidence. We strongly believe in these moral notions. But only if Jefferson, Lincoln, and King were right that they are God-given, can we meaningfully say that they are true.

---

53. Lewis, *Mere Christianity*, 30.
54. Quoted Gingerich, *God's Universe*, 81.

At this point in our argument, I would ask you to notice what we have observed about ourselves so far—*we are conscious creatures in an unconscious world, rational creatures in a non-rational world, free creatures in an unfree world, and moral creatures in an amoral world. How has this come about?"* Has nature given us something it does not have? I believe the evidence strongly points to the conclusion that men are not only natural beings. We are conscious, rational, free, moral souls, created by a supernatural God in His image.

Chapter 6

"We Have Met the Enemy and He Is Us!"

Evidence from Human Moral Failings

> "The hand of Vengeance found the Bed
> To which the Purple Tyrant fled,
> The iron hand crushd the Tyrant's head
> And became a Tyrant in his Stead."
>
> —WILLIAM BLAKE.[1]

IN 1813, AFTER DEFEATING the British fleet in the Battle of Lake Erie, Commander Oliver Hazard Perry reported, "We have met the enemy and he is ours." A few years ago, the comic-strip character Pogo reworded that quote: "We have met the enemy and he is us!"[2]

The next thing we should notice about human beings is that there is something wrong with us. Mark Twain suggested, "Man was made at the end of the week's work when God was tired!"[3] In 1908, the *London Times* asked a number of writers to submit essays on the question, "What is wrong with the world?" G. K. Chesterton submitted by far the shortest response: "Dear sirs: I am. Sincerely yours, G. K. Chesterton."[4]

But if we are what is wrong with the world, what is wrong with us? I would suggest that our problem is moral. We strongly believe in certain

---

1. Blake, "The Gray Monk," 209.
2. Kelly, Walt, *Pogo*, Earth Day, 1971.
3. Quoted Payne, *Mark Twain, A Biography*, Vol. 3 & 4, 1195.
4. Quoted Kreeft, *Making Sense Out of Suffering*, 14.

moral standards, but we regularly violate those same standards. Until recent times, most all men have recognized this fact. In the fifth century, BC, Confucius wrote, "This is the Tao [moral law]. I do not know if any one has ever kept it."[5] Ancient religions almost all involved sacrifices, because ancient man understood that he had offended the gods.[6]

In modern times, it has become popular to talk only of the "goodness" of man. But this view cannot explain human history. In 1922, English author H. G. Wells wrote:

> "Can we doubt that presently our race will more than realize our boldest imaginations, that it will achieve unity and peace . . . [that our] children . . . will live in a world made more splendid and lovely than any palace or garden that we know, going on from strength to strength in an ever-widening circle of achievement?"[7]

But in 1946, after the horrors of World War II and the holocaust, Wells wrote:

> "A series of events has forced upon the intelligent observer the realization that the human story has already come to an end and that 'Homo Sapiens,' as he has been pleased to call himself, is in his present form played out."[8]

Before World War II, Wells was a believer in the optimistic idea that man is gradually progressing toward perfection. The events of that war gave him a more pessimistic view of human nature, but it was also a more realistic view. World War I was supposed to have been "the war to end all wars," but World War II began only twenty-one years later.

Warfare is as old as mankind. My wife and I have had the chance to travel in Europe several times, and I love to visit the old castle ruins. As you drive along the Rhine Valley in Germany, every six or eight miles you come to another romantic little town, each guarded by its ancient walls, and on the hill above, by its castle. Why were those walls and castles built? Was there some terrible invading army at one time that caused all the towns to build defenses? No. *They were built in each little town to defend themselves against each other, because one was always attacking the other.* Peter Kreeft

---

5. Quoted Vanauken, *A Severe Mercy*, 90.

6. Jeyachandran, "Tough Questions about Hinduism and Transcendental Meditation," 159–160.

7. Wells, *A Short History of the World*, 427.

8. Wells, *A Mind at the End of its Tether*, 18. The idea of juxtaposing these two quotes is borrowed from Keller, *The Reason for God*, 165.

wrote, "War is the stupidest idea in history: 'We have problems. Let's solve them by killing each other.' Yet history is full of this brilliant idea, and peace is the exception."[9]

Why do we kill one another? Why do we lie, cheat, or steal? Why do we not do what we know to be right? Why has no one ever fully done so? *It appears that there is a real moral law, which is both universally recognized and universally disobeyed.* C. S. Lewis called these two facts, that we know the moral law and that we break it, "the foundation of all clear thinking about ourselves and the universe we live in."[10]

Cures That Don't Work

"Nothing straight was ever made out of the crooked timbers of humanity."

—IMMANUEL KANT[11]

Many ideas have been tried, to solve what is wrong with the world, but all have failed. The greatest of these in the last century was Marxism. Karl Marx taught that the source of our problems was material—economic realities such as the profit motive were behind all the greed, envy and hatred in the world. So communist societies were established, where everything was owned by the state and distributed, theoretically, according to need. But instead of utopias, these societies became economic and social wrecks. Those in charge hoarded the wealth and power for themselves. The leaders of several of these countries became some of the greatest mass murderers in history. Instead of solving the problems of mankind, Marxism produced the Soviet Gulag, the purges under Chairman Mao, and the killing fields of Cambodia. *Marxism failed because greed did not result from bad economic systems. Rather, the economic systems, including communism, were corrupted by greed.*

George Orwell understood this in the 1940s, when many still looked to Marxism as the hope for the future. In his classic, *Animal Farm*, the animals overthrow the cruel, drunken humans and take over the farm. The pigs, being the smartest, take charge. They promise to see that everyone gets his "fair share." But the pigs soon prove to be just as greedy, dishonest, and cruel as the humans had been. The seven "commandments" they establish in the beginning are all changed, one by one, to benefit the pigs. Finally the most

---

9. Kreeft, *The Philosophy of Jesus*, 143.

10. Lewis, *Mere Christianity*, 7.

11. Kant, "Idea for a General History with a Cosmopolitan Purpose," 1784; quoted McGrath, *Mere Apologetics*, 189, n26.

important one of all is changed, from "All animals are equal," to "All animals are equal, but some animals are more equal than others."[12]

In this country, every politician of both parties will tell you that "education is the answer." In the early twentieth century, Columbia University psychologist John Dewey helped shape the modern American educational system. He believed that society's problems resulted from ignorance—if we taught our children how to deal with situations more intelligently, we could solve our social problems.[13] In contrast, Theodore Roosevelt said, "A man who has never gone to school may steal from a freight car; but if he has a university education, he may steal the whole railroad."[14] Who was right? After a century of universal education, do we make better choices than we did one hundred years ago? The problem has never been a shortage of good advice on how we ought to act; the problem is that we do not follow that advice. Education is a good thing, but it is not the answer.

Today we put our faith in science and technology. We have made more scientific advances in the last century than in the entire previous history of mankind. But while our technology has given us incredible medical advances and put a man on the moon, it has also given us deadlier weapons with which to kill one another, from the caveman's club to nuclear missiles. Technology is morally neutral—it can be used for either good or evil. Men invented gas ovens so that we could cook our food faster, and the Nazis used them to kill 6,000,000 Jews. We invented jet airplanes so that we could travel around the world faster, and used them to drop atomic bombs.[15]

All these attempted solutions have been well-meant, but all have failed. We still need our "castles," dead-bolt locks on our doors and expensive security systems. In fact, these things are more necessary in the so-called "developed" world than in the "third world."

Howard's Law #8 is: If your philosophy cannot explain why you need locks on your doors, your philosophy is probably wrong.

---

12. Orwell, *Animal Farm*, 123.

13. Dewey wrote that a teacher is "the prophet of the true God and the usherer in of the true kingdom of God." Dewey, "My Pedagogic Creed," 235.

14. Quoted Pine, *Wit and Wisdom of the American Presidents*, 38.

15. Kreeft, *Socrates Meets Descartes*, 236.

The Old Testament Answer

"If God lived on earth, people would break His windows."
—YIDDISH PROVERB[16]

"It is becoming more and more obvious that it is not starvation, nor microbes, nor cancer, but man himself who is mankind's greatest danger."
—CARL JUNG[17]

At the 1961 trial of Adolf Eichmann, one of the architects of the holocaust, concentration camp survivor Yehiel Dinur was called to testify. As soon as he entered the courtroom, he began to sob uncontrollably and then fainted. Years later, he explained to Mike Wallace on *60 Minutes* that what so upset him was seeing Eichmann in the courtroom and realizing that he was just an ordinary man. Dinur said, "I was afraid about myself . . . I saw that I am capable to do this. I am . . . exactly like he."[18]

What is wrong with the world? The answer is found in the Old Testament. Genesis 6:5 says, *"Then the LORD saw that the wickedness of man was great in the earth, and that every intent of the thoughts of his heart was only evil continually."* Jeremiah 6:13 says, *"From the least to the greatest, all are greedy for gain."* Communism failed because Karl Marx did not understand this. It is ironic, because Marx was raised in a Jewish family which converted to Christianity when he was a child.[19] But he forgot the teachings of the Old Testament.

I would suggest that our attempted solutions have all failed because we have misdiagnosed the problem, and bad diagnoses always lead to cures which do not work. The problem is not with human institutions, but with human nature. Jesus said, *"Out of the heart proceed evil thoughts, murders, adulteries . . . [and] theft."*[20]

President Obama, in his speech accepting the 2009 Nobel Peace Prize, said:

> "[M]ake no mistake: Evil does exist in the world. A nonviolent movement would not have halted Hitler's armies . . . To say that

---

16. Quoted Behe, *The Edge of Evolution*, 239.
17. Jung, "Epilogue," *Modern Man in Search of a Soul*; quoted McDowell and Stewart, *Answers to Tough Questions Skeptics Ask about the Christian Faith*, 124.
18. Quoted Colson, *Who Speaks for God?* 136–137.
19. Geisler, *Baker's Encyclopedia of Christian Apologetics*, 440.
20. Matthew 15:19.

force may sometimes be necessary is not a call to cynicism—it is a recognition of history, the imperfections of man and the limits of reason."[21]

Let me ask you to conduct a quick thought experiment. Imagine that in any major city in the world, all law enforcement were suddenly removed. What would happen? English author Francis Spufford wrote, "[P]eace is not the default state of human beings."[22]

The idea of evil has become very unpopular in Western cultures. When you and I talk about guilt, we usually just mean guilt *feelings*. We talk of "overcoming" our guilt. But our ancestors meant true guilt. They believed in a real moral law which we have really broken. When a jury returns a verdict of guilty, they are not commenting on the defendant's feelings; they are saying that he did it. When Scripture says we are guilty, it means the same thing—God said, *"Thou shalt not,"* and we did. Shakespeare expressed this understanding when he wrote in "The Merchant of Venice," "[I]n the course of justice, none of us should see salvation. We do pray for mercy."[23]

If the problem is with us, the solution must start with us. Confucius said:

> "If there is harmony in the heart, there will be harmony in the family.
> If there is harmony in the family, there will be harmony in the nation.
> If there is harmony in the nation, there will be harmony in the world."[24]

But as Russian novelist Leo Tolstoy wrote, "[E]verybody thinks of changing humanity, and nobody thinks of changing himself."[25] Joy Davidman was raised a Jew, then became a communist in her youth. Ultimately, she became a Christian. She wrote:

> "The ideal solution, of course, would be to remake our . . . society into a sound and safe one. But, let's admit it; we don't know how; and if we knew, we have not the power; and if we had the power, as long as we are sinners we should lack the love."[26]

---

21. Obama, "Remarks by the President at the Acceptance of the Nobel Peace Prize."

22. Spufford, *Unapologetic: Why, Despite Everything, Christianity Can Still Make Surprising Emotional Sense,* 12.

23. Shakespeare, "The Merchant of Venice," Act IV, Scene 1, 95.

24. Quoted Kreeft, *Back to Virtue,* 16. Similarly, the Trappist monk, Thomas Merton said, "Man is not at peace with his fellow man because he is not at peace with himself. He is not at peace with himself because he is not at peace with God." Quoted Kreeft, *Before I Go,* 124.

25. Tolstoy, "Three Methods of Reform," 29.

26. Davidman, *Smoke on the Mountain,* 69.

It's All About Me

This is the Old Testament answer—we are sinners. What does that mean? In the sixteenth century, Martin Luther defined sin with a Latin phrase, *"cor incurvatus ad se,"* "the heart turned in upon itself."[27] When our hearts turn inward, when we put our own interests ahead of others, when we insist on being in control of our own lives rather than yielding our wills to God's control, that is sin. The nineteenth-century Scottish writer, George MacDonald, wrote, "[T]he one principle of hell is—'I am my own.'"[28] John Milton wrote the best expression of sin I have ever read in the words he put into the mouth of Satan in *Paradise Lost*: "Better to reign in Hell than serve in Heaven."[29]

The sad truth is, while we agree that the essence of morality is to "love your neighbor as yourself," we are self-centered, self-absorbed, and just plain selfish. We are greedy, lustful, and envious of others who have good things. We lie, we cheat, we break our most solemn promises, just to get something we want. We are angry with, we hate, we look down on, we use and exploit our fellow man. We have broken every one of God's commandments, at least in spirit. And if we are honest with ourselves, we know that we are not the least bit likely to do any better tomorrow. It seems that the essence of our character is our self-centeredness. In other words, we are sinners.

You may have heard the old joke, "My momma called me 'son' because the world revolved around me!" But we all look at life that way—"It's all about me." *If you and I have problems, it's because you don't understand that it's all about me. You think it's about you!*[30] In all seriousness, I would suggest that this simple fact about human nature, not economics, education, politics, or anything else, is the cause of human conflict.

The Most Unpopular Doctrine of the Church

"Certainly nothing offends us more rudely than this doctrine [of original sin]; and yet, without this mystery, the most incomprehensible of all, we are incomprehensible to ourselves."

—BLAISE PASCAL[31]

---

27. Quoted Kinlaw, *We Live as Christ*, 32.
28. MacDonald, "Kingship," *Unspoken Sermons*, 264.
29. Milton, *Paradise Lost*, Book 1, Line 262, 10.
30. From a sermon by Dr. John Oswalt, Visiting Distinguished Professor of Old Testament, Asbury Theological Seminary.
31. Pascal, *Pensees*, #434, 121.

> "[I]t is not hard for me to believe that you are fallen. My problem comes when I must believe that I am fallen."
>
> —DENNIS KINLAW[32]

The Biblical teaching is that God made us good, but we rebelled against Him, in the persons of Adam and Eve, and became corrupted. We are no longer the way God made us. We are now *inclined* to be selfish, dishonest, greedy, and cruel. The story of how we got this way, told in Genesis chapter 3, is hard to understand, but as Pascal wrote, if we reject it, we cannot understand ourselves.

Malcolm Muggeridge, a twentieth-century British writer, said that this teaching, known as "the fall" or "original sin," is the most unpopular doctrine of the Church—and the only one that can be proven every day just by reading the newspaper![33] Mark Twain was an agnostic and a cynic, but he understood human nature:

> "Adam was but human—this explains it all. He did not want the apple for the apple's sake; he wanted it only because it was forbidden. The mistake was in not forbidding the serpent; then he would have eaten the serpent."[34]

One of Aesop's fables, written in the sixth century, BC, told of a man who was extremely jealous of his neighbor. The gods offered him anything he wanted, on the condition that his neighbor would receive twice as much. In his jealousy, he asked only to be made blind in one eye![35] The ancient Greeks understood human nature. We, on the other hand, have made ourselves naïve and seek the explanation for human conflict everywhere except where it can be found, in our own sinfulness.

This understanding, that we are sinners, is the true basis for democracy—no man can be trusted to rule over another. The American founding fathers understood this. In the Federalist Papers, James Madison wrote, "If men were angels, no government would be necessary. If angels were to govern men . . . [no] controls on government would be necessary."[36]

---

32. Kinlaw, *This Day with the Master*, May 18.

33. Quoted Kreeft, *C. S. Lewis for the Third Millennium*, 19.

34. Quoted Benardete, *Mark Twain's Wit and Wisecracks*, 1. Of course, the Biblical teaching is that this characteristic is a result of the fall, not the cause of it. Perhaps Twain understood human nature better than he understood Christian doctrine!

35. Aesop, "Avarice and Envious," quoted Davidman, *Smoke on the Mountain*, 120.

36. Madison, *The Federalist Papers*, #51, 322.

"What I Hate, That I Do"

> "[T]he ordinary condition of man is not his sane or sensible condition... the normal itself is an abnormality."
>
> —G. K. CHESTERTON[37]

We can see this tendency toward evil in ourselves. The Apostle Paul wrote:

> "[W]hat I am doing, I do not understand. For what I will to do, that I do not practice, but what I hate, that I do... I know that in me (that is, in my flesh), nothing good dwells, for to will is present with me, but how to perform what is good I do not find."[38]

The ancient Roman poet, Ovid, observed the same characteristic in himself:

> "One way desire, another reason calls;
> The better course I see and do approve—
> The worse I follow."[39]

The inclination to evil is not something we learn; it comes naturally to us. There is another characteristic which children show, from the time they can first express themselves: "I want it!" "It's mine!" "I want to do it my way!" Human selfishness starts young and so does human cruelty. G. K. Chesterton said that the greatest problem in philosophy is "why little Tommy loves to torture the cat."[40] I heard a preacher say once that he had no trouble understanding the Genesis story of Cain and Abel—he raised two boys![41]

Howard's Law #9 is: If your philosophy cannot explain why children fight, your philosophy is probably wrong.

Our fiction teaches us the same lesson. J. R. R. Tolkien, the long-time professor of literature at Oxford, said, "[A]ll stories are ultimately about the fall."[42] That is, we know that nothing, in us or in nature, is what it should be. To "ring true," a story must start with a problem. Like a good story must have characters making free choices, it must also include people and circumstances which have gone wrong.

---

37. Chesterton, *Orthodoxy*, 150.
38. Romans 7:15, 18.
39. Ovid, *Metamorpheses*, Book 7, 144.
40. Quoted Kreeft, *Making Sense out of Suffering*, 42.
41. From a sermon by John Oswalt.
42. Tolkien, *The Letters of J. R. R. Tolkien*, #131, 147.

Even the characteristics in us which reflect God's image are corrupted. Our sense of self is turned to selfishness, our reason confused, our free will limited by "slavery to sin,"[43] and our sense of right and wrong clouded. We cannot do what we want, want what we should, or think clearly.[44] We are fallen, no longer the way God made us.

The Dual Nature of Man

"Hitler is your relative . . . So is Mother Teresa."

—PETER KREEFT AND RONALD TACELLI[45]

But to say we are sinners is not to say that there is no good in us. In fact, Christians think far more highly of men than materialists do. We are not just accidental arrangements of atoms, but the height of God's creation. The Psalmist wrote that God made man *"a little lower than the angels . . . crowned . . . with glory and honor."*[46] The Biblical teaching is that we were made good, but we have gone bad. Man is like the Venus de Milo—ruined, but still a masterpiece.[47]

We should not confuse the teaching that we are both good and evil with the idea that we are both bodies and souls. It was the ancient Greeks who said that the soul is good and the body evil. Christians say that both are good, because God made both, but both are corrupted by the fall.

It is hard to overstate either half of this equation, the greatness of man as he was created, or the depths to which he has fallen. In C. S. Lewis' greatest sermon, "The Weight of Glory," he said:

> "It is a serious thing to live in a society of possible gods and goddesses, to remember that the dullest and most uninteresting person you talk to may one day be a creature which, if you saw it now, you would be strongly tempted to worship, or else a horror and corruption such as you now meet, if at all, only in a nightmare. All day long we are, in some degree, helping each other to one or other of those destinations. It is in the light of these overwhelming possibilities . . . that we should conduct all

---

43. Romans 6:6, 17–19; 7:15–20.

44. But as St. Thomas Aquinas wrote, "[S]in cannot entirely take away from man the fact that he is a rational being, for then he would no longer be capable of sin." Aquinas, *Summa Theologica*, Vol. 1, part 2, q85, 967.

45. Kreeft and Tacelli, *Handbook of Christian Apologetics*, 124.

46. Psalm 8:4–5.

47. Kreeft, *You Can Understand the Bible*, 236.

our dealings with one another, all friendships, all loves, all play, all politics. There are no ordinary people. You have never talked to a mere mortal. Nations, cultures, arts, civilizations—these are mortal, and their life is to ours as the life of a gnat. But it is immortals who we joke with, work with, marry, snub and exploit—immortal horrors or everlasting splendours."[48]

In the second of Lewis' Chronicles of Narnia, *Prince Caspian*, the title character learns that he is descended from a band of South Seas pirates. He tells the great lion, Aslan:

> "'I was wishing that I came of a more honorable lineage.' 'You come of the Lord Adam and the Lady Eve,' said Aslan. 'And that is both honor enough to erect the head of the poorest beggar and shame enough to bow the shoulders of the greatest emperor in earth.'"[49]

Russian Nobel Peace Prize-winner Aleksandr Solzhenitsyn wrote, "[T]he line dividing good and evil cuts through the heart of every human being."[50] We are, each one of us, able to rise to great heights of nobility or sink to extreme depths of cruelty and depravity.

The Dual Nature of Nature

The Bible also teaches that nature has a dual nature—*it is both beautiful and broken.*[51] In Genesis, after God finished creating, He described everything He had made as "very good."[52] As the old country preacher said, "God don't make no junk!"

But we know that something is badly wrong with the world. "Like in a broken mirror, every image is distorted."[53] The universe contains great love, beauty, and joy, but also great cruelty, ugliness, and sorrow. How can we reconcile these facts? The Old Testament answer is that God made the world good, but that nature, like man, is corrupted as a result of the fall. Our experience tells us the same thing. This world has exactly the appearance of something made good and beautiful, but then corrupted. Lewis wrote,

---

48. Lewis, "The Weight of Glory," 14–15.
49. Lewis, *Prince Caspian*, 211–212.
50. Solzhenitsyn, *The Gulag Archipelago*, Vol. 1, 168.
51. Ordway, *Not God's Type*, 104.
52. Genesis 1:31.
53. This is a paraphrase of John Calvin. See Chalke and Watkis, *Intelligent Church*, 55.

"Nature, like us but in her different way, is much alienated from her Creator, though in her, as in us, gleams of the old beauty remain."[54]

I love strawberries. I believe my wife's strawberry pie is the best dessert in the world, and I like desserts! I once jokingly proposed that strawberries were not affected by the fall, but were perfect. A friend pointed out that they spoil. But strawberries represent very well the entire universe in this respect—it is full of joys of every kind, but all material objects decay.

Is Sin an Argument for God?

It sounds odd to suggest that sin is an argument for the existence of God. But only the Judeo-Christian tradition, with its twin doctrines of a perfect creation followed by a catastrophic fall, can explain both good and evil.

For a pantheist, good and evil are just a matter of how we look at things. We call cancer evil because it kills a man. We could just as well call chemotherapy evil because it kills a cancer.[55]

For a materialist, everything is the result of either chance or natural laws. Good and evil are only human concepts. But even on these terms, while natural selection might lead to what we call evil—selfishness, violence, deception, and treachery seem to be behaviors which would promote survival—it will never lead to what we somehow know to call good. True altruism, looking out for the interests of the other person, family, or tribe, cannot be explained by natural selection.

But if materialism cannot explain good, I would suggest that modernist or liberal Christianity, when it ignores the unpopular teaching of the fall, cannot explain evil. If a good God made a good world, why is there evil? *This world appears to be designed. But in its present state, it does not appear to be designed by a perfect, loving, and all-powerful designer.* It is intricately and beautifully put together, but it is fundamentally and fatally flawed. If we reject God, we cannot explain the design. If we reject the doctrine of the fall, we cannot explain the flaws. We will discuss the question of evil and suffering in more depth later, but I would submit that the only explanation for both good and evil, in both men and nature, is that we were made good, but we are fallen. Peter Kreeft wrote:

> "The human lock is weirdly shaped. The Biblical key is also weirdly shaped: a story of radical tragedy at our very roots. There are all sorts of difficulties with the story. But it fits—the key fits

---

54. Lewis, "On Living in an Atomic Age," 79.
55. Lewis, *Mere Christianity*, 30.

the lock. *What happened in Eden may be hard to understand, but it makes everything else understandable.*"[56] (emphasis added)

There Is Hope!

The doctrine of the fall not only explains what is wrong with the world; it says that there is hope. Sin is "our disease, not our design."[57] If violence and cruelty are our natural state, Stephen Hawking's plan, to move men to various planets so that we cannot wipe ourselves out all at once, may be the best answer. But if we are only sick, we might be cured! The Biblical story is in three stages—we were made good, we have gone bad, and we will one day be redeemed. Christianity teaches that the entire Bible is the story of God's plan for our salvation and our cure from sin, substantially in this life and totally in the life to come.

On Christmas Day, 1863, while America was mired in the Civil War, and after hearing that his oldest son had been wounded in battle, Henry Wadsworth Longfellow wrote a poem which he called, "Christmas Bells." He intended it as a commentary on war. That anti-war poem was later put to music, and we know it today as the Christmas carol, "I Heard the Bells on Christmas Day." The third verse reads:

> "Then in despair I bowed my head.
> There is no peace on earth, I said.
> For hate is strong and mocks the song
> Of peace on Earth, good will to men."

But Longfellow had hope, because he believed in God. The fourth verse says:

> "Then rang the bells, more loud and deep:
> God is not dead nor doth He sleep.
> The wrong shall fail, the right prevail,
> With peace on Earth, good will to men."[58]

A Christian can be an optimist. A materialist must ultimately be a pessimist.

You will notice that we have made a turn in this chapter, from human characteristics which we would call "normal" or "good," to something

---

56. Kreeft, *Heaven: The Heart's Deepest Longing*, 216.
57. Kreeft, *Christianity for Modern Pagans*, 148.
58. Longfellow, Henry Wadsworth, "Christmas Bells." 1863.

which is wrong with us. We will look in the next two chapters at two other characteristics which seem not to be what they should be. But this piece of evidence may be the strangest of them all—that we humans, born with strong moral notions, all fail to follow them. The Judeo-Christian tradition, with its old-fashioned teachings of sin and the fall, offers the only explanation for this odd fact.

Chapter 7

"I Can't Get No Satisfaction"

Evidence from Human Desire

"I have now reigned above fifty years in victory or peace; beloved by my subjects, dreaded by my enemies and respected by my allies. Riches and honors, power and pleasure, have waited on my call . . . In this situation I diligently numbered the days of pure and genuine happiness which have fallen to my lot; they amount to fourteen. O man, place not thy confidence in this present world!"

—ABD AL-RAHMAN, EIGHTH-CENTURY EMIR OF CORDOVA.[1]

SOME YEARS AGO MY wife and I had the chance to visit Switzerland. We spent several days in the beautiful Alpine village of Wengen, accessible only by mountain railroad. We stood on our balcony and looked out over the Lauterbrunnen Valley, almost a thousand feet below us. We could see waterfalls tumbling down the other side. There was a mountain rising straight up behind us and in almost every direction, some of the highest peaks in the Alps, snow-capped year 'round. We declared it "the most beautiful place on earth." But while we were there, we visited a doctor's office, and as I sat in the waiting room, I noticed something—the pictures on the walls were all of beaches! In "the most beautiful place on earth," a mile high in the Swiss Alps, they dream of the beach!

Before Sharon and I were married, I had read several books on marriage. Our pastor had counseled with us. I had heard all the wise sayings:

---

1. Quoted Gibbon, Edward, *The History of the Decline and Fall of the Roman Empire*; quoted Robertson, *Handbook of Preaching Resources from Literature*, 85.

"There is no such thing as a perfect marriage between two imperfect people;" "To make a happy marriage, you need two people who have already learned how to be happy;" and so forth. I had very realistic expectations, I thought. I did not expect her to make me happy all the time. But it had never occurred to me that being married to me was not going to make her happy all the time! The first time she was unhappy with me, I was stunned. How could she be married to the world's greatest husband and not be happy? But I discovered that sometimes, she is really hard to satisfy! And so am I, and so are you.

This is part of human nature—*we are not happy*. Very few people are truly and deeply happy, and no one is totally satisfied. While we have moments of great joy, we all have, deep in our hearts, an unfulfilled desire which we cannot name, but which always leaves us wanting something more. This theme is repeated again and again in popular music. Mick Jagger lamented, "I Can't Get No Satisfaction."[2] Peggy Lee asked, "Is That All There Is?"[3] The Irish band, U-2, sang, "I Still Haven't Found What I'm Looking For."[4]

But we want to be happy. Aristotle said that the search for happiness is the primary goal of every man.[5] And we seek happiness for its own sake—we seek everything else, including money, sex, and power, in order to be happy. We have all heard the expression, "Money can't buy happiness." No one ever said, "Happiness can't buy money."[6]

The Grass Is Always Greener

"This world is wonderful and rich; it sets before us countless treasures; it enchants us; it attracts both our reason and our will. But in the end, it does not satisfy our spirit."

—POPE JOHN PAUL II[7]

---

2. Jagger, Mick and Richards, Keith, "I Can't Get No Satisfaction," ABKCO Music, 1963.

3. Leiber, Jerry and Stoller, Mike, "Is That All There Is?" Jerry Leiber and Mike Stoller Music, 1966.

4. Bono and The Edge, "I Still Haven't Found What I'm Looking For," Universal-Polygram Music, 1987.

5. Mitchell, *Ethics and Moral Reasoning*, 59. For Aristotle and the ancient Greeks, happiness was not merely a feeling. It was a deep sense of well-being, or "human flourishing." Ibid.

6. Kreeft, *Because God Is Real*, 189–190.

7. John Paul II, "Message for World Youth Day, 1997;" quoted *Pope John Paul II: His Essential Wisdom*, 43.

We have many ways of expressing this desire. We call it restlessness. We say that the grass is always greener on the other side of the fence. When John D. Rockefeller was asked how much money was enough, he answered, "Just a little bit more."[8] Aldous Huxley said, "There comes a time when one asks even of Shakespeare, even of Beethoven, is this all?"[9]

Many things in life promise to satisfy this longing. When we were children, we thought some new toy would bring true happiness. Some adults still think this! When we are falling in love, beginning a new career, even starting a vacation, we feel the excitement. But none of these things ever keep their promise. This is true not only of bad marriages or bad careers; even the best ones fall short.[10] As we get older, we look back on our youth, and it almost seems that we had it back then. We call the longing for those times "nostalgia." But if we remember well enough, we know that we were not satisfied in our youth, only hopeful that we would find satisfaction in the future. Benjamin Franklin wrote, "The Golden Age never was the present Age."[11] Or as someone said, "Nostalgia just ain't what it used to be!"

C. S. Lewis illustrated the illusiveness of this desire in one of the Chronicles of Narnia, *The Voyage of the Dawn Treader*. A little girl, Lucy, is in a magician's house and reads a magical book. One story is "the most beautiful story she had ever read." But she immediately forgets the story and cannot recall it, no matter how hard she tries. Lewis adds, "And she never could remember; and ever since that day, what Lucy means by a good story is a story which reminds her of the forgotten story in the Magician's Book."[12]

Sigmund Freud wrote that ancient man invented the gods to fulfill his "fairy-tale wish" for power. He said that modern man, through technology, "has almost become a god himself." But he also observed, "[P]resent-day man does not feel happy in his God-like character."[13]

If happiness came from material possessions, twenty-first-century Americans should be the happiest people in history, but we are not. Joy Davidman wrote:

> "Modern men . . . have for two hundred years or so looked for the earthly paradise ahead of them . . . With power and machines, one could stuff every man's belly with chicken, drape

---

8. Quoted Cockerill, *Christian Faith in the Old Testament*, 117.
9. Quoted Smith, *The Religions of Man*, 23.
10. Lewis, *Mere Christianity*, 105.
11. Franklin, *Poor Richard's Almanac*, 48.
12. Lewis, *The Voyage of the Dawn Treader*, 133.
13. Freud, *Civilization and its Discontents*, 28–29.

every woman's shoulders with silk, fill every child's heart with laughter . . .

As far as material goods go, our earthly paradise has given us more, far more, than the first progress worshipers ever dreamed possible. Yet there is one indispensable condition of paradise lacking. We are not happy in the place."[14]

We now have, in almost every town in America, storage units for rent, where we can put all the "stuff" we do not need and have no room for. Yet we suffer from more depression than any society in history.[15] Our material possessions have not made us happy.

In fact, some of the unhappiest people are those who "have it all." After Jack Higgins became a best-selling author, he said the main thing he had learned was, "When you get to the top, there's nothing there."[16] This is why suicide rates are higher among the rich than the poor, and why we see so much self-destructive behavior among movie stars, popular musicians, and professional athletes. The rest of us can tell ourselves that if we could just fulfill one more dream or obtain one more possession, we would be happy. The rich and famous know better.

"Preach to the Broken-Hearted"

Not only are we not satisfied when things are going well; things do not always go well. We experience real heartbreak. We lose loved ones. We face health problems, career disappointments, and financial setbacks. We have dreams that do not come true. The story is told of an old preacher who spoke to a group of young pastors. He gave them this advice: "When you preach, preach to the broken-hearted. You will find them every Sunday in every pew."

This is the human experience. I do not mean to be depressing, but we hear repeated, again and again, the claim that we can find happiness in the things of this world. We hear it most often, I suspect, from people trying to sell us something. But it is not true. If there is any hope for real joy, it will not come from a McDonalds hamburger or even a BMW automobile, although "Joy" was a recent advertising slogan for both of those companies. Real joy will not come from this world at all.

---

14. Davidman, *Smoke on the Mountain*, 116, 118.
15. Seligman, *Authentic Happiness*, 117–118.
16. Quoted Zacharias, *Can Man Live Without God?* 56.

Why Does Nature Feel Unnatural?

> "A fish feels at home in the water. If we 'belonged here,' we should feel at home here... If this world is the only world, how did we come to find its laws either so dreadful or so comic? If there is no straight line elsewhere, how did we discover that nature's line is crooked?"
>
> —C. S. LEWIS[17]

Why are we not satisfied? Why does nature feel unnatural? We not only want more; we feel that we should have more, that things are not what they should be. Blaise Pascal asked, "Who indeed is unhappy at not being a king except a dispossessed king?... Who is unhappy at having only one mouth? And who is not unhappy at having only one eye?"[18]

Materialism cannot explain this odd fact. It can only say that our longing for something more must result from some chance mutation in the genes of one of our remote ancestors, which was passed down to us, in spite of the fact that it does not seem to be useful.

Pantheism offers a lot of good advice about how to handle our dissatisfaction, but no explanation of where it comes from, nor any hope that satisfaction is possible. Buddha rightly observed that getting what we want does not make us happy; it only makes us fearful that we will lose what we have wished for and obtained.[19] But his only solution was to learn not to want anything, so that we would not be disappointed.

Howard's Law #10 is: If your philosophy cannot explain why Mick Jagger "can't get no satisfaction," nor why you and I can't either, your philosophy is probably wrong.

Paradise Lost

"All men seek happiness. This is without exception... [Yet] all men complain ...A trial so long, so continuous, and so uniform, should certainly convince us

---

17. Lewis, "On Living in an Atomic Age," 78.
18. Pascal, *Pensees*, #409, 109.
19. Kreeft, *Christianity for Modern Pagans*, 170.

of our inability to reach the good by our own efforts... the infinite abyss can only be filled by an infinite and immutable object, that is to say, God Himself."

—BLAISE PASCAL[20]

Christianity, on the other hand, explains both why we have this longing and what it is we are seeking. St. Augustine argued that our unfulfilled desire is a clue to the existence of God. He wrote, "Thou hast formed us for Thyself, and our hearts are restless till they find rest in Thee."[21] St. Thomas Aquinas wrote, "Man cannot live without joy. That is why a man deprived of spiritual joys goes over to carnal pleasures."[22] There is a quote which has been attributed to Pascal which says, "There is in every human heart a God-shaped vacuum that only He can fill."[23]

No one has ever described this desire better than C. S. Lewis. He wrote:

> "There was something we grasped at, in that first moment of longing, which just fades away in the reality. I think everyone knows what I mean. The wife may be a good wife, and the hotels and scenery may have been excellent, and chemistry may be a very interesting job; but something has evaded us."[24]

But Lewis believed that we can eventually find what we are seeking. In the last of The Chronicles of Narnia, *The Last Battle*, the main characters find themselves in Heaven, and then:

> "It was the unicorn who summed up what everyone was feeling. He stamped his right fore-hoof on the ground and neighed and then cried: 'I have come home at last! This is my real country! This is the land I have been looking for all my life, though I never knew it till now. The reason why we loved the old Narnia is that it sometimes looked a little like this.'"[25]

Lewis also provided the answer to the objection that desiring something does not prove we will obtain it:

---

20. Pascal, *Pensees*, #425, 113.
21. Augustine, *Confessions*, Book 1, §1, Pilkington, 1.
22. Aquinas, *Summa Theologica*, §II: II, q35, a4; quoted Kreeft, *Ecumenical Jihad*, 55.
23. The attribution to Pascal, though often repeated, is apparently erroneous. See McGrath, *Mere Apologetics*, 109.
24. Lewis, *Mere Christianity*, 105.
25. Lewis, *The Last Battle*, 171.

"A man's physical hunger does not prove that man will get any bread; he may die of starvation on a raft in the Atlantic. But surely a man's hunger does prove that he comes of a race which repairs its body by eating and inhabits a world where eatable substances exist. In the same way, though I do not believe (I wish I did) that my desire for Paradise proves that I shall enjoy it, I think it is a pretty good indication that such a thing exists and that some men will. A man may love a woman and not win her; but it would be very odd if the phenomenon called 'falling in love' occurred in a sexless world."[26]

Lewis summarized his argument this way: "If I find in myself a desire which no experience in this world can satisfy, the most probable explanation is that I was made for another world."[27]

The Christian teaching is that our secret, inconsolable desire can only be satisfied by God, because it is the desire for Him. George MacDonald wrote, "He that is made in the image of God must know Him or be desolate."[28] Dennis Kinlaw said, "He made us for companionship with deity."[29] But that companionship was lost in the fall. Our longing is for what our lives were meant to be. We have born into us a hint, a memory, of the way things were in Eden and will be in Heaven. As the gospel song says:

"I'm kind of homesick for a country
To which I've never been before."[30]

So I would suggest that the desire for something this world does not offer did not come from this world. It is evidence that we are not only natural beings, but were made by a supernatural Creator with a longing for Him, if we would only recognize it. Our next piece of evidence is this unfulfilled desire, present in every human being and satisfied in none. Only Christianity can explain where it comes from or what it is we are seeking.

---

26. Lewis, "The Weight of Glory," 32–33.
27. Lewis, *Mere Christianity*, 106.
28. MacDonald, "The Word of Jesus on Prayer," *Unspoken Sermons*, 126.
29. Kinlaw, *Let's Start with Jesus*, 45.
30. Parsons, Squire, "Sweet Beulah Land," Bridge Building, 1973.

"I'm Married to the Wrong Person"

> "Made for joy, we settle for pleasure."
> —N. T. WRIGHT[31]

Before we go on, let me ask, how should we respond to this dissatisfaction? One response is to blame our circumstances: "I'm married to the wrong person;" "I'm in the wrong career;" "If I only had more money." This response seems to be most prevalent in wealthy societies like ours. We see it in many of the rich and famous, who go from one lover to another or one "cause" to another.

We see it in ourselves when we look for short-term pleasures or thrills, whether in sex, drugs, or anything else. Where I live, the number one problem, both for law enforcement and for family courts, is methamphetamine abuse. It is a horrible drug, a poison, destroying people's bodies, lives, and families. Why would anyone put such a thing into his body? I am told that the number one "selling point" for meth is the claim that it will increase sexual pleasure.

On a lesser level, it seems to me that the "extreme" sports which have become popular with young people fall into this category. I am a sports fan, and I am not against extreme sports. So long as a person does not put himself in real danger, there is nothing that I know of wrong with any of them. But if he thinks they are going to satisfy the deepest longing of his heart, he is mistaken. Not even Kentucky basketball can do that!

It is not only the youth who are looking for thrills. A friend of mine is a pastor in New Jersey. He says that the largest age group gambling in the casinos of Atlantic City is senior citizens. These people represent the experience and wisdom of our society. What does it say when they take that wisdom and experience and put it into a slot machine?[32] I believe it says that we are a restless people, and we often respond to that restlessness foolishly, no matter what our age.

In my law practice, I am constantly amazed at how many people I see who leave their spouses, families, or jobs, just because, "I'm not happy." But they are rarely any happier a few years later. Second marriages end in divorce more often than first marriages do. *This is because the problem is not primarily with the wife or the husband or the job. The problem is that we are asking them*

---

31. Wright, *Simply Christian*, 202.

32. From a sermon by Dr. Ronald E. Smith, Pastor, St. John's United Methodist Church, Blackwood, New Jersey.

for something they can never give. Even the best things in this world were never meant to satisfy our deepest longing. Only God can do that.

Of course, the same formula applies here as elsewhere—we can experience this satisfaction substantially in this life, but fully only in the life to come. This is because we cannot fully experience the joy God has for us until we are in perfect relationship with Him. We cannot have that relationship until sin no longer gets in the way, until we are "perfect as [our] Father in heaven is perfect."[33] But the great saints report that even in this life, the closer to God we live, the more of His joy we will experience.

We have been talking about the best things in life. If you look to short-term pleasures or thrills for true happiness, you will always be disappointed. Not only can these things never satisfy you; they operate on the law of diminishing returns. The second time is not as great a thrill as the first, the third high is not as high as the second, and so forth. So you constantly look for something new. But you will never find satisfaction in these things.

Don't Think About It

"As men are not able to fight against death, misery, ignorance, they have taken it into their heads, in order to be happy, not to think of them at all."

—BLAISE PASCAL[34]

Another way we respond to our unhappiness is to avoid thinking about it. We dull our minds with drugs or alcohol. (Most substance abuse is not for thrills, but for escape.) We turn to diversions—work, sports, hobbies, even television. We will watch almost *anything*. How else can you explain the Kardashians? Then we ask, "Where did all our time go?" We have hundreds of labor-saving devices our parents and grandparents did not have, yet we seem to have less free time than they did. Peter Kreeft suggests the reason:

> "We *want* to complexify our lives. We don't *have* to; we *want* to. We want to be harried and hassled and busy . . . For if we had leisure, we would look at ourselves and listen to our hearts and see the great gaping hole in our hearts and be terrified, because that hole is so big that nothing but God can fill it."[35] (emphasis in original)

---

33. Matthew 5:48.
34. Pascal, *Pensees*, #168, 49.
35. Kreeft, *Christianity for Modern Pagans*, 168.

But ultimately, the diversions do not work. Ralph Barton was one of the leading American cartoonists of the twentieth century. He left this note on his pillow before taking his life:

> "I have had few difficulties, many friends, great successes; I have gone from wife to wife and from house to house, visited great countries of the world, but I am fed up with inventing devices to fill up twenty-four hours of the day."[36]

"That's All There Is"

A third way we may respond is by becoming cynics. We learn to just accept life, with all its sorrows. We answer Peggy Lee's question by saying, "Yes, that's all there is." If real satisfaction is not possible, this may be the best approach to life. I suspect it allows the one who adopts it to get through life better, and I am sure it makes him easier to get along with for the rest of us!

Most of the pantheistic religions seem to teach a version of this response. The most basic teaching of Buddhism is found in the "Four Noble Truths"—1) All life is suffering; 2) The cause of suffering is desire; 3) The way to end suffering is to end desire; and 4) The way to end desire is through the Noble Eight-fold Path.[37]

A few years ago, after Tiger Woods was caught in his sex scandal, he stated at a press conference that he had "drifted away" from his Buddhist upbringing, which taught him "to stop following every impulse and to learn restraint." Most of us agreed that he needed to learn that lesson. But Boston University professor Stephen Prothero, writing in *U.S.A. Today*, suggested that Woods had taught America that other religions besides Christianity offer "redemption." The only difference, according to Dr. Prothero, is that Christianity offers redemption from what it calls "sin," and Buddhism from what it calls "cravings."[38] But to what end does Buddhism teach restraint? So that we can get to the point of having no desires at all? Is this the redemption we desperately want?

---

36. Quoted Bright, *Jesus and the Intellectual*, 33.
37. Quoted Kreeft, *Making Sense Out of Suffering*, 3–4.
38. Prothero, "A Buddhist Moment in America," 11A.

"Your Heart Will Rejoice"

The Christian way is different—Scripture promises us real joy. Jesus said, *"I came . . . that they might have life and have it more abundantly;"*[39] *"These things I have spoken to you . . . that your joy may be full;"*[40] and *"Your heart will rejoice, and your joy no one will take from you."*[41]

The promise is not that our circumstances will change, but that we can find joy in those circumstances. In Philippians, the Apostle Paul wrote, *"Make my joy complete;"*[42] *Rejoice in the Lord always, and again I say, rejoice;"*[43] and *"I have learned in whatever state I am, therein to be content."*[44] (This is how we know Paul was not from Kentucky!) Paul wrote Philippians from a Roman prison, facing possible execution, but he wrote about joy.

At its heart, Christianity is not about suppressing our desires, but fulfilling them. It is not about self-denial, but joy. Please do not misunderstand me—Christianity talks a great deal about self-denial. Jesus said, *"If anyone desires to come after Me, let him deny himself, and take up his cross, and follow Me."*[45] But almost every promise of what will result if we do so contains an appeal to desire.[46] Christian self-denial is always the denial of the lesser, in order that God can give us something greater. The old Christian teachers said that the pleasures of earth are just weak reflections of the pleasures of Heaven, and that if we were to experience those Heavenly pleasures in this life, they would kill us! Lewis said:

> "The faint, far-off results of those energies which God's creative rapture implanted in matter when He made the worlds are what we now call physical pleasures; and even thus filtered, they are too much for our present management. What would it be to taste at the fountain-head that stream of which even these lower reaches prove so intoxicating? Yet that, I believe, is what lies before us. The whole man is to drink joy from the fountain of joy."[47]

---

39. John 10:10.
40. John 15:11.
41. John 16:22.
42. Philippians 2:2.
43. Philippians 4:4.
44. Philippians 4:11.
45. Matthew 16:24.
46. Lewis, "The Weight of Glory," 26.
47. Ibid., 44.

"[I]t would seem that Our Lord finds our desires not too strong, but too weak. We are half-hearted creatures, fooling about with drink, sex and ambition when infinite joy is offered us."[48]

If Christianity is true, we are meant to experience this "infinite joy," real satisfaction of the deepest longing of our hearts. Would it not be a shame to find out too late that real joy was possible, and we missed it?

---

48. Ibid., 26.

Chapter 8

"The Most Urgent Wish of Mankind"
Evidence from the Human Desire for Immortality

"Life is real! Life is earnest!
And the grave is not its goal;
Dust thou art, to dust returnest
Was not spoken of the soul."

—HENRY WADSWORTH LONGFELLOW.[1]

I AM ON THE board of trustees of a seminary. After a board meeting a few years ago, I had the chance to play golf with another board member, a wonderful Christian man and a successful businessman. But a few months earlier, his doctors had told him that he had inoperable cancer. As the afternoon went on, I discovered that I had trouble finding things to talk about. I did not want to make him uncomfortable, but I was uncomfortable. I got by, I think, making small talk, but it was difficult. As I wondered about this later, I thought, "I guess I have never played golf before with someone who is dying." But the truth is, I have never played golf with anyone who is not dying, including myself. As they said in the old Westerns, "Nobody gets out of this place alive." But we live in denial. We go days, even weeks or months or years, without thinking about death, until the doctor gives us the diagnosis, and the reality becomes unavoidable.

Another unique characteristic of human beings is that we think about the past, which is no longer real (it is gone forever), and we imagine the future, which is not yet real. We also want the future to last. But it will not last,

---

1. Longfellow, "A Psalm of Life," 266.

not for us, not in this life. The death rate of the human race never changes—it is one hundred per cent.

A friend of mine was a pall bearer in a funeral. It is customary where I live for one of the pall bearers to ride to the cemetery in the front of the hearse. By oversight, no one did. My friend apologized to the funeral director: "I'm sorry. I should have ridden with you in the hearse." The funeral director responded with a slight smile, "Don't worry, you will."

Throughout history, from the ancient cave-man to today's new-born baby, from emperors to slaves, from Mother Teresa to Adolph Hitler, all have lived their brief time on earth and departed, or will. Some have died violently, some "naturally," some young, and some old, but we all die.

"No One Believes in His Own Death"

All animals die—man is unique in that he knows it. But we do not want to die. Woody Allen said, "I don't want to live on in the hearts of my countrymen; I want to live on in my apartment!"[2] *In fact, we want to live forever.* The strange thing is, we naturally believe that we should live forever. Sigmund Freud wrote:

> "We cannot, indeed, imagine our own death; whenever we try to do so we find that we survive ourselves as spectators . . . [A]t bottom no one believes in his own death, which amounts to saying: in the unconscious every one of us is convinced of his immortality."[3]

Freud was right. Do you remember the scene in *Tom Sawyer*, when everyone thinks Tom and Huck Finn have drowned, and the boys sneak into the gallery of the church and watch their own funeral?[4] If we try to imagine being dead, we see ourselves still conscious, still watching, like Tom and Huck.

This desire to live forever is as old as human history. The Babylonian "Epic of Gilgamesh," dating from the eighteenth century, BC, tells of the hero's life-long search for immortality. Finally he is told by the gods that his search is hopeless; only they can live forever: "When the gods created man they allotted to him death, but life they retained in their own keeping."[5]

The alchemists of the middle ages did not merely attempt to turn base metals into gold. Their greatest hope was to find the "elixir of life," which

---

2. Quoted Lopatin, "Indestructible Dream," 38.
3. Freud, "Reflections on War and Death."
4. Twain, *The Adventures of Tom Sawyer*, 106–110.
5. Sanders, "The Epic of Gilgamesh," 17.

would make them immortal. The sixteenth-century Spanish explorer, Ponce de Leon, sailed to Florida searching for the "fountain of youth." In the twentieth century, Walt Disney found a fountain of money in Florida, but no one has ever found a fountain of youth! And no matter how much money we have, we still grow old, we still die, and we still can't take it with us.

A few years ago, there was a popular movie called "Cocoon," about a group of senior citizens who were visited by space aliens. They were given the chance to go with the aliens on their spaceship. If they did, they would never be able to return to Earth or see their families again, but they would never grow any older and never die. The drama was how each individual struggled to make that choice. All but one chose to go.[6]

Most men have concluded that this life, with its inevitable suffering, should not go on forever, but have believed there will be life after death. A few years ago, my family and I visited the Field Museum of Natural History in Chicago. One of the featured exhibits was the Egyptian Collection, room after room of fabulous treasures from ancient Egypt, *all originally preserved in tombs, for the benefit of the dead*. Mankind's oldest book is believed to be *The Egyptian Book of the Dead*, written to prepare a person for death and the life thereafter.

We consider those ancient cultures naïve. We believe in science. But a few years ago, we witnessed the sad story of Ted Williams, the baseball great. After he died, his family engaged in a botched attempt to freeze his body in the hope that someday science would find a way to bring him back to life.[7] Whatever form it has taken, men from the beginning of history have had an innate belief either that we should not die, or that we should live again after death.

Is Nature Wrong?

Nothing is more natural than death. Why do we find it unnatural? We not only fight against dying; we are offended by it. *When it comes to death, it is human nature to believe that nature is wrong*, that we should not die. Freud called the various beliefs in life after death "illusions," but he also called them, "fulfillments of the oldest, strongest and most urgent wishes of mankind."[8] Old Testament scholar Sandra Richter wrote, "Adam remembers

---

6. "Cocoon," 20th Century Fox, 1985.
7. Montville, *Ted Williams: The Biography of an American Hero*, 455–469.
8. Freud, *The Future of an Illusion*, 26.

... Humanity somehow knows that it should not die, even though in all remembered experience, humanity has died."[9] Peter Kreeft wrote:

> "It is a remarkable fact that all the myths throughout the world see death not as natural but as unnatural, as an accident, a fall, a mistake, a catastrophe that could have been averted but wasn't. The myth of paradise lost is universal, appearing in many forms. Adam eats forbidden fruit; Pandora opens a box; a bird drops the magic berry of immortality; Primal Woman throws a stone at the sky and chases the gods away. Only then does death appear. Why do all the variations insist on this single theme of paradise lost, of death as an accident? Because death does not feel natural, however biologically necessary it may be ... Man does not feel like recycled fertilizer."[10]

Howard's Law #11 is: If your philosophy cannot explain why the ancient Egyptians, Sigmund Freud, and you and I all find death unnatural, your philosophy is probably wrong.

In 2011, *Time* magazine ran a cover story about optimism. The subheading read, "Hope isn't rational—so why are humans wired for it?"[11] The article did not really answer the question, just suggesting a few ways optimism may help us live longer, so as to be favored by natural selection, and other ways it may be harmful. But whether or not *Time* can explain it, we are "wired" for hope.

Yet this hope seems futile. Nothing in this world lasts. The best careers end with a retirement party and a few gifts. The best marriages end with one spouse grieving at the grave of the other. Eventually the last generation of all will die, and you and I will not even be a memory in this world, because no one will be left to remember us. One day the sun will burn out and the dead, frozen earth will go spinning off into space. The second law of thermodynamics says that eventually the entire universe will run down. Bertrand Russell wrote, "[T]he whole temple of man's achievement must inevitably be buried beneath the debris of a universe in ruins."[12]

---

9. Richter, *The Epic of Eden*, 116.
10. Kreeft, *Love Is Stronger than Death*, 3.
11. Sharot, "The Science of Optimism," 40.
12. Russell, *A Free Man's Worship*; reprinted in *Why I Am Not a Christian*, 107.

Who Is Naïve?

Christians are sometimes ridiculed for believing in "pie in the sky." The world considers us naïve, believing in children's stories. Karl Marx said, "Religion is the opium of the people."[13] Former Minnesota Governor Jesse Ventura called religion "a crutch for weak-minded people."[14]

But we are wired for hope, so materialistic philosophies inevitably try to convince us that we can find hope in this life. Marx's colleague, Frederick Engels, wrote, "[M]aterialists . . . believe in man, in his capacity to transform the world by his own hand."[15] The Humanist Manifesto II said, "No deity will save us; we must save ourselves."[16] *But we cannot save ourselves.* So let me suggest that Christians are not the naïve ones. The naïve ones are those who believe there is real hope in this world, when all human experience says it is not so.

Neither pantheism nor materialism can explain this innate desire to live forever, nor offer any hope that it will be fulfilled. The ultimate goal for a pantheist is *nirvana*, in which one is swallowed up in the ultimate, impersonal reality, "as a drop of rain, which falls into the sea."[17] In 2010, the leaders of several religions, seeking to promote cooperation, sponsored a "Festival of Faiths" in Louisville, Kentucky. A group attended representing the Dalai Lama. Among that group were several artists, who created a beautiful "sand mandala," a circle of many different colors of sand, as an artistic centerpiece for the gathering. But on the last day of the festival, the artists destroyed their work, symbolizing their Buddhist belief that nothing lasts.[18]

Materialism says that the belief in life after death is just wishful thinking. Irish playwright Samuel Becket expressed this view memorably: "They gave birth astride a grave. The light gleams an instant, then it's night once more."[19] Richard Dawkins wrote, "Religion teaches the dangerous nonsense that death is not the end."[20]

A materialist may fight against dying, but he cannot say that death is wrong. It is natural and for him, what is natural is right. A Christian, who believes in the Biblical story of Eden and the fall, can say that death is neither natural nor right. It has not always been our fate, and it will not always be so.

---

13. Marx, *Critique of Hegal's Philosophy of Right*, 131.
14. Coonradt, "Religion and Governor Ventura."
15. Quoted Sleeper, *A Lexicon of Marxist-Leninist Semantics*, 168.
16. Kurtz, "Humanist Manifesto II," 16.
17. Spidle, Simeon, "The Belief in Immortality," Vol. 5, 8.
18. The *Louisville Courier Journal*, November 1, 2010, A6.
19. Becket, *Waiting for Godot*, 89.
20. Dawkins, "Religion's Misguided Missiles."

If there is no life after death, the universe is a fraud. It has given us the desire to live forever, without any possible fulfillment of that desire. It has also given us a longing for justice. We want to believe what Plato taught, that good always triumphs over evil in the end.[21] But this is clearly false if this life is all there is. Everywhere we look, we see the evil prosper and the righteous suffer, as in the Book of Job. Only if there is life after death can there be ultimate justice.

"I Go to Prepare a Place for You"

"[We] shall live to remember the galaxies as an old tale."

—C. S. LEWIS[22]

Scripture teaches that we want to live forever because we were made to live forever. The writer of Ecclesiastes wrote that God has *"set eternity in the human heart."*[23] The prophet Isaiah wrote, *"Eye has not seen, ear has not heard, nor has it entered into the heart of man, the things God has prepared for those who love Him."*[24] Jesus promised, *"I go to prepare a place for you."*[25]

I have attended many funerals over the years, and I have concluded that there is nothing in the world sadder than a non-Christian funeral. If this life is all there is, death is the end, and we have no hope. But a Christian can be hopeful, even in a world that is dying. Nature says that the moment we are born, we begin to die. Christianity says that the moment we die, we will begin to truly live!

C. S. Lewis was asked by a reporter during World War II what his last thought would be if the Germans got an atomic bomb and he saw it falling directly on him. He responded that he would stick out his tongue and think, "Pooh! You're only a bomb. I'm an immortal soul."[26]

---

21. Plato wrote, "[I]njustice is never more profitable than justice." Plato, *The Republic*, Book I, §354a, 35.
22. Lewis, "Membership," 173.
23. Ecclesiastes 3:11 (NIV).
24. Isaiah 64:4; quoted by the Apostle Paul in I Corinthians 2:9.
25. John 14:2.
26. Quoted Kreeft, *Christianity for Modern Pagans*, 56.

What Is Heaven Like?

What will Heaven be like? The only honest answer is that we do not know. It has not *"entered into the heart of man"* to imagine *"the things God has prepared for [us]."* It is totally beyond our experience, and therefore we do not have words for it. The Biblical descriptions are surely imagery, because a literal description would be impossible in our feeble, inadequate languages.

But Scripture does tell us some things about Heaven. The first is that we will be with God, worshipping Him.[27] So Heaven will be the fulfillment of that secret longing we discussed in the last chapter. Second, all the things that are wrong in this life will be made right. There will be no more sin, evil, injustice, or oppression;[28] no more pain, suffering, sickness, or death; no more separation from loved ones, sorrow, or tears.[29] *That world will be what we know this world should be.* Third, we will live forever.[30] So our most basic human desires, for God, for justice, for companionship, and for eternal life, will all be fulfilled.

Beyond that, I believe Lewis gave us the best answer to all our "What will Heaven be like?" questions. In his last book, *Letters to Malcolm*, he tried to describe his ideas of Heaven and then concluded, "Guesses, of course, only guesses. If they are not true, something better will be."[31] So what will Heaven be like? Think of the most wonderful things you can imagine, and then remind yourself, "If they are not true, something better will be."

My favorite picture of Heaven also comes from Lewis. At the end of the Chronicles of Narnia, the children find themselves in "Aslan's Country." As they walk, they recognize places they loved in Narnia, but all are more beautiful than ever before. They meet old friends who have died. They begin to suspect that they might be in Heaven, but are afraid they will be sent back. Then the great lion, Aslan, who represents Christ, appears and tells them:

> "'There was a real railway accident . . . Your father and mother and all of you are—as you used to call it in the Shadow-Lands—dead. The term is over; the holidays have begun. The dream is ended; this is the morning' . . .
>
> And as He spoke, He no longer looked to them like a lion; but the things that began to happen after that were so great and beautiful that I cannot write them. And for us this is the end

---

27. Revelation 4:8–11, 15:2–4.
28. Revelation 22:15.
29. Isaiah 65:19; Luke 20:36; Revelation 21:4.
30. John 3:16, 6:47; Revelation 22:5.
31. Lewis, *Letters to Malcolm: Chiefly on Prayer,* 123–124.

of all the stories, and we can most truly say that they all lived happily ever after. But for them it was only the beginning of the real story. All their life in this world and all their adventures in Narnia had only been the cover and the title page; now at last they were beginning Chapter One of the Great Story, which no one on earth has read; which goes on forever; in which every chapter is better than the one before."[32]

Our next piece of evidence is this universal desire to live forever. Every other innate human desire has a possible fulfillment somewhere. Is the deepest one of all the only exception? I would suggest that this longing, the "oldest, strongest and most urgent wish . . . of mankind," is not unnatural, but supernatural. *Death is unnatural.* Our desire to live forever is evidence that this world is fallen, but we are creatures of a race that transcends this world and belongs to another.

---

32. Lewis, *The Last Battle*, 183–184.

Chapter 9

"The Good, the True, and the Beautiful"
Evidence from Human Values and Beliefs

"When ultimate ends disappear, toys remain . . . There are many pleasant recreations on the deck of the Titanic."

—PETER KREEFT[1]

IN THE MOVIE, "CITY SLICKERS," Billy Crystal's character, suffering from a mid-life crisis, goes on a western cattle drive. He asks Curly, the rough old cowboy played by Jack Palance, what is the meaning of life? Curly holds up his forefinger and says, "One thing," but never tells him what that one thing is. It is a Hollywood movie, so in the end Crystal "learns" that he has to find his own meaning in life—the one thing is whatever he chooses it to be. Crystal finds his "meaning" in a baby calf that he helps to deliver and takes home as a family pet.[2]

Our last piece of evidence from human nature is a collection of ideas in which almost all of us believe. We say that life has meaning. We believe in human dignity, equality, and rights. We seek, even fight for freedom. We believe in love and love beauty. Where do these ideas come from? Are they true, or just accidental products of nature?

Mankind is naturally religious. From our earliest beginnings, we have sought meaning in life and found it through a belief in something higher than ourselves. Princeton philosopher Walter Kaufmann calls man "the God-intoxicated ape."[3] In the twenty-first century, many believe there is nothing

---

1. Kreeft, *Three Philosophies of Life*, 21.
2. "City Slickers," Castle Rock, 1991.
3. Kaufmann, *Critique of Religion and Philosophy*, 359.

higher than ourselves. But we still seek meaning and purpose, so we each try to make our own meaning. Even the United States Supreme Court has said, "At the heart of liberty is the right to define one's own concept of existence, of the meaning of the universe and the meaning of human life."[4]

"The Firm Foundation of Unyielding Despair"

> "The purpose of man is like the purpose of the pollywog—to wiggle along as far as he can without dying."
>
> —CLARENCE DARROW[5]

But if we make our own meaning, it is not real. We are just playing psychological tricks on ourselves, and those tricks are futile. Baby calves do not satisfy us. Henric Ibsen, the Norwegian playwright, said that if you take away a man's "life-lie," you take away his hope.[6] Bertrand Russell wrote, "[O]nly on the firm foundation of unyielding despair, can the soul's habitation . . . be safely built." Russell's conclusion is unavoidable, if you accept his view of what man is. Earlier in the same paragraph, he wrote, "[Man's] origin, his growth, his hopes and fears, his loves and his beliefs, are but the outcome of accidental collocations [arrangements] of atoms."[7] If we are only atoms, true meaning is impossible, and our only choices are Ibsen's self-deception or Russell's despair.

Materialistic thinkers understand this. Jean Paul Sartre wrote, "Man is a useless passion."[8] German philosopher Martin Heidegger said, "I know we are all on this ship and that the ship is going down. But I am going to stand on the deck and salute because it looks better."[9]

This same idea is expressed in literature. Ernest Hemingway described life as "a short day's journey from nothingness to nothingness."[10] Shakespeare caused Macbeth, a cynic, to say:

> "Life's but a walking shadow, a poor player
> That struts and frets his hour upon the stage,

---

4. *Planned Parenthood v Casey*, 505 U.S. 833 (1992).

5. Darrow, "Living," 154.

6. Quoted Schaeffer, *The God Who Is There*, 95; see also Encyclopedia Jrank, "The Life-Lie."

7. Russell, *Why I Am Not a Christian*, 107.

8. Sartre, *Being and Nothingness*, 615.

9. Quoted Zacharias, *Can Man Live Without God?* 67.

10. Quoted *Time*, "The Hero of the Code," 87–88.

And then is heard no more. It is a tale
Told by an idiot, full of sound and fury
Signifying nothing."[11]

Modern art expresses the same idea. Traditionally, art was meant to communicate truth or beauty. Modern art attempts only to communicate feelings, most often the feelings of meaninglessness or lostness, as in Edvard Monch's painting, "The Scream" (the source for the popular Halloween mask). Or it is "art for art's sake," with no meaning at all.

But art without meaning does not satisfy us. Willem de Kooning died in 1997, the last of his generation of great abstract painters, which included Pablo Picasso, Jackson Pollock, and others. An article in *U. S. News* after his death told of an interview in which he talked about his admiration for Titian, a sixteenth-century Venetian painter. Titian painted Madonnas his entire life. But when he was ninety, so arthritic that he had to have his paint brushes tied to his hand, Titian produced paintings of the Virgin Mary and other holy figures that de Kooning called "luminous," "as if he'd just heard about them."[12] de Kooning wanted that sort of passion in his painting. If I may say so with no disrespect, the difference is that Titian painted something which had real meaning because it was true.

Peter Kreeft provides a great illustration of the emptiness of making our own meaning. He says, imagine two men shipwrecked on an island. They send out a number of messages in bottles, hoping someone will find one and rescue them. One day they see a bottle floating toward them and rush into the surf to grab it. Excitedly, they open it. But all their hope turns to despair as one looks at the other and says, "It's only from us."[13]

Almost three thousand years ago, the writer of Ecclesiastes observed, *"I have seen all the works that are done under the sun; and indeed, all is vanity and grasping for the wind."*[14] So he concluded that we should simply *"eat, drink and be merry."*[15] If what is done *"under the sun"* is all there is, we just live until we die, and the best we can do is *"eat, drink and be merry."*

Ravi Zacharias wrote, "[I]f life is random, we have climbed the evolutionary ladder only to find nothing at the top."[16] If life is random—an accidental arrangement of atoms—our "search for meaning" is just a search

---

11. Shakespeare, "Macbeth," Act V, Scene V, 184.
12. Horn, "America's Old Master," 16.
13. Kreeft, *A Refutation of Moral Relativism*, 154.
14. Ecclesiastes 1:14.
15. Ecclesiastes 8:15.
16. Zacharias, *The End of Reason*, 39.

for diversions, trying to stay amused. But if the universe is meaningless, why has it produced creatures like us, who long for meaning?

Christianity says that life has true meaning, and that it comes from "one thing." But that one thing is not of our choosing; it is the will of God. History has meaning because it is "His story," from creation to the final judgment. We have purpose because God has a purpose for us, to love and serve Him. Human beings are meaningful because we were made in God's image, because God became man, because Christ died for us, because we alone were given the freedom to accept or reject His plan for us, and because our ultimate destiny is to be with Him.

Where Did We Come From?

> "Modern man thought that when he had gotten rid of God, he had freed himself from all that repressed and stifled him. Instead, he discovered that in killing God, he had only succeeded in orphaning himself. For if God does not exist, then man's life becomes absurd."
>
> —WILLIAM LANE CRAIG[17]

True meaning or purpose must relate to where we came from and where we are going. If our origin was a cosmic accident, how can we have any meaning? If we are going nowhere, how can we have any purpose? Biochemist Michael Denton wrote that when Darwin's theory of evolution "broke man's link with God," it "set him adrift in the cosmos without purpose."[18]

Michelangelo's famous painting, "The Creation of Adam," is one panel of the ceiling of the Sistine Chapel. In that painting, we see God reaching out to Adam, with His hand and forefinger extended, and Adam weakly reaching back. In that moment, a spark of God's divine life passes from God to Adam, and Adam is made human. He is stamped with God's image and given the supernatural gifts which distinguish him from the rest of creation.

I read a newspaper article a few years ago which described this scene as "Michelangelo's famous image of God and Adam pointing at each other." That description so gloriously misunderstood the painting that it made me angry. But if Adam—if man—is only a product of nature and if God is merely a human invention, Michelangelo believed a fable. We might as well describe the scene as "God and Adam pointing at each other," because it has no real meaning.

---

17. Craig, *Reasonable Faith*, 71.
18. Denton, *Evolution: A Theory in Crisis*, 67.

On the other hand, if Christianity is true, this painting tells me who I am. It tells me that I am not an accident, but was created for a purpose. It tells me why I have consciousness, reason, free will, and an understanding of right and wrong—these are reflections God has placed within me of His own nature. For our lives to have meaning, our origin must have had meaning. If Scripture is true, we know where we came from: *"So God created man in His own image; in the image of God He created him; male and female He created them."*[19]

Where We Are Going?

"[L]ife is either totally meaningful or totally meaningless, depending on what death is."

—PETER KREEFT[20]

For our lives to have meaning, we must also know where we are going. *If we will end in nothing, we are nothing.*[21] Even doing for others does not provide meaning, if their lives are meaningless as well. William Lane Craig wrote that if death is the end:

> "The contributions of the scientist to the advance of human knowledge, the researches of the doctor to alleviate pain and suffering, the efforts of the diplomat to secure peace in the world, the sacrifices of good people everywhere to better the lot of the human race—all these come to nothing."[22]

But if Christianity is true, we know where we are going. In addition to the ceiling of the Sistine Chapel, Michelangelo painted a fresco titled "The Last Judgment" on the front wall of the chapel. It shows Christ returning in the clouds, and the saints being raised from the dead and taken up into Heaven with Him. In the lower right-hand corner, it also shows some people going the other direction. One high Vatican official had given Michelangelo a great deal of trouble. When the painting was unveiled, there was a scandal as people recognized the face of this priest, carefully painted, on a naked body covered only by a snake coiled around his loins, and headed to hell![23] Do not get into a feud with an artist! But the point of the painting is hope.

---

19. Genesis 1:27.
20. Kreeft, *Love Is Stronger than Death*, xvi.
21. Craig, *The Existence of God and the Beginning of the Universe*, 16.
22. Ibid., 15.
23. Michelangelo Gallery, "The Last Judgment."

For a Christian, death is not the end; it is a door to eternal life. Blaise Pascal wrote that he defined life backwards and lived it forwards.[24] He defined death first—he knew where he was going—and it gave meaning to his life.

"A Barnyard of Pigs"

> "[A]ll human life . . . is sacred, because human life is created in the image and likeness of God. Nothing surpasses the greatness or dignity of a human person."
>
> —POPE JOHN PAUL II[25]

In Western cultures, we talk a great deal about human "dignity," "equality," and "rights." But materialism provides no reason to believe that these qualities are real. What does human dignity mean if we are just accidents who will soon die? Craig wrote:

> "Mankind cannot be more significant than a swarm of mosquitos or a barnyard of pigs, if their end is all the same. The same blind cosmic process that coughed them up in the first place will eventually swallow them all up again."[26]

Other cultures, not based on Biblical teachings, do not share the belief in the dignity or importance of an individual. In 1994, American student Michael Fay was sentenced to "caning" in Singapore for a minor theft. There was an outcry in the United States over the brutality of this method of punishment. Lee Kwan Yew, the former Prime Minister of Singapore, tried to explain to American journalists the difference in cultures between East and West: "To us in Asia, an individual is an ant. To you, he's a child of God. It is an amazing concept."[27]

But many materialistic thinkers in the West also deny that human beings have any inherent dignity. B. F. Skinner's most famous book was titled, *Beyond Freedom and Dignity*. Steven Pinker wrote an article titled, "The Stupidity of Dignity."[28] Bioethicist Ruth Macklin wrote, "Dignity is a Useless

---

24. Quoted Zacharias, *Can Man Live Without God?* 53.
25. John Paul II, Homily, Washington D.C., 1979; *Pope John Paul II: His Essential Wisdom*, 66.
26. Craig, *The Existence of God and the Beginning of the Universe*, 16.
27. Boston Globe, April 29, 1004; quoted Keller, *The Reason for God*, 296, n5.
28. Pinker, "The Stupidity of Dignity."

Concept."²⁹ We can only claim true dignity if we are children of God. If we are only ants—or atoms—the concept of human dignity has no meaning.

Thomas Jefferson wrote, "[A]ll men are created equal." What does that mean? We are certainly not equal in talents, intelligence, or looks. I have long been frustrated because I love sports but have no athletic ability. In that sense, Michael Jordan and I were not created equal! I appreciate both art and music, but have no talent for either one. Forget Michelangelo—I can't draw a straight line! Beethoven?—I can't carry a tune! If there is no Creator, the idea of equality is a useful political fiction, but nothing more. Only if we were equally created by God as human souls and are of equal value to Him, do Jefferson's words have any meaning. *A materialist could never have written the Declaration of Independence.*

Howard's Law #12 is: If your philosophy cannot explain how you and Michael Jordan were "created equal," your philosophy is probably wrong.

Do Laboratory Rats Have "Inalienable Rights?"

"Another Christian concept, no less crazy . . . the concept of this equality of souls before God. This concept furnishes the prototype of all theories of equal rights."

—FRIEDRICH NIETZSCHE[30]

We believe in "human rights," such as "life, liberty and the pursuit of happiness." But there is also a currently-popular movement promoting "animal rights." The idea is that we are just animals, and we have no more rights than any other animal. If we claim that humans are special, we are accused of "speciesism."[31] These people are right in a sense. If we are only animals, other animals do have just as many rights as we have—none. If humans and laboratory rats are both just accidental arrangements of atoms, what basis is there to claim that either of us has any rights?

There are no rights in the animal kingdom. The lion and the shark eat what they want; the zebra and the tuna have no right to object. The animal rights advocates say that we are only animals, but they hold us responsible for violating the rights of other animals. They do not hold those other animals responsible for violating our rights or each other's. But the whole idea of rights came from the theistic religions, which taught that God

---

29. Macklin, "Dignity is a Useless Concept."
30. Nietzsche, *The Will to Power*, 401.
31. Singer, *Animal Liberation*, 213.

gave certain rights (and responsibilities) to humans. I would suggest that the error of the animal rights folks is that they subconsciously remember the teachings of a once Judeo-Christian culture and mix those teachings with their secular beliefs. Animals do not have rights, but men, as stewards of God's creation, have obligations in how we must treat animals.

We believe in freedom. Israeli statesman Natan Sharansky, who lived until he was thirty-eight years old in the Soviet Union, wrote that all men, even those who have never known freedom, desire it.[32] But where does the right to freedom come from, if not from God? For that matter, if our actions are all determined, either by our DNA or our environment, what is freedom? If there is no Creator who made us free, the "right to freedom" is a meaningless phrase.

Biblical theism provided the historical foundation and still provides the only logical basis for the ideas of human dignity, equality, or rights. Only if we were "endowed by [our] Creator" with these characteristics do they truly exist.

"All You Need Is Love"

"[T]he largest problem a convinced materialist ha[s] to explain [is] the problem of love. Love has no place in a purely materialistic . . . world, yet here it is."

—HARRY LEE POE[33]

More than anything else, we believe in love. The Beatles sang, "All You Need is Love,"[34] and then broke up! But if materialism is true, what we call love is just a biochemical reaction, brought about by a random genetic mutation in one of our remote ancestors, which caused that organism to live longer or breed more, and thus was passed down to us. As to romantic love, this seems plausible. But what about love of our neighbors? What about any love which causes one person to sacrifice his life for another? Charles Darwin wrote, "Natural selection will never produce in a being anything injurious to itself."[35]

Did love emerge by chance from an impersonal and loveless nature? Does "I love you," only mean, "My chemicals are attracted to yours?" Is that the explanation for all those whom you love, or who love you?

---

32. Sharansky, *The Case for Democracy*, 18–38.
33. Poe, *The Inklings of Oxford*, 153.
34. Lennon, John, "All You Need is Love," Lennon/McCartney, 1967.
35. Darwin, *On the Origin of Species*, 223.

Rodney Brooks is head of the Computer Science and Artificial Intelligence Laboratory at MIT. He argues that men are just "living machines." In a debate, he said, "I am a robot . . . I view myself as a living machine." He said that his wife and children are robots as well. But then he added, "I have this completely different way of interacting with them, with unconditional love, which is not part of that scientific view." He acknowledged that these two views are "inconsistent."[36] Once again, materialism can only be preached, not practiced.

What about a mother's love? Ravi Zacharias tells an old Indian fable about a young man who fell in love. He wanted to marry the young woman, but she insisted on more and more extreme proofs of his love. Finally she demanded, "If you love me, you must take your mother's life and bring me her heart as a trophy of my victory over your love for her." The young man resisted, but she was insistent. Finally he consented. He killed his mother and removed her heart. As he ran through the jungle, taking it to his lover, he tripped and fell, dropping the heart. As he picked it up from among the leaves, he heard his mother's voice coming from it: "Son, are you hurt?"[37] Zacharias says that he has told this story all over the world, and he has never found a culture where the idea of a mother's sacrificial love is not immediately recognized. Is a mother's love only chemicals?

Yet materialism has to explain all love (and all of life) as just chemicals. Joy Davidman, an adult convert from atheism to Christianity, described her philosophy in her youth this way: "Life is only an electrochemical reaction. Love, art and altruism are only sex. The universe is only matter. Matter is only energy. I forgot what I said energy is only."[38]

We say that love lasts forever. But if there is no God, when the last human dies, that will be the end of love. A materialist wants to say that love is real, and that it will last, but he has no logical basis for either belief. A theist can say that love is at the heart of ultimate reality, because God is Love. A Christian can say that love is eternal, because God is Love, within the Trinity, from all eternity and for all eternity. But these things are only true if the God of the Bible is real.

Howard's Law #13 is: If your philosophy cannot say that love is real, your philosophy is probably wrong.

---

36. Brooks, "Living Machines," 196, 210.
37. Zacharias, *Can Man Live without God?* 110.
38. Lewis, C. S., "Forward," Davidman, *Smoke on the Mountain*, 7.

"Breathtaking Rightness"

"There is no way in which a man can earn a star or deserve a sunset."

—ST. FRANCIS OF ASSISI[39]

We appreciate, even love, beauty. We are poets and mystics. "Men look on the starry heavens with reverence; monkeys do not."[40] Only humans create art, but we have done so since our earliest ancestors. Almost as soon as men learned to make clay pots or wooden spears, we began to decorate them. Similarly, from our earliest history, men have loved music. But why? Such loves are not useful, something natural selection would have preserved. Stephen Pinker once told an audience of music students that their music was "worthless" in terms of human evolution. He called it, "auditory cheesecake."[41] But beauty thrills us and inspires us, and we believe it is real. Famed conductor Leonard Bernstein wrote:

> "Beethoven . . . turned out pieces of breathtaking rightness. Rightness—that's the word! When you get the feeling that whatever note succeeds the last is the only possible note that can rightly happen at that instant, in that context, then chances are, you're listening to Beethoven. . . . Our boy has the real goods, the stuff from Heaven, the power to make you feel at the finish: Something is right in the world."[42]

Albert Einstein, after listening to 14-year old violin prodigy Yehudi Menuhin perform with the Berlin Philharmonic in 1930, said to the young man, "Now I know there is a God in heaven!"[43]

But if materialism is true, there is no such thing as real beauty. Nature is not a work of art, but merely an accident which, by another accident, we are chemically programmed to appreciate. A Michelangelo sculpture is just a piece of marble, and a Titian painting merely paint on canvas. A Shakespearian sonnet is nothing but ink marks on paper, and a Beethoven symphony just random sounds. What we call beauty is only a coincidence. We happen to respond positively to certain combinations of light or sound, but it means nothing. This is the logical conclusion of materialism, but our human nature tells us that it is not true.

---

39. Quoted Chesterton, *Saint Francis of Assisi*, 189.
40. Lewis, "Dogma and the Universe," 41.
41. Quoted Plantinga, *Where the Conflict Really Lies*, 132.
42. Bernstein, *The Joy of Music*, 29.
43. Jammer, *Einstein and Religion*, 19.

Howard's Law #14 is: If your philosophy cannot say that a Michelangelo sculpture or a Beethoven symphony is truly beautiful, your philosophy is probably wrong.

Christianity says that there is real beauty and that it is art, because there is a divine artist. The universe is "God's art and man's science."[44] St. Thomas Aquinas wrote, "The beautiful is the same as the good, but with a difference of accent."[45] We seek beauty because we seek God, whether we know it or not. *He is Beauty.* St. Augustine called Him, "Beauty so ancient and so new."[46] We make art and music, we love beauty of every kind, because we are made in God's image.

Things We Believe In

Our ancestors taught that the three things which make life meaningful are "the good, the true, and the beautiful."[47] We believe in these things. We believe that life has meaning; that humans have dignity, equality, and rights such as freedom; and that love and beauty are real. None of these beliefs seem to be useful for survival, so that they would be preserved by natural selection. Materialism says they are all subjective, just matters of opinion. But why do we naturally believe in them? Why are we so made that we would we be miserable if we did not? *If there is no God, these beliefs are not true.* I would submit that they are another piece of evidence that we are more than just natural beings, but were made in the image of a supernatural Creator.

So these are my eight arguments from human nature for the existence of God—consciousness, reason, free will, and our sense of right and wrong; the facts that we do not do what we know is right, we are never satisfied, we want to live forever, and we share the values and beliefs which we have discussed in this chapter. I do not claim that these are absolute proofs, so that reasonable men could never disagree. But taken together, I believe they make a powerful case. Put simply, Christianity can explain human nature, and materialism cannot. The Biblical view of man fits—it explains the reality we all experience. Lewis wrote, "I believe in Christianity as I believe the sun has risen. Not only because I see it, but because by it I see everything else."[48]

---

44. Kreeft, *The Philosophy of Jesus*, 61.
45. Aquinas, *Summa Theologica*, §II: II, q35, a4; as quoted by Oden, *The Living God*, Vol. 1, 170.
46. Augustine, *Confessions*, Book X, §27, Boulding, 222.
47. Reynolds, *When Athens Met Jerusalem*, 22.
48. Lewis, "Is Theology Poetry?" 140.

Chapter 10

Nothing Comes from Nothing
Why Does Anything Exist?

"[A]t this moment it seems as though science will never be able to raise the curtain on the mystery of creation. For the scientist who has lived by his faith in the power of reason, the story ends like a bad dream. He has scaled the mountains of ignorance; he is about to conquer the highest peak; as he pulls himself over the final rock, he is greeted by a band of theologians who have been sitting there for centuries."

—ROBERT JASTROW, ASTROPHYSICIST AND DIRECTOR OF NASA'S GODDARD INSTITUTE OF SPACE STUDIES.[1]

WE HAVE BEEN CONSIDERING evidence for the existence of God which can be found in human nature. Now I want to look briefly at the larger picture. G. K. Chesterton, many years ago, identified three questions facing anyone trying to make sense of the world we live in: "[T]he origin of the universe . . . the origin of the principle of life . . . [and] the origin of man himself."[2] In the next three chapters, we will discuss each of these questions, primarily from the standpoint of science. I am not a scientist, but I believe I can accurately summarize what the scientists tell us, and that science, when looked at apart from the materialistic philosophy which often accompanies it, provides compelling evidence to support the belief in a Creator.

We will discuss evolution later, but we should note for now that Darwinian evolution, based on natural selection, does not claim to be a

---

1. Jastrow, *God and the Astronomers*, 107.
2. Chesterton, *The Everlasting Man*, 26.

complete answer to these questions. In fact, Darwinism, as opposed to a materialistic philosophy, only attempts to answer the third question, how the first one-cell organisms evolved into all the currently existing life-forms, including man. It has nothing to say to the first two questions, why anything exists or why life exists.

Some materialists talk of the physical universe "evolving," but this can only mean they believe that once it existed in some form, it developed into its current form by natural processes. *The universe could not have evolved from nothing into something.* Nor could it have evolved into its current form by natural selection. Natural selection operates through reproduction. You must have living organisms, capable of reproducing themselves, before natural selection comes into play. Theodosius Dobzhansky of Columbia University, one of the leading evolutionary biologists of the twentieth century, said, "Pre-biological [before life] natural selection is a contradiction in terms."[3]

Why Does Anything Exist?

"Philosophy stares, but brings no reasoned solution, for from nothing to being there is no logical bridge."

—HARVARD PHILOSOPHER WILLIAM JAMES[4]

"What is it that breathes fire into the equations and makes a universe for them to describe? . . . Why does the universe go to all the bother of existing?"

— STEPHEN HAWKING[5]

Chesterton's first question is "the origin of the universe." Seventeenth-century German philosopher Gottfried Leibniz asked, "Why is there something

---

3. Dobzhansky's longer statement, made as part of a panel discussion, was, "I would like, however, to express the belief that the words 'natural selection' must be used carefully. Dr Schramm has so used them. In reading some other literature on the origin of life, I am afraid that not all authors have used the term carefully. Natural selection is differential reproduction, organism perpetuation. In order to have natural selection, you have to have self-reproduction or self-replication and at least two distinct self-replicating units or entities. Now, I realize that when you speak of origin of life, you wish to discuss the probable embryonic stages, so to speak, of natural selection. What these embryonic stages will be is for you to decide. *I would like to plead with you, simply, please realize you cannot use the words 'natural selection' loosely. Pre-biological natural selection is a contradiction in terms.*" (emphasis added) Quoted Fox, *The Origins of Pre-Biological Systems*, 310.

4. James, *Some Problems of Philosophy*, 40.

5. Hawking, *A Brief History of Time*, 142.

rather than nothing?"[6] Twentieth-century philosopher Martin Heidegger called this "the first of all questions."[7] Carl Sagan said, "If you wish to make an apple pie from scratch, you must first invent the universe."[8] By the way, did you hear about the young bride who wanted to surprise her husband with a homemade pie, so she went to the grocery store and asked for some "scratch?" But materialism has no answer to this question, nor does our society. Historian Arnold Toynbee wrote that of twenty-one great civilizations in history, ours is the first which has no answer to why we exist.[9]

Howard's Law #15 is: *If your philosophy cannot explain where the "scratch" to make an apple pie came from, your philosophy is probably wrong.*

Theists say that God created the universe *"ex nihilo"* (Latin for "from nothing"). According to the laws of nature, nothing comes from nothing—everything must have a cause. No matter how far back we go in time, no matter how many natural causes we come to, each must be caused by another. But where did this system of natural causes come from? Either it had no beginning and no cause, or eventually we must come to a "first cause," an uncaused event or object or being. Christians say that God is that first cause. He is not subject to the laws of nature; He established them.

Some ask, if God created the universe, where did He come from? The answer is that God is, by definition, the eternal, uncaused being. Christian apologist Josh McDowell says, "The great I AM has no birthday and will have no funeral."[10] You may like that answer or not, but if something exists (it does), and if something cannot come from nothing (it cannot), then something or someone has always existed. The only two real choices are God or nature. If the natural universe, in some form, is not eternal and uncaused, God must be. *But this question can never be answered scientifically, based on the laws of nature. Those laws can no more explain an uncaused universe than they can explain an uncaused God.*

Eleventh, Twelfth, and Thirteenth Century Wisdom

Many great thinkers over the last 3500 years have concluded that God is self-existent and eternal, and that He created the universe. Historically, the most popular of these arguments for a Creator was called the *Kalam*

---

6. Leibniz, *Leibniz Selections*, 527.
7. Heidegger, *An Introduction to Metaphysics*, 1.
8. Sagan, *Cosmos*, 218.
9. Quoted Kreeft, *Three Philosophies of Life*, 20.
10. McDowell and McDowell, *The Unshakable Truth*, 54.

argument. As put forward by the Muslim philosopher Al-Ghazali in the eleventh century, it went like this:

1. Whatever begins to exist has a cause.
2. The universe began to exist.
3. Therefore, the universe had a cause.[11]

Generally speaking, no one has ever questioned the first statement, that whatever begins to exist must have a cause. Plato wrote that everything which moves is moved by something, and everything which changes is changed by something.[12] This is one of the fundamental principles of science. The weakness of the *Kalam* argument was always believed to be with the second statement, that the universe began to exist. Historically, this was where the battle-lines were drawn—did the universe have a beginning, or not?

The twelfth-century Jewish philosopher Moses Maimonides was a great admirer of Aristotle. But he struggled with the fact that Aristotle taught the universe was eternal, while Genesis said God created the universe from nothing. Maimonides concluded that Scripture was right, because if the universe had always existed, it had no purpose. Only if God created the universe was there a purpose for its existence, that purpose being that men should know God.[13]

The thirteenth-century Christian philosopher St. Thomas Aquinas, for purposes of his argument for the existence of God, accepted Aristotle's view that the universe had always existed. Asked why, he said that if he assumed the universe had a beginning, it made his argument too easy![14]

BANG!

The question of what has always existed, God or the universe, is not a scientific question. But there has been a major scientific development in the last century which affects how we look at this question. Despite theistic thinkers such as Al-Ghazali, Maimonides, and Aquinas, most men, from ancient pagans to scientists at the turn of the twentieth century, believed that the universe—and matter, the stuff of which the universe is made—had existed forever. When Darwin published *On the Origin of Species* in 1859, that was

---

11. Kreeft and Tacelli, *Handbook of Christian Apologetics*, 58.
12. Plato, *Laws*, Book X; 333–341.
13. Novak, "The Mind of Maimonides," 23–24.
14. Craig, William Lane; Strobel, *The Case for a Creator*, 107–108.

still the accepted scientific view. *Until the twentieth century, only the Bible taught that the universe had a beginning.*

But one of the most important scientific discoveries of the last century was that the universe as we know it began in what is called the "big bang." Some scientists concluded, theoretically, that the universe had a beginning from Einstein's theory of relativity.[15] But the proof came in 1929 when astronomer Edwin Hubble discovered a "red shift" in the light from other galaxies, meaning that those galaxies were moving away from us. Astronomers already knew that if a source of light is moving toward us, the light has a blue cast and if it is moving away, it has a red tint.[16] Hubble concluded that the entire universe is expanding. This conclusion has since been confirmed many times. Astrophysicist Robert Jastrow succeeded Hubble as director of the Mount Wilson Observatory and later became founding director of NASA's Goddard Institute of Space Studies. He wrote:

> "Regardless of the direction in which we look out into space, all the distant objects in the heavens are moving away from us and from one another. The universe is blowing up before our eyes, as if we are witnessing the aftermath of a gigantic explosion."[17]

What is more, the astronomers say that if you could cause the galaxies to retrace their paths, they would all come back to roughly the same point at roughly the same time, about fourteen billion years ago.[18] Thus, the big bang theory developed.

This theory was further confirmed when scientists predicted that if it were true, we should find low-level heat and light throughout the universe, the "afterglow" from the big bang. In 1964, Nobel Prize-winning astronomers Arno Penzias and Robert Wilson found this "cosmic background radiation," with the exact wave-lengths that would result from a huge cosmic explosion.[19]

---

15. Willem de Sitter, a Dutch astronomer, proposed an expanding universe in 1917, working only from Einstein's equations. Jastrow, *God and the Astronomers*, 18–20. Similarly, the Belgian astronomer Georges Lemaitre, who was also a Roman Catholic Priest, proposed an expanding universe and a beginning very similar to the big bang, in 1927. National Academy of Sciences, *Science, Evolution and Creationism*, 18. But most scientists, including Einstein, rejected these conclusions, until the observation of the galaxies, by Hubble and others, made it unavoidable. Jastrow, *God and the Astronomers*, 32–33.

16. Jastrow, *God and the Astronomers*, 12–13. Astronomer Vesto Slipher first noticed this "red shift" as early as 1913, but it was Hubble, together with his colleague, Milton Humason, who realized that this proved the universe was expanding. Ibid., 11, 26–33.

17. Ibid., 12.

18. Collins, *The Language of God*, 64.

19. Geisler, *Baker Encyclopedia of Christian Apologetics*, 277.

Other cosmologists then said, if all the galaxies resulted from the big bang, we should find slight temperature variations in this background radiation, indicating where the matter in the universe collected into galaxies, due to gravity, after the big bang. In 1989, NASA launched the COBE (Cosmic Background Explorer) satellite and in 1992, NASA scientists found exactly such "ripples" in the cosmic background radiation.[20] These ripples are so precisely what would be expected to result from the formation of galaxies that George Smoot, director of the COBE project, called them, "machining marks from the machine that tooled the universe" and "fingerprints from the maker."[21]

The result, as Stephen Hawking has written, is that "[A]lmost everyone now believes that the universe, and time itself, had a beginning at the Big Bang."[22]

Science now agrees with theology that at a point in space and time, the universe began to exist. There was a beginning! Robert Jastrow calls himself an agnostic, but he wrote:

> "Now we see how the astronomical evidence leads to a biblical view of the origin of the world. All the details differ; but the essential element in the astronomical and biblical accounts of Genesis is the same; the chain of events leading to man commenced suddenly and sharply, at a definite moment in time, in a flash of light and energy."[23]

At first, many scientists did not want to accept the idea that the universe had a beginning, because of the obvious religious implications. Albert Einstein described himself as "irritated" by the concept and tried to prove it wrong.[24] Astrophysicist Arthur Eddington wrote, "Philosophically, the notion of a beginning of the present order of Nature is repugnant to me ... I should like to find a genuine loophole."[25] Elsewhere, he insisted, "We [must] allow evolution an infinite time to get started."[26] But ultimately, both Einstein and Eddington were forced by the evidence to conclude that the universe did indeed have a beginning in the big bang.

---

20. Geisler and Turek, *I Don't Have Enough Faith to Be an Atheist*, 82–83.
21. Heeren, *Show Me God*, 142.
22. Hawking and Penrose, *The Nature of Space and Time*, 20.
23. Jastrow, *God and the Astronomers*, 14.
24. Ibid., 21.
25. Eddington, "The End of the World: From the Standpoint of Mathematical Physics," 450.
26. Eddington, "On the Instability of Einstein's Spherical World," quoted Ross, *The Creator and the Cosmos*, 51.

"Beyond Physics"

> "[The] Big Bang was not an explosion in space but the explosion of space. It was not an explosion in time but the beginning of time. It was not an explosion of pre-existing matter but the creation of matter itself."
>
> —FRANK TUREK[27]

If the big bang caused the universe to come into being, what caused the big bang? Scientists say that all the matter in the universe exploded in an unbelievable burst of energy from what they call a "singularity." *And they define this singularity as an event which cannot be explained by scientific laws.* Jastrow described the big bang theory as, "the discovery that the world had a beginning under conditions in which the known laws of physics are not valid."[28]

Arizona State physicist Paul Davies wrote:

> "[I]t is not possible to attribute the big bang to anything that happened before it, as is usually the case in discussions of causation. Does this mean that the big bang was an event without a cause? If the laws of physics break down at the singularity, there can be no explanation in terms of those laws. Therefore, if one insists on a reason for the big bang, then this reason must lie *beyond physics*."[29] (emphasis added)

What existed before the universe? For years I imagined the big bang as an explosion in which pre-existing matter or energy was changed in form. Einstein taught that matter could be converted to energy and *vice versa*. But the scientists say that the big bang was an event before which *nothing* existed—neither matter, energy, space, time, nor scientific laws. Physicists John Barrow of Cambridge and Frank Tipler of Tulane wrote:

> "At this singularity, space and time came into existence; literally nothing existed before the singularity, so, if the Universe originated at such a singularity, we would truly have a creation *ex nihilo* . . .
>
> [T]here is a temptation to ask the question 'what happened before the singularity?' . . . the answer is that nothing happened 'before' because there is no 'before.'"[30]

---

27. Turek, "The Cosmological Argument," 422.
28. Jastrow, *God and the Astronomers*, 105–106.
29. Davies, *The Mind of God*, 57.
30. Barrow and Tippler, *The Anthropic Cosmological Principle*, 442.

Particle physicist Victor Stenger, an atheist, wrote, "[T]he universe exploded out of nothingness."[31] Oxford philosopher Anthony Kenny wrote, "A proponent of this theory, at least if he is an atheist, must believe that the matter of the universe came from nothing and by nothing."[32]

Evolution ex Nihilo?

"[T]here is always something really unthinkable about the whole evolutionary cosmos . . . because it is something coming out of nothing; an ever-increasing flood of water pouring out of an empty jug.

—G. K. CHESTERTON"[33]

How could the universe have come from nothing? Materialists are left having to question the first premise of the *Kalam* argument, that if something begins to exist, it must have a cause. MIT physicist Alan Guth called the universe "the ultimate free lunch."[34] Philosopher Bertrand Russell said, "[T]he universe is just there and that's all."[35] Popular author Bill Bryson wrote, "It seems impossible that you could get something from nothing, but the fact that once there was nothing and now there is a universe is evident proof that you can."[36] *If there was a beginning, a materialist must believe in "evolution ex nihilo,"*[37] evolution from nothing, in spite of all human experience and scientific evidence, both of which say that such is impossible.

Scientists have struggled to find an answer to this dilemma. Some have suggested an "oscillating" universe—an infinite series of big bangs, each followed billions of years later by a "big crunch," where the universe collapses back into a point, only to explode again. Most scientists have rejected this idea because the evidence does not appear to support it,[38] but the bigger

---

31. Stenger, "The Face of Chaos," 13.
32. Kenny, *The Five Ways: St. Thomas Aquinas' Proofs of God's Existence*, 66.
33. Chesterton, *St. Thomas Aquinas / St. Francis of Assisi*, 159.
34. Quoted Hawking, *A Brief History of Time*, 129.
35. Russell and Copleston, "A Debate on the Existence of God," 175.
36. Bryson, *A Short History of Nearly Everything*, 13.
37. Morris, "Evolution Ex Nihilo," 4–5.
38. Robert Jastrow wrote, "[T]he evidence is against [the oscillating universe], because the latest word is that there is not enough matter in the universe to halt the expansion and bring the universe together again." Jastrow, "What Forces Filled the Universe with Energy Fifteen Billion Years Ago?" 46. See also Townes, *Making Waves*, 181.

problem is that it does not answer the question—where did the oscillating universe come from?

Stephen Hawking has proposed a theoretical model which he claims avoids a beginning (it makes time circular). But it involves the idea of "imaginary time" using "imaginary numbers." Hawking admits that if you substitute real time for the imaginary time, the beginning reappears.[39]

And again, Hawking has no answer for why anything exists. *Any materialistic theory of the origin of the universe must start with something which already existed and with some form of natural laws which guided its development.* But in that case, it is not an explanation of the *origin* of the universe at all. Even natural laws are not "nothing." Where did they come from?

Beyond Nature

"The big bang cries out for a divine explanation. It forces the conclusion that nature had a defined beginning. I cannot see how nature could have created itself. Only a supernatural force that is outside of space and time could have done that."

—FRANCIS COLLINS[40]

So the question remains—we know that in nature, everything must have a cause. Did nature itself have none? Many of the greatest scientists in the world have concluded that the answer must indeed lie "beyond physics" (metaphysical) and beyond nature (supernatural). Arthur Eddington wrote, "The beginning seems to present insuperable difficulties unless we agree to look at it as frankly supernatural. We may have to let it go at that."[41]

Allan Sandage of the Carnegie Observatories was one of the world's leading cosmologists. He discovered quasars and was the first to establish the uniformity of the expansion of the universe, out to nearly ten billion light years. Sandage said:

> "It was my science that drove me to the conclusion that the world is much more complicated than can be explained by science . . . It is only through the supernatural that I can understand the mystery of existence."[42]

---

39. Hawking, *A Brief History of Time*, 138–139.
40. Collins, *The Language of God*, 67.
41. Eddington, *The Expanding Universe*, 125.
42. Quoted Begley, "Science Finds God," 44.

"God to me is a mystery but is the explanation for the miracle of existence, why there is something instead of nothing."[43]

Arno Penzias, one of the co-discoverers of the cosmic background radiation, wrote:

"Astronomy leads us to a unique event, a universe which was created out of nothing, one with the very delicate balance needed to provide exactly the conditions required to permit life, and one which has an underlying (one might say 'supernatural') plan. Thus, the observations of modern science seem to lead to the same conclusions as centuries-old intuition."[44]

Stephen Hawking is not a theist, but he wrote, "It would be very difficult to explain why the universe would have begun in just this way [the big bang] except as the act of a God who intended to create beings like us."[45] More recently, at a conference held to celebrate his seventieth birthday, Hawking said, "A point of creation would be a place where science broke down. One would have to appeal to religion and the hand of God."[46]

Maybe the scientists will one day change their minds and replace the big bang with another theory, although that presently seems unlikely. We should not base our faith in God on any scientific theory, no matter how widely accepted. But as the scientific consensus now stands, the logical conclusion seems unavoidable—*if space, time, matter, energy, and scientific laws were all caused by the big bang, then the big bang (and the universe as we know it) must have been caused by something beyond space, time, matter, energy, or scientific laws.*[47]

Howard's Law #16 is: *If your philosophy says that the big bang resulted from things which resulted from it, your philosophy is probably wrong.*

Notice how dramatically the argument has changed in the last century. As William Lane Craig commented:

"[O]ne hundred years ago . . . Christians had to maintain by faith in the Bible that despite all appearances to the contrary, the universe was not eternal but was created out of nothing a finite time ago. Now, the situation is exactly the opposite.

---

43. Quoted Wilford, "Sizing Up the Cosmos: An Astronomer's Quest," b9.
44. Penzias, "Creation Is Supported by All the Data So Far," 83.
45. Hawking, *A Brief History of Time*, 144.
46. Quoted Flam, Faye, *The Philadelphia Enquirer*; reprinted *The (Louisville) Courier Journal*, January 30, 2012, D3.
47. Geisler and Turek, *I Don't Have Enough Faith to Be an Atheist*, 89.

> It is the atheist who has to maintain, by faith, despite all the evidence to the contrary, that the universe did not have a beginning . . . but is in some inexplicable way eternal after all."[48]

"The Universe Is Running Down Like a Clock"

There are other scientific reasons to believe that the universe had a beginning. The Second Law of Thermodynamics has been said to "hold . . . the supreme position among the laws of nature."[49] This law says that both heat and energy eventually spread out evenly. If you pour hot water into one end of your bath and cold water into the other end, after a while the temperature of the entire bath will become the same. Eventually, it will become room temperature.

Applied to the universe as a whole, this means that it is winding down, moving toward such an equilibrium of temperature and energy and becoming less ordered. *But the universe has not yet reached that point, so it cannot have been winding down forever.* This understanding fits perfectly with the big bang theory and with the Biblical teaching of creation, but not with the idea that the universe is eternal. Jastrow wrote:

> "[T]he second law of thermodynamics, applied to the Cosmos, indicates the universe is running down like a clock. If it is running down, there must have been a time when it was fully wound up."[50]

Paul Davies wrote:

> "[The Second Law of Thermodynamics] is not reversible: it imprints upon the universe an arrow of time, pointing the way of unidirectional change . . . [T]he universe is engaged in a one-way slide toward a state of thermodynamic equilibrium . . . The fact that the universe has not yet so died—that is, it is still in

---

48. Craig, William Lane; Strobel, *The Case for a Creator*, 120–121.

49. Arthur Eddington wrote, "The law that entropy always increases—the second law of thermodynamics—holds, I think, the supreme position among the laws of nature. If someone points out to you that your pet theory of the universe is in disagreement with Maxwell's equations—then, so much the worse for Maxwell's equations. If it is found to be contradicted by observation—well, these experimentalists do bungle things sometimes. But if your theory is found to be against the second law of thermodynamics I can give you no hope; there is nothing for it but collapse in deepest humiliation." Eddington, *The Nature of the Physical World*, 74.

50. Jastrow, *God and the Astronomers*, 32–33.

a state of less-than-maximum entropy—implies that it cannot have endured for all eternity."[51]

Furthermore, the stars consume hydrogen but they do not create it. The universe contains a fixed supply of hydrogen, and when the stars run out, they burn out.[52] Jastrow wrote:

> "Now three lines of evidence—the motions of the galaxies, the laws of thermodynamics, and the life-story of the stars—pointed to one conclusion; all indicated that the universe had a beginning."[53]

So we are back to our original question—if the universe had a beginning, and whatever begins to exist has a cause, what caused the universe? Norman Geisler and Frank Turek set out the only options: "Either someone created something out of nothing (the Christian view), or no one created something out of nothing (the atheist view). Which view is more reasonable?"[54]

Before Time

Do you want to hear a 1600-year-old joke that is still funny? St. Augustine wrote that someone once asked him, what did God do with His time before He created the universe? Augustine answered that God was busy making hell for people who ask such questions! He then gave the serious answer that he believed time is part of the created order and that God is not in time.[55]

This idea, that time and space exist only within the created universe, was introduced by the ancient Greek philosophers and popularized by Augustine in the fifth century. He wrote:

> "The distinguishing mark between time and eternity is that the former [time] does not exist without some movement and change, while in the latter [eternity] there is no change at all. Obviously, then, there could have been no time had not a creature been made whose movement would effect some change . . . [T]he world was not made in time, but together with time."[56]

51. Davies, *The Mind of God*, 46–47.
52. Jastrow, *God and the Astronomers*, 84–85.
53. Jastrow, *God and the Astronomers*, 1st edition, 111.
54. Geisler and Turek, *I Don't Have Enough Faith to be an Atheist*, 26.
55. Augustine, *Confessions*, Book XI, §12, Boulding, 254.
56. Augustine, *The City of God*, Book X1, 188.

God, according to Augustine and many other Christian teachers, exists in eternity, not in time. This is usually described by picturing time as a line and God being above or outside that line, observing all of it at once. Therefore, He does not *foresee* the future. He simply *sees* it, as he sees both the past and the present.

Again, it appears that the scientists now agree with the theologians. I do not pretend to fully understand Einstein's theory of general relativity, but part of that theory holds that space, time, and matter are mutually dependent, or "relative." You cannot have one without the others. According to Einstein, time arises from the movement of material objects.[57] Einstein must have read Augustine!

To "the first of all questions," why anything exists, materialism has no answer. By definition, it never could. Materialism says that everything is explainable by natural causes, but natural causes cannot explain why there is a universe at all, or why there are natural causes. The only answer on the market, other than simply calling it a mystery, is the Biblical answer: *"In the beginning, God created the heavens and the earth."* Our next piece of evidence is the undeniable fact that *something exists*.

---

57. Jammer, *Einstein and Religion*, 247–250. According to Einstein, space, time, and matter are all relative to the speed of light.

Chapter 11

The Miracle of Life
Why Does Life Exist?

"An honest man, armed with all the knowledge available to us now, could only state that in some sense, the origin of life appears at the moment to be almost a miracle, so many are the conditions which would have had to have been satisfied to get it going."

—FRANCIS CRICK, NOBEL PRIZE-WINNING MOLECULAR BIOLOGIST[1]

MOST EVERYONE HAS HEARD of Pinocchio, the boy whose nose grew longer every time he told a lie. But the story is really about a small wooden puppet which comes to life and becomes "a real boy." He then learns various lessons that a boy needs to know, such as not to lie. It is a nice story, but only a small child would believe such a thing could happen. In all of human experience, non-living things have never come to life.

The second of G. K. Chesterton's three questions is "the origin of the principle of life."[2] Why does life exist? Jacques Monod, a Nobel Prize-winning French molecular biologist, expressed the standard materialistic view:

"[C]hance alone is at the source of every innovation, of all creation in the biosphere. Pure chance, absolutely free but blind . . . The universe was not pregnant with life nor the biosphere with man. Our number came up in the Monte Carlo game."[3]

---

1. Crick, *Life Itself*, 88.
2. Chesterton, *The Everlasting Man*, 26.
3. Monod, *Chance and Necessity*, 112–113, 145–146.

The title of Monod's book was *Chance and Necessity*. Even if you skip the question of why there is a universe at all, these are the only two possible materialistic explanations for anything, whether life, humans, or basketballs—they either result from blind chance or they are "necessary," inevitable from the very nature of the universe. Only a theist can add a third possibility, that they are intelligently designed and freely created.

Was Monod right? Was the appearance of life just a fluke, a one-in-a-gazillion shot in a game of chance? This brings us to another question—how *could* life arise by chance? The difficulty is the same, whether you are talking about a wooden puppet or a few tiny particles of matter in Darwin's "warm little pond"[4] (or in either of two currently-popular suggestions, the edge of a volcano or an underwater ocean vent). It is still *non-living* matter in a *non-living* pond or volcano or ocean vent. No one believes that the first matter resulting from the big bang contained life. *If materialism is true, at some point in the distant past, one or more particles of non-living matter had to come to life.* But both human experience and scientific evidence say that life only comes from life.

Again, Darwinism, based on natural selection, is of no help here. It only explains how living things change over time. Harvard biologist E. O. Wilson wrote, "Evolution by natural selection is perhaps the only one true law unique to biological systems, as opposed to non-living physical systems."[5]

How did the first living cell, from which every more advanced form of life evolved, get here in the first place? Materialists sometimes talk of the first life-forms evolving—they call it "chemical" or "molecular" evolution—but there is no generally-accepted theory for how it could have occurred. The National Academy of Sciences, in a 2008 publication, said:

> "Constructing a plausible hypothesis of life's origins will require that many questions be answered. Scientists who study the origin of life do not yet know which sets of chemicals could have begun replicating themselves. Even if a living cell could be made in the laboratory from simpler chemicals, it would not prove that nature followed the same pathway billions of years ago on the early earth."[6]

Colorado State microbiologist Franklin Harold is a Darwinist, but he wrote:

---

4. 1871 letter to Joseph Hooker, quoted *The Telegraph*, "Darwin Proved Right on Origin of Life on Earth."
5. Wilson, "Intelligent Evolution."
6. National Academy of Sciences, *Science, Evolution and Creationism*, 18.

"We should reject, as a matter of principle, the substitution of intelligent design for the dialogue of chance and necessity; but we must concede that there are presently no detailed Darwinian accounts of the evolution of any biochemical system, only a variety of wishful speculations."[7]

Atheist philosopher Thomas Nagle wrote:

"[N]o viable account, even a purely speculative one, seems to be available of how a system as staggeringly functionally complex and information-rich as a self-reproducing cell, controlled by DNA, RNA, or some predecessor, could have arisen by chemical evolution alone from a dead environment."[8]

Charles Darwin did not claim that his theory explained the origin of life. In the last paragraph of *On the Origin of Species*, he wrote:

"There is grandeur in this view of life, with its several powers, *having been originally breathed into a few forms or into one*; and that, whilst this planet has gone cycling on according to the fixed law of gravity, from so simple a beginning endless forms most beautiful and most wonderful have been, and are being, evolved."[9] (emphasis added)

In the second edition of *On the Origin of Species*, in 1860, Darwin added three words, making this line read, "having been originally breathed *by the Creator* into a few forms or into one."[10] (emphasis added) *Darwin started with the existence of life and then explained "descent with modification."*[11] A materialist may use the word "evolution" when talking about the origin of life, but Darwinian evolution cannot explain it.

Believing the Impossible

"[The] break between the living and non-living world . . . represents the most dramatic and fundamental of all the discontinuities in nature. Between a living

---

7. Harold, *The Way of the Cell*, 205.
8. Nagle, *Mind and Cosmos*, 123.
9. Darwin, *On the Origin of Species*, 526.
10. Darwin, *On the Origin of Species*, 2nd edition, 1860; quoted Ross, *A Matter of Days*, 26. All the current editions I have seen go back to Darwin's original language, in the first edition.
11. Darwin, *On the Origin of Species*, 141.

cell and the most highly ordered non-biological system, such as a crystal or a snowflake, there is a chasm as vast and absolute as it is possible to conceive."

—BIOCHEMIST MICHAEL DENTON[12]

Some scientists are attempting to find a way that the simplest forms of life might have developed on their own. They call this "abiogenesis." It used to be called "spontaneous generation." By any name, these efforts have so far been unsuccessful. In fact, the more science learns, the less likely such success appears. It may have been possible in Darwin's time to imagine a "simple" one-cell organism developing by chance. One of Darwinism's early advocates, the German biologist Ernst Haeckel, described the simplest living cell as a "homogeneous and structure-less globule of protoplasm."[13] Translated, that means a glob of Jell-O! *But we now know that there are no simple living cells.* The simplest known living organism, *Mychoplasma genetalium*, a tiny one-cell bacterium which lives in the human urinary tract, requires 482 proteins to perform its functions and 562,000 bases in its DNA to assemble those proteins.[14] Michael Denton wrote:

> "Although the tiniest bacterial cells are incredibly small . . . each is in effect a veritable micro-miniaturized factory containing thousands of exquisitely designed pieces of intricate molecular machinery, made up altogether of one hundred thousand million atoms, far more complicated than any machine built by man and absolutely without parallel in the non-living world."[15]

Scientists in Darwin's time believed in spontaneous generation, that maggots developed spontaneously from rotting meat or mold from aging bread. French scientist Louis Pasteur later proved that flies only come from eggs laid by other flies. Mold only comes from living, air-borne spores which settle on the bread and grow. *Life only comes from life.*

Materialistic scientists have long recognized this difficulty. In 1954, Harvard biologist and Nobel Prize-winner George Wald wrote:

> "One has only to contemplate the magnitude of this task to concede that the spontaneous generation of a living organism is impossible. Yet, here we are—the result, I believe, of spontaneous generation."[16]

12. Denton, *Evolution: A Theory in Crisis*, 249–250.
13. Haeckel, *The Wonders of Life*, 130.
14. Meyer, *Signature in the Cell*, 201.
15. Denton, *Evolution: A Theory in Crisis*, 250.
16. Wald, "The Origin of Life," 46. Wald wrote that he was using the term

It is impossible but he believed it, because there is no other option without a Creator. Wald could only speculate that while spontaneous generation is impossible under present conditions, it might have been possible—he could not explain how—under conditions present on the early earth.[17] But the sixty years since Wald wrote this have not produced any discoveries which would make such an event seem any more possible, even in the distant past.

In 1983, Cambridge astronomer Fred Hoyle gave a colorful illustration of how unlikely it is that the first life could have arisen by chance:

> "A junkyard contains all the bits and pieces of a Boeing 747, dismembered and in disarray. A whirlwind happens to blow through the yard. What is the chance that after its passage a fully assembled 747, ready to fly, will be found standing there?"[18]

In 2007, Harvard chemist George Whitesides, accepting the Preistley Medal for lifetime achievement, said, "Most chemists believe, as I do, that life emerged spontaneously from mixtures of molecules in the prebiotic earth. How? I have no idea ... *We need a really good new idea.*"[19] (emphasis added) This is the second great dilemma for a materialist. He still has to believe, against all the evidence, in some form of spontaneous generation—at least once, in the beginning.

The discovery of DNA multiplied this problem many times over. One of the most important scientific advances of the twentieth century was the discovery of the structure of the DNA molecule (a double-helix ladder), by biologists James Watson and Francis Crick in 1953. This tiny molecule, found in the nucleus of every living cell, has an outer backbone of simple phosphates and sugars, but Watson and Crick discovered that it contains vast amounts of *information* in the arrangement of the chemical compounds, called nucleotide bases, which make up the rungs of its ladder.[20] DNA directs the makeup of the cell—the entire body—by communicating this information to the proteins in a coded language. There are four different bases, or "letters," in this genetic alphabet, usually represented as A, C, G,

---

"impossible" in a "colloquial, practical sense." Ibid.
   17. Ibid.
   18. Hoyle, *The Intelligent Universe*, 19.
   19. Whitesides, "Revolutions in Chemistry."
   20. Watson and Crick wrote, "The phosphate-sugar backbone of our model is completely regular, but any sequence of the pairs of the bases can fit into the structure. It follows that in a long molecule many different permutations are possible, and it therefore seems likely that the precise sequence of the bases is the code which carries the genetic information." Watson and Crick, "Genetic Implications of the Structure of Deoxyribonucleic Acid," 965.

and T. Each bit of instruction, known as a gene, is made up of hundreds or thousands of these letters, in precise sequence.[21]

If materialism is true, not only did the first living cell have to develop spontaneously from non-living matter; DNA or some similar molecule, complex enough to direct the cell's organization, had to do so as well.

The Science of Life—Amino Acids, Proteins, and DNA

Let us look more closely at some of the scientific questions involved in the origin of life. The popular notion that life arose from a "pre-biotic soup" originated with two biologists, Russian A. I. Oparin and Englishman J. B. S. Haldane, in the 1920s. They proposed that simple chemicals came together to form organic compounds such as amino acids, the organic compounds collected to form proteins, and the proteins combined to form the simplest living cells.[22] But they could not demonstrate how any of this occurred.

One of the most famous scientific experiments of the twentieth century was conducted by two University of Chicago chemists, Harold Urey and Stanley Miller, in 1953. They started with a chemical mixture intended to represent the atmosphere of the early earth, applied an electrical charge to represent lightning, and got some of the twenty amino acids necessary to produce the proteins which make up a living cell.[23] Similar experiments were done in following years, some involving ultraviolet light instead of electricity, and these also produced amino acids. It was widely reported that these experiments demonstrated how life could have arisen spontaneously on the early earth. Many believed it would only be a few years before scientists would create life in the laboratory.

But that has not happened. In fact, scientists have concluded that the chemicals used in these experiments (hydrogen, methane, ammonia, and water vapor) were not the chemicals likely to have existed in the early atmosphere at all (the current consensus is carbon dioxide, nitrogen, and water vapor). Unintentionally, Urey and Miller and their colleagues used a combination of chemicals much more likely to produce amino acids.[24]

In 2007, Jeffrey Bada of the Scripps Institute of Oceanography, a former student of Miller's, claimed to have produced amino acids from a realistic

---

21. Collins, *The Language of God*, 102–103.
22. Dembski and Wells, *The Design of Life*, 213.
23. Meyer, Stephen; Strobel, *The Case for a Creator*, 228. There are hundreds of amino acids in nature, but only twenty specific amino acids are present in proteins. Ibid.
24. Wells, Jonathan; Strobel, *The Case for a Creator*, 37.

"primordial soup." But Bada first failed, like the many others who have tried to recreate these experiments using the correct chemicals. He succeeded only after adding certain metals which acted as antacids.[25]

But even if the problems with these experiments could be overcome, producing amino acids is only one small step, almost certainly the easiest step, toward creating life. Next you would have to construct each of the thousands of proteins which make up a living cell. These proteins decode information received from the DNA and then carry out all the tasks of assembling the cell. They are so amazing that Jacques Monod referred to their "demoniacal functions."[26]

Each protein molecule is so tiny that it has to be magnified a million times just to be visible to the human eye.[27] But each consists of between fifty and 1000 amino acids (the twenty different amino acids which are found in proteins, in various sequences) in complex, three-dimensional structures.[28] These sequences and structures are different for each type of protein—approximately 250 different types in a typical living cell.[29]

Experiments have shown that the ordering of the amino acids does not occur spontaneously.[30] To get the necessary proteins, one would not only have to produce all the right amino acids, he would have to precisely arrange them, for each different type of protein. Could they all have come together in nature, in just the right sequences, by chance? The odds against this are enormous. Fred Hoyle wrote, "[T]he number of ways in which even a single enzyme [protein] could be wrongly constructed [is] greater than the number of all the atoms in the universe."[31] Hoyle and his colleague at Cambridge, Chandra Wickramasinghe, calculated the odds of all the proteins in a typical living cell developing spontaneously to be one in ten to the 40,000th power. They called this "an outrageously small probability that could not be faced even if the entire universe consisted of organic soup."[32]

If all the proteins could be properly constructed, the process would then become even more difficult. The thousands of proteins would have to be precisely arranged to make a cell capable of life. Non-living matter is not organized in cells. No one has explained how even the simplest living cell,

---

25. Bailey, *Do Scientists Understand the Origin of Life?*
26. Quoted Denton, *Nature's Destiny*, 171.
27. Denton, *Evolution: A Theory in Crisis*, 234.
28. Behe, *Darwin's Black Box*, 52; Dembski and Wells, *The Design of Life*, 208.
29. Bradley, Walter; Strobel, *The Case for Faith*, 102.
30. Dembski and Wells, *The Design of Life*, 235.
31. Hoyle, "The Universe: Past and Present Reflections," 8.
32. Hoyle and Wickramasinghe, *Evolution from Space*, 24.

with hundreds of specific proteins and multiple component parts, including a nucleus, cell membrane, and cytoplasm, could come together on its own or organize itself.

Very Tiny Floppy Discs

Then you come to DNA, which is even more complex. A typical DNA molecule contains millions of pairs of nucleotide bases (in humans, more than three billion pairs), all precisely arranged in a long string. If it were stretched out, the human DNA chain would be roughly two meters long. Tightly coiled, it makes up one tiny molecule, contained in every living cell.[33]

But DNA is not just its chemical bases any more than Darwin's *On the Origin of Species* is just letters on a page. In both cases, it is the *arrangement* of the bases or letters which communicates information—in DNA, the instructions necessary for the assembly of the cell. Specific sequences of bases in the DNA cause specific arrangements of amino acids, which form specific proteins, each of which performs specific functions in the cell.[34]

This idea of information or instruction is not just a metaphor. Richard Dawkins wrote:

> "It is raining DNA outside. On the bank of the Oxford canal at the bottom of my garden is a large willow tree, and it is pumping downy seeds into the air . . . The whole performance, cotton wool, catkins, tree and all, is in aid of one thing and one thing only, the spreading of DNA around the countryside. Not just any DNA, but DNA whose coded characters spell out specific instructions for building willow trees . . . It is raining instructions out there; it's raining programs; it's raining tree-growing, fluff-spreading, algorithms. That is not a metaphor, it is the plain truth. It couldn't be any plainer if it were raining floppy discs."[35]

When Watson and Crick discovered the structure of the DNA molecule, they solved one mystery—how genetic information is passed down from one generation to another. *But they uncovered an even greater mystery, which continues to defy explanation to this day—where that very specific genetic information came from in the first place.*[36]

---

33. Lennox, *God's Undertaker*, 137.
34. Meyer, *Signature in the Cell*, 113, 365–367.
35. Dawkins, *The Blind Watchmaker*, 157–158.
36. Meyer, *Signature in the Cell*, 14.

DNA presents other problems as well. Its formation requires that the proteins from which it is made already exist, but the amino acids are arranged, so as to form the right proteins, based on instructions contained in the DNA. The two appear to be mutually dependent on one another. Jacques Monod called this a "veritable enigma,"[37] and Karl Popper, philosopher of science at the University of London, referred to it as "a vicious circle."[38] No wonder Hoyle and Wickramasinghe called the creation of DNA, "too complex to set numbers to."[39]

There is also the issue of reproduction. There is no reason to expect that first living cell would have arrived with the ability to reproduce itself, but it would have had to possess this ability before it could begin to evolve into more complicated forms of life.[40]

Furthermore, scientists can only speculate that the first living cell must have developed by "chemical evolution." But this would require non-living chemicals to replicate themselves, and scientists have been unable to identify any chemicals which might have done so, to begin the process. Richard Dawkins could only suggest:

> "At some point a particularly remarkable molecule was formed by accident. We will call it the Replicator. It may not have been the biggest or most complex molecule around, but it had the extraordinary property of being able to create copies of itself."[41]

Dawkins cannot identify this "remarkable molecule," offer any evidence for its existence, or explain how it acquired this "extraordinary property." He just asserts that it happened.

Chandra Wickramasinghe is not a theist, but in an interview, he stated, "[T]he earth's atmosphere was never of the right character to form an organic soup;" and "[I]t doesn't follow that if you have an organic soup it could get life started."[42] He concluded that the origin of life can only be explained "in terms of a statistical miracle or in terms of an intelligence intervening. It's one or the other."[43] Elsewhere, he said:

---

37. Quoted Bedau and Cleland, *The Nature of Life*, 141.
38. Popper, "Scientific Reduction and the Essential Incompleteness of all Science," 270.
39. Hoyle and Wickramasinghe, *Evolution from Space*, 30.
40. Conway, *The Rediscovery of Wisdom*, 125; Antony Flew, *There Is a God*, 125–126.
41. Dawkins, *The Selfish Gene*, 16.
42. Wickramasinghe, "Science and the Divine Origin of Life," 25.
43. Ibid., 34.

> "The emergence of life from a primordial soup on earth is merely an article of faith that scientists are finding difficult to shed. There is no experimental evidence to support this at the present time. Indeed, all attempts to create life from non-life, starting from Pasteur, have been unsuccessful."[44]

How Much Faith Do You Have?

> "The miracle stands 'explained'; it does not strike us as any less miraculous... As Francois Maurice wrote, 'What this professor says is far more incredible than what we poor Christians believe.'"
>
> —JACQUES MONOD[45]

We are discussing some incredible numbers, the odds of the necessary steps for random molecules of matter to form a living cell, all happening by chance. It is hard to grasp how minuscule one in ten to the 40,000th power is. This is not one divided by 40,000; it is one divided by one with 40,000 zeroes after it. If I were to type that number, it would take twenty pages, just for the zeroes!

For comparison, the odds of winning a major prize in the lottery are "only" about one in ten to the eighth power (one in 100 million). The total number of seconds since the big bang is approximately ten to the sixteenth power.[46] The total number of living cells which have ever existed on earth is roughly ten to the fortieth power.[47] The total number of atoms in the universe is about ten to the seventieth power.[48] The total number of elementary particles (protons, neutrons and electrons) is approximately ten to the eightieth power.[49]

Howard's Law #17 is: If your philosophy requires you to believe in something far less likely than picking one particular atom at random, from all the atoms in the universe, your philosophy is probably wrong.

No one would consider such odds in ordinary life. If you are playing cards, how many times in a row can someone deal themselves four aces,

---

44. Quoted Geisler and Turek, *I Don't Have Enough Faith to be an Atheist*, 121.
45. Monod, *Chance and Necessity*, 138.
46. Meyer, *Signature in the Cell*, 216.
47. Behe, *The Edge of Evolution*, 135.
48. Denton, *Evolution: A Theory in Crisis*, 310.
49. Meyer, *Darwin's Doubt*, 175.

before you conclude that it is not an accident?[50] How about trillions of times every second, since the big bang? Yet some very intelligent people believe in Monod's "Monte Carlo game." Dawkins wrote, "However improbable the origin of life might be, we know it happened . . . because we are here."[51] No wonder Norman Geisler and Frank Turek wrote, *I Don't Have Enough Faith to be an Atheist.*

Was the Universe Predisposed Toward Life?

Since the 1960s, many scientists have looked for explanations other than chance for the origin of life. If chance is ruled out, the only other option for a materialist is necessity. So almost all these explanations are based on some variation of the idea that the universe is *predisposed* toward life. But for a materialist, everything must result from blind, natural causes. There can be no intelligence, no design, no purpose involved. So any such predisposition must result from chance. These suggestions do not solve the mystery; they only push it back another level.

There are other problems with these theories. Dean Kenyon, a biologist at San Francisco State University, developed one of the more popular proposals. In 1969, he authored a much-used college textbook called *Biochemical Predestination,* teaching this theory. But after years of conducting and observing experiments, Dr. Kenyon was forced to conclude that he had been mistaken. He said:

> "[O]ne thing that stands out is that you do not get ordered sequences of amino acids. Nor do you get ordered sequences of nucleotides, the building blocks of DNA . . . If we thought we were going to see a lot of spontaneous ordering, something must have been wrong with our theory."[52]

50. Craig, "Tough Questions about Science," 65.

51. Dawkins, *The God Delusion,* 137.

52. Quoted Pearcey and Claxton, *The Soul of Science,* 230. Stephen Meyer points out two other difficulties with any hypothesis based on necessity. First, natural laws produce endlessly repeating patterns, as in a crystal. But if DNA were arranged in such patterns, it could not convey meaningful information. To communicate information, there must be "contingency," the possibility of many different sequences of the nucleotide bases. Second, the only apparent natural mechanism for any specific arrangement of the bases would be some attraction between the bases, causing certain ones to attach to others, or an attraction between specific bases and the "ladder" to which they attach. But there is no chemical bond at all between the bases, and the bonds connecting them to the sugar molecules in the ladder (and the sugar molecules themselves) are all the same, and will bond with any of the four bases. Chemically speaking, any arrangement is equally likely. Meyer, *Signature in the Cell,* 240–243, 250.

Furthermore, these theories all assume that if the ingredients for life are present, all properly assembled, life will necessarily result. But this has never been demonstrated to be true. The assumption arises because for a materialist, it *has* to be true. But when we die, all the chemicals are still present, but life is not. *Apparently, life is more than its chemicals.*

The most popular hypothesis today is that RNA, the "messenger molecule" which carries information from the DNA to the proteins, developed first and eventually evolved into a cell containing both DNA and proteins. There are a host of unanswered questions as to how this could have occurred.[53] But it also does not solve the problem. RNA is structured as a single strand rather than a double helix, but it consists of thousands of nucleotide bases in precise arrangement.[54] Jeffrey Bada acknowledged in an interview with the New York Times, "We know that RNA is too complex to have arisen out of the simple molecules of the primordial soup."[55]

We Need More Time!

There is yet another difficulty. The best estimates are that the earth is about 4.5 billion years old. But there is fossil evidence of abundant single-cell life on earth 3.85 billion years ago.[56] After you allow time for the earth to cool, develop an atmosphere, and become hospitable for life, this leaves very little time for life to develop. Francis Collins wrote:

> "Four billion years ago, the conditions on this planet were completely inhospitable to life as we know it. 3.85 billion years ago, life was teeming. That is a very short period—150 million years—for the assembly of macromolecules into a self replicating form. I think even the most bold and optimistic proposals for the origin of life fall well short of achieving any real probability for that kind of event having occurred."[57]

In the nineteenth century, when scientists still believed that the universe had always existed, perhaps all these unlikely events might have seemed possible. In an infinite amount of time, theoretically anything could happen. But science now says that there was a beginning. In a finite period

---

53. For a scientific discussion of some of the problems with the "RNA world" hypothesis, see Meyer, *Signature in the Cell*, 296–323.
54. Denton, *Evolution: A Theory in Crisis*, 239–240.
55. Dreifus, "A Marine Chemist Studies How Life Began."
56. Collins, *The Language of God*, 88–89.
57. Collins, "Faith and the Human Genome," 152.

of time, even billions of years, the chance hypothesis simply does not hold up. And even an infinite amount of time would not help, unless the laws of physics were changed. The Second Law of Thermodynamics says that nature is moving from order to disorder. If we allow more time, do we not just get more disorder? Would a junk-yard ever transform itself into a 747, even in an infinite amount of time?

In an effort to provide more time, Chandra Wickramasinghe, Francis Crick, and others have suggested that perhaps microscopic life was "seeded" on earth from some older part of the universe. Wickramasinghe proposes that this was done accidently, by a comet,[58] and Crick that it was done intentionally, by space aliens, sending microscopic life to earth on a spaceship.[59] These are very intelligent men. But not only is there a lack of evidence to support these ideas; they do not answer the question—how did life come from non-life, whether on earth, another planet, or a comet? Where did the space aliens come from?

Howard's Law #18 is: *If your philosophy causes you to say that life was planted on earth by space aliens, your philosophy is probably wrong.*

Materialism cannot explain the origin of life. Even materialistic scientists call a natural origin "impossible," "almost a miracle," or "a statistical miracle." Once again, the only answer on the market is the Biblical answer, that the living God created life. The existence of life is our next piece of evidence, because o*nly a theist can say that life came from life.*

We Live in a Scientific Age!

"Somehow or other an extraordinary idea has arisen that the disbelievers in miracles consider them coldly and fairly, while believers in miracles accept them only in connection with some dogma. The fact is quite the other way. The believers in miracles accept them (rightly or wrongly) because they have evidence for them. The disbelievers in miracles deny them (rightly or wrongly) because they have a doctrine against them."

—G. K. CHESTERTON[60]

Before we conclude this chapter, let me suggest that for many people today, the greatest obstacle to believing in a Creator, or in the supernatural

58. Quoted Geisler and Turek, *I Don't Have Enough Faith to Be an Atheist*, 121.

59. *Scientific American*, "Profile: Francis Crick—The Mephistopheles of Neurobiology," 33.

60. Chesterton, *Orthodoxy*, 142.

generally, is that we are so programmed in favor of naturalistic explanations that we cannot bring ourselves to consider anything else. "We live in a scientific age!" But science can neither prove nor disprove the supernatural. How can you do a scientific experiment to determine if there is something beyond the scope of scientific experiment? If there is a Creator God, He is by definition beyond the realm of science.

But many scientists have adopted a principle called "methodological naturalism." This is a rule which says that only natural causes will be considered; anything else is dismissed as "unscientific." George Wald illustrated this, in the same article in which he said the spontaneous generation of life was "impossible," but he believed it occurred. He wrote:

> "About a century ago the question, How did life begin?, which has interested men throughout their history, reached an impasse. Up to that time, two answers had been offered: one that life had been created supernaturally, the other that it arises continually from the non-living. *The first explanation was outside science*; the second was shown to be untenable [by Pasteur and others]." (emphasis added)[61]

Having rejected the supernatural explanation simply because it was "outside science," and despite writing that spontaneous generation was both "impossible" and "untenable," Wald concluded, "I think a scientist has no choice but to approach the origin of life through a hypothesis of spontaneous generation."[62] But he based this conclusion not on any scientific evidence, only on the philosophical assumption that everything must have a natural cause.

It all comes back to the God question. If God exists, is it unlikely that He created the universe, or life, or man? If God created both water and grapes, and designed the natural process of fermentation, is it unbelievable that on one occasion He might skip that process and change water directly into wine?

The question is not whether there are laws of nature—there are. If we did not believe in the laws of nature, we could not say that anything was a miracle. The question is whether those laws are all that exist. If there is a Creator, why should we think it unlikely that He might intervene in what He created? If God performed the big miracle of creation, why should we object to the little ones? I would submit that our difficulty in believing in the supernatural is more emotional, based on the "spirit of the age," than it is logical or scientific.

---

61. Wald, "The Origin of Life," 45.
62. Ibid.

Chapter 12

"A Creator as well as a Creature"
Why Does Intelligent Life Exist?

"[W]ith the arrival on earth of symbol-centered, behaviorally modern *Homo sapiens*, an entirely new order of being had materialized on the scene. And explaining just how this extraordinary new phenomenon came about is at the same time both the most intriguing question and the most baffling one in all of biology."

—IAN TATTERSALL, PALEOANTHROPOLOGIST,
AMERICAN MUSEUM OF NATURAL HISTORY[1]

"[I]f you wish to ask the question of the ages—Why do humans exist?"
—STEPHEN JAY GOULD, HARVARD PALEONTOLOGIST[2]

MATERIALISM CANNOT EXPLAIN WHY anything exists. It can offer only highly improbable speculations as to how the first life began. Now we come to the third of G. K. Chesterton's three questions, "the origin of man himself."[3] We will look primarily at one aspect of this question, intelligence. Biologist Julian Huxley wrote, "The essential character of man . . . is conceptual thought."[4] So this question may be worded, why does intelligent life exist?

1. Tattersall, "How We Came to be Human," 58.
2. Gould, *Wonderful Life*, 323.
3. Chesterton, *The Everlasting Man*, 26.
4. Huxley, *The Uniqueness of Man*, 15.

We should notice again two undeniable facts about humans. The first is that we are animals. We share all our basic biological systems with other animals. At the molecular level we are almost exactly the same, with the same basic amino acids, proteins, and DNA structure, the same assembly processes for the cell. But *men are different*. Our brains are physically much like those of other animals, and many animals have some basic intelligence. But we are conscious, rational, free, and moral, in ways that no other animal is. Other animals have breath and vocal cords, but only humans can speak meaningfully. Other animals have hands which could hold a paintbrush, but no other animal can produce meaningful art. Other animals suffer, but only man asks, "Why?"

Men have long noticed these differences. Cicero, the Roman statesman and philosopher of the first century, BC, wrote:

> "This animal, foreseeing, sagacious, various, acute, gifted with memory, full of method and design, which we call man, was produced by the supreme Deity under remarkable circumstances; for this alone of so many kinds and natures of animals, partakes of judgment and reflection, when all other animals are destitute of them."[5]

Chesterton wrote:

> "[It] sounds like a truism to say that the most primitive man drew a picture of a monkey and . . . it sounds like a joke to say that the most intelligent monkey drew a picture of a man . . . Art is the signature of man . . . This creature was truly different from all other creatures; because *he was a creator as well as a creature*."[6] (emphasis added)

Christianity and Evolution

How did these differences come about? Here we are finally at the point where Darwin's theory of evolution has something to say. An overwhelming majority of scientists, including many who are Christians, accept this theory. But did man, with the ability to perform calculus, develop scientific theories, and invent spaceships, evolve from lower life-forms solely by blind, natural causes? Did microbes just develop into microbiologists?[7] Before we

---

5. Cicero, "Laws," Book I, 174.
6. Chesterton, *The Everlasting Man*, 34–35.
7. Mortenson and Ury, *Coming to Grips with Genesis*, 18.

attempt to answer these questions, let us take two brief detours. First we should define the word, "evolution." It may be used in at least four different ways.

First, it may mean gradual changes within a given species, as in the beaks of the finches Darwin observed in the Galapagos Islands, changing over several generations to adapt to the different food supplies on each island. This is called *micro-evolution,* and everyone agrees that it occurs.

Second, evolution may mean the theory, drawn from such observations, that all current life-forms are the result of millions of such changes—that all living things, plants or animals, descended from the first simple, one-cell organisms. This is sometimes called *macro-evolution.*

Third, the word may be used for Darwin's particular theory—that the mechanism for all evolution, both micro and macro, is small, accidental changes, or "mutations" (now understood to be in the DNA), which help an organism adapt better to its environment, gain a competitive advantage in the struggle for survival, live longer or breed more, and therefore produce more offspring, so that the changes are preserved in future generations by what he called "natural selection." This is the way we will use the term, *Darwinism.*

Finally, the word evolution is sometimes used for the philosophical statement that the evolutionary process is entirely the result of chance, with no plan, no design, and no purpose, what we will call *undirected evolution.* Steven Jay Gould expressed this view:

> "[W]ind back life's tape to the dawn of time and let it play again—and you will never get a human a second time . . .
>
> We are here because one odd group of fishes had a peculiar fin anatomy that could transform into legs for terrestrial creatures; because comets struck the earth and wiped out dinosaurs, thereby giving mammals a chance not otherwise available . . . because the earth never froze entirely during an ice age; because a small and tenuous species, arising in Africa a quarter of a million years ago, has managed, so far, to survive by hook and by crook. We may yearn for a 'higher' answer—but none exists."[8]

Evolution in the first sense, micro-evolution, is uncontroversial. Evolution in the last sense, undirected evolution, is not a scientific position but a philosophical one, and is totally contrary to Christian beliefs. It is with the second and third uses of the word, macro-evolution (common ancestry)

---

8. Gould, *The Meaning of Life: Reflections in Words and Pictures of Why We Are Here,* 33.

and Darwinism (the mechanism of random mutation and natural selection), that there is disagreement among Christians.

I would suggest that a Christian can (but does not have to) believe in evolution in either of these two senses, so long as he sees it as being divinely directed, part of God's creative plan. The largest Christian church, the Roman Catholic Church, officially declared Christianity and evolution to be compatible in 1950, and reaffirmed that position in 1996. However, both Pope Pius XII and Pope John Paul II also stated, "If the origin of the human body comes through living matter which existed previously, the spiritual soul is created directly by God."[9] Christians hold different views on the questions of how, and how long ago, God *"created the heavens and the earth"* and all His living creatures. These debates are interesting, and I have my own views. But I would urge that what is important is that God is the creator, not how or when He created.[10]

On the other hand, to be consistent with Christian teachings (or, I believe, to explain the scientific evidence), we must reject the idea that there is no Creator and that everything which exists is an accident. I will submit

---

9. Pius XII, "Humani Generis;" quoted John Paul II, Message to the Pontifical Academy of Sciences: "Magisterium Is Concerned With the Question of Evolution for It Involves Conception of Man."

10. From the discussion which follows, the reader will gather that while I believe it is possible for a Christian to accept evolution in any of the first three senses—God could have designed the Darwinian process so that it would eventually produce humans—I am not a Darwinist. I am not a scientist, and I recognize the overwhelming support for Darwinism among scientists. But I also am not a materialist, and therefore I am not compelled to accept Darwinism on philosophical grounds. And as I understand the scientific evidence, I find Darwin's mechanism for evolution, random mutation and natural selection, to be insufficient. I have no particular problem with the idea that God may have used directed evolution in His creative process, but I will leave that debate for other, more qualified, writers.

I also recognize that many intelligent Christians believe that Scripture requires a rejection of almost all evolutionary theory. This is based primarily on a literal reading of the early chapters of Genesis. But a review of church history will reveal many different (and often non-literal) interpretations of these early chapters. To cite only two examples, St. Iraneus of Lyon, in the second century, wrote that the first six days of the Genesis creation account were each 1000 years long, and the seventh day was still going on. Iraneus, "Against Heresies," quoted Ross, *A Matter of Days*, 43. Both St. Augustine in the fifth century and St. Thomas Aquinas in the thirteenth century taught that God, who is not in time, created everything "simultaneously," and that the Genesis account of six days was a literary device to help us, who are in time, to understand. Augustine, "The Literal Meaning of Genesis," Book I, §18.36, 185, Book V, §3.6, 279; and Aquinas, "The Work of the Six Days of Creation, 90–91. See also Fiedrowicz, Introduction to Augustine, "The Literal Meaning of Genesis," 166; and Richter, *The Epic of Eden*, 99. I do not see how I can claim any one interpretation of these passages to be the only acceptable reading, given the many different interpretations held by devout and wise Christians over the last 2000 years.

that this is where we should draw the line, because here we are not rejecting science, only materialistic philosophy. For a Christian, science is the study of God's creation. Evolution is a scientific theory, and we can argue for or against it, based on the evidence. But the philosophical statement that the process was undirected, that "no higher answer exists," is incompatible with Christian beliefs, and it is a claim which I believe we are entirely justified in rejecting, based on the arguments we have already discussed.

Who Is Free To Follow the Evidence?

Our second detour is historical. The philosophies of naturalism, holding that nature is all there is, and humanism, teaching that man is the highest being which exists, became popular between the sixteenth and eighteenth centuries. Darwinism followed in the nineteenth century. These first two ideas left no room for God. But men, being men, still asked, "Where did we come from?" The belief that everything came from nature was not new. Neither was the general idea of evolution, gradual changes over time. Both had been around at least since the fifth century, BC.[11] But no one could explain how we could have evolved by natural causes alone. Darwin gave a plausible answer with his theory of natural selection, and made these philosophies more acceptable. Richard Dawkins wrote, "Although atheism might have been logically tenable before Darwin, Darwin made it possible to be an intellectually fulfilled atheist."[12] On another occasion, Dawkins commented, "I could not imagine being an atheist at any time before 1859, when Darwin's *Origin of Species* was published."[13]

The result of this is that a Christian is free to follow the evidence wherever it leads, but a materialist is not.[14] He has to believe in some form of evolution, because if everything is brought about by natural causes, there is no other option. Harvard biologist Richard Lewontin wrote:

> "We take the side of science in spite of the patent absurdity of some of its constructs, in spite of its failure to fulfill many of its extravagant promises of health and life, in spite of the tolerance of the scientific community for unsubstantiated just-so stories, because

---

11. Both of these ideas were proposed by the very early Greek philosophers known as Atomists, such as Democritus and Epicurus. Denton, *Evolution: A Theory in Crisis*, 39–40.

12. Dawkins, *The Blind Watchmaker*, 10.

13. Dawkins quotes himself as having made this statement in a conversation with a fellow atheist. Ibid.

14. Craig, "Tough Questions about Science," 67.

we have *a prior commitment, a commitment to materialism*. It is not that the methods and institutions of science somehow compel us to accept a material explanation of the phenomenal world, but, on the contrary, that we are forced by our *a priori* commitment to material causes to create an apparatus of investigation and a set of concepts that produce material explanations, no matter how counter-intuitive, no matter how mystifying to the uninitiated. *Moreover, that materialism is absolute, for we cannot allow a Divine Foot in the door.*"[15] (emphasis added)

Richard Dawkins, having rejected in advance any supernatural explanation, wrote:

"The theory of evolution by cumulative natural selection is the only theory we know of that is in principle capable of explaining the existence of organized complexity. *Even if the evidence did not favor it, it would still be the best theory available.* In fact the evidence does favor it, but that is another story."[16] (emphasis added)

Again, this is "methodological naturalism," refusing in advance to consider anything other than natural causes. Please do not misunderstand me—it is perfectly appropriate for a scientist, in his laboratory, to look for natural causes. Science is the study of nature. However, when he says that nothing exists outside of nature, he has gone beyond science. He has turned a rule of scientific methodology into a philosophy. But if he makes such a "prior commitment to materialism," he *will* end up a Darwinist—"even if the evidence [does] not favor it"—because it is his only option.

Where Does Intelligence Come From?

"[I]t is as impossible to conceive that ever pure incogitative [unthinking] matter should produce a thinking intelligent being, as that nothing should of itself produce matter."

—JOHN LOCKE, SEVENTEENTH-CENTURY PHILOSOPHER[17]

As with our previous questions, the more science learns, the more difficult it is to explain the origin of intelligence naturally. The crucial question is the same,

---

15. Lewontin, "Billions and Billions of Demons," 31.
16. Dawkins, *The Blind Watchmaker*, 452.
17. Locke, *Essays Concerning Human Understanding*, Book 4, §X, 315.

as to human intelligence, animal intelligence, or the intelligent information contained in DNA—*how does intelligence arise by chance from matter?*

Let us look again at DNA. Putting aside the question of how it developed in the first place, how was it modified so as to produce complex, intelligent organisms? The Darwinian answer is random mutation and natural selection. According to the current scientific consensus, evolution works entirely through gradual changes in our DNA. It is DNA which determines that we are humans, rather than amoebas or turtles or monkeys, and it is DNA which determines our individual differences.[18] There are more than three billion base pairs of DNA in the human genome. Each pair is made up of two chemical bases, two of the four "letters" in the genetic alphabet.[19] These bases are precisely arranged to make up thousands of bits of intelligent information, called genes.

Every living cell has a DNA molecule. In a given individual, they are all identical. Although a DNA molecule weighs only a few trillionths of a gram, each one contains all the information necessary to build a copy of the entire body. We inherit our DNA from our parents. Ordinarily, ours will be a combination of theirs. But every now and then, one or more letters in an organism's DNA will be different—nature occasionally makes copying errors. The vast majority of these "random mutations" will be either meaningless or harmful, like viruses in a computer. It has been estimated that only one in every 20,000 will be beneficial.[20] But as Francis Collins describes:

> "[O]n rare occasions, a mutation will arise by chance that offers a slight degree of selective advantage. That new DNA 'spelling' will have a slightly higher likelihood of being passed on to future offspring. Over the course of a very long period of time, such favorable rare events can become widespread in all members of the species, ultimately resulting in major changes in biological function."[21]

---

18. This is an over-simplification. There are gene-switching, gene-splicing, and error-correcting mechanisms, along with other "epigenetic" sources of information in the cell, all of which contribute to our individual characteristics, but do not appear to be directly determined by our DNA. Lennox, *God's Undertaker*, 140–143; Meyer, *Darwin's Doubt*, 275–286.

19. The bases always occur in matched pairs—"a" is always paired with "t," and "c" with "g." But any letter may occur at any point on the chain, so long as its partner is the appropriate match. Meyer, *Signature in the Cell*, 79–82.

20. Simmons, *What Darwin Didn't Know*, 306.

21. Collins, *The Language of God*, 131.

"An Enormous Lottery, Blindly Picking the Rare Winners"

> "[N]atural selection operates upon the products of chance and can feed nowhere else."
>
> —JACQUES MONOD[22]

This "slightly higher likelihood of being passed on"[23] is what Darwinists mean by "natural selection." It is common sense—if a mutation gives an organism a competitive advantage and helps it survive, that mutation is more likely to be passed on to future generations. But natural selection does not produce anything—it only selects from existing genes, and mutations which arise by chance. It does not have any plan or purpose. It does not look to the future or consider the greater good. Only conscious, rational minds can do those things. Natural selection is simply a natural process by which an organism with a beneficial genetic change produces more, or more competitive, offspring.[24] Richard Dawkins wrote:

> "Natural selection, the blind, unconscious, automatic process which Darwin discovered . . . has no purpose in mind. It has no mind and no mind's eye. It does not plan for the future. It has no vision, no foresight, no sight at all. If it can be said to play the role of a watchmaker in nature, it is a blind watchmaker."[25]

It is also entirely dependent on random mutations. Dawkins argues that while natural selection is "blind," it is not just a matter of chance—it selects what promotes survival.[26] *But it only selects from mutations which arise by chance.* Darwin wrote, "[N]atural selection can do nothing until favorable variations chance to occur."[27] Jacques Monod described evolution as "an enormous lottery presided over by natural selection, blindly picking the rare winners from among numbers drawn at utter random."[28]

---

22. Monod, *Chance and Necessity*, 118.

23. Statistically, these mutations occur about once in every hundred million nucleotides. Behe, *The Edge of Evolution*, 11, 66. Since a human genome has some six billion nucleotides (three billion pairs), we would expect roughly sixty such random mutations in a typical human being. Collins, *The Language of God*, 131. But if only one in every 20,000 mutations is beneficial, the overwhelming likelihood is that no beneficial mutation will occur in any given individual.

24. Behe, *The Edge of Evolution*, 1.

25. Dawkins, *The Blind Watchmaker*, 9.

26. Ibid., 61–62.

27. Darwin, *On the Origin of Species*, 198.

28. Monod, *Chance and Necessity*, 138.

Biochemist Michael Denton points out that natural selection is an example of what, in areas other than biology, we call "trial and error."[29] Nature accidentally "tries" a new genetic spelling, and if it is advantageous, it is more likely to be preserved in succeeding generations. But because the entire system is based on random mutations, it is *random* trial and error.

When I was a boy, I loved to build models—airplanes, ships, cars, anything I could find. Occasionally, I would try to put one together without using the instructions. If it was simple enough, I might succeed. But I never thought of trying to build a model blindfolded or with no plan at all. How could living organisms develop that way?

This is an even greater problem when we consider that complex living organisms contain thousands of inter-related biological systems. If you change one, it affects many others. Did multiple favorable changes in DNA randomly happen at once, so that these inter-related systems could develop together? How could the different biological systems have evolved so as to work together, if their evolution was not simultaneous (or planned)? In real life, has anyone ever heard of a *blind* watchmaker? Some activities require sight!

Bill Gates said, "Human DNA is like a computer program, but far, far more advanced than any software ever created."[30] It takes highly-trained engineers to develop computer programs. Did the most advanced software in the universe arrange itself? It takes intelligence to decode intelligent messages, such as to map the human genome. Did it take none to encode them?[31]

All of human experience says that detailed, intelligent messages, such as those contained in DNA, only come from intelligent minds. Late in his life, George Wald suggested that the intelligence inherent in life also came from "mind:"

> "How is it that, with so many other apparent options, we are in a universe that possesses just that particular nexus of properties that breeds life? It has occurred to me lately—I must confess with some shock at first to my scientific sensibilities . . . that [perhaps] mind, rather than emerging as a late outgrowth in the evolution of life, has existed always as the matrix, the source and condition of physical reality . . . It is mind that has composed a physical universe that breeds life, and so eventually evolves creatures that know and create."[32]

29. Denton, *Evolution: A Theory in Crisis*, 314.
30. Gates, *The Road Ahead*, 188.
31. Varghese, *The Wonder of the World*, 32.
32. Wald, "Life and Mind in the Universe," 219.

Philosopher Thomas Nagle recently made a similar proposal, that "mind is not just an afterthought or an accident or an add-on, but a basic aspect of nature."[33] Both Nagle and Wald are or were naturalists, attempting to find an explanation in necessity rather than chance. But I would suggest that to say the universe was "composed" by mind is awfully close to saying, *"In the beginning, God created the heavens and the earth."*

"Thinking Man"

"The naturalists have been engaged in thinking about nature. They have not attended to the fact that they were thinking."

—C. S. LEWIS[34]

If the intelligent information in DNA is difficult to explain, what about human intelligence? We are rational, thinking creatures. The name *homo sapiens* means "thinking man." Our ability to perceive truth cannot be explained solely by our physical brains, but it is also true that the brain is beyond our understanding. Science writer Isaac Asimov said, "In man is a three-pound brain, which, as far as we know, is the most complex and orderly arrangement of matter in the universe."[35]

Some animals have larger brains than humans, but none are so intricately developed. *One neuron (nerve cell) in the human brain is more complex than any computer ever built,*[36] *and there are ten trillion neurons in a human brain.*[37] Each one connects with about 10,000 other neurons, so there are more connections in your brain than stars in the Milky Way or grains of sand on all the beaches in the world.[38] During early fetal development, the brain adds more than 250,000 neurons per minute and sends them out to the appropriate parts of the body. Each one seems to know where to go, how to get there and where to connect.[39] Owen Gingerich wrote, "[T]he laws of

---

33. Nagle, *Mind and Cosmos*, 16.
34. Lewis, *Miracles*, 1947, 65.
35. Asimov, "In the Game of Energy and Thermodynamics, You Can't Even Break Even;" quoted Dembski and Wells, *The Design of Life*, 10.
36. Simmons, *What Darwin Didn't Know*, 92.
37. Denton, *Nature's Destiny*, 322.
38. Ibid., 347; Gingerich, *God's Universe*, 29–30.
39. Simmons, *What Darwin Didn't Know*, 252, 282.

nature are rigged, not only in favor of complexity, or just in favor of life, but also in favor of mind."[40]

The materialistic explanation for all this is that intelligence is useful for survival and therefore favored by natural selection. But this leaves two huge unanswered questions. First, natural selection only preserves; it does not create, and no one has explained how the simplest animal intelligence developed in the first place. Charles Darwin wrote, "In what manner the mental powers were first developed in the lowest organisms is as hopeless an inquiry as how life itself originated."[41]

Second, while practical animal intelligence might aid in survival, it does not appear that the abstract or theoretical reasoning which is unique to man would do so. MIT philosopher and linguist Noam Chomsky, an atheist, wrote:

> "Some have argued that [the validity of theoretical human reasoning] isn't blind luck but rather a product of Darwinian evolution . . . but this argument is not compelling. It is possible to imagine that chimpanzees have an innate fear of snakes because those who lacked this genetically determined property did not survive to reproduce, but one can hardly argue that humans have the capacity to discern quantum theory for similar reasons."[42]

How did the ability to perform math, study the galaxies, or come up with a theory of human origins, contribute to the survival of the earliest man or help him find a mate? What good would such abilities have been, "when the chief aim of human existence was to avoid being eaten?"[43] Or as Alvin Plantinga asked, "What prehistoric woman would be [more] interested in some guy who prefers thinking about set theory to hunting?"[44]

The idea that natural selection would preserve basic animal intelligence, once it existed, seems reasonable. But as a total explanation for the development of human minds, from non-rational matter to animal intelligence and from animal intelligence to abstract human reasoning, it is simply insufficient. How could a mindless process produce minds?

---

40. Gingerich, *God's Universe*, 38.
41. Darwin, *The Descent of Man*, 96.
42. Chomsky, *Language and the Problems of Knowledge*, 157–158.
43. Ferguson, "The Heretic," 28.
44. Plantinga, *Where the Conflict Really Lies*, 133.

¿Habla Ingles?

One aspect of human intelligence is our use of language. We both think and communicate using either written symbols or verbal sounds to represent meaning. This was true in even the most ancient human civilizations.[45] Small children can learn and understand language, but humans are the only animals with this ability. Noam Chomsky, sometimes called the "father of modern linguistics," wrote, "When we study human language, we are approaching what some might call the 'human essence,' the distinctive qualities of mind that are, so far as we know, unique to man."[46]

How can this ability be explained naturally? Richard Dawkins acknowledged:

> "Nobody knows how [language] began. There doesn't seem to be anything like syntax in non-human animals and it is hard to imagine evolutionary forerunners of it. Equally obscure is the origin of semantics, of words and their meanings."[47]

Philosopher Anthony Kenny observed that to explain the development of human language based on natural selection, one has to say that the first language-user had a survival advantage over non-language-users. But "[T]he difficulty [is in] seeing how anyone could be described as a language-using individual at all before there was a community of language-users."[48]

Ian Tattersall, a paleoanthropologist and the curator of the American Museum of Natural History, writes that it was the use of language which made us human. But his only suggestions for how language originated are that a language instinct was "hard-wired" (apparently by chance) into our ancestors, and that the actual use of language may have begun as a game, played by children![49]

Furthermore, Tattersall points out that human brains, of the same size and structure as in present-day man, existed for many thousands of years before humans began to think or communicate in symbols. The same is true of vocal cords—they existed "half a million years before we have evidence our forebears used language."[50] But he makes no attempt to explain why these structures would have developed or have been preserved by natural selection for hundreds of thousands of years, before they became useful.

---

45. Ibid., 57.
46. Chomsky, "Form and Meaning in Natural Languages," 100.
47. Dawkins, *Unweaving the Rainbow*, 294.
48. Kenny, *From Empedacles to Wittgenstein*, 186–187.
49. Tattersall, "How We Came to be Human," 60
50. Ibid., 62.

Only theists can explain human language—it is a gift from God, given to enable us to communicate with Him and with one another. Christians believe that, "Humans were language users from the beginning . . . and the initial language they heard and understood was God speaking to them."[51]

Can Matter Produce Mind?

"How is it that inanimate matter can organize itself to contemplate itself?"

—ALLAN SANDAGE[52]

Many people, as children, have played with Quija Boards. These are flat boards of wood or pasteboard, with letters, numbers, and a few words, such as "yes" and "no" printed on them. You place your hand on an object called a "planchette" and ask a question. The planchette supposedly floats to various letters to spell out an answer. Some claim that it is guided by a supernatural power. Many Christians oppose the use of these games for this reason. In fact, the game is only a trick—the person with his hand on the planchette either consciously or unconsciously guides it to the appropriate answer.

But what if a Quija Board began spelling out intelligent messages without anyone touching it? We would be strongly inclined to believe that there was something supernatural about it, because we know that matter—wood or paper or plastic—cannot on its own form words or communicate meaning. *But if materialism is true, this is what has to happen in the human brain.* Mindless molecules must arrange themselves to "spell out" complicated, intelligent messages, messages which are true about the world outside of the brain.

Karl Marx once observed that there are only two possibilities—either mind produced matter, or matter produced mind.[53] But how could non-rational matter produce a rational mind? This is the third fundamental problem for a materialist. I would submit that this leap, from atoms to intelligence, from molecules to meaning, is so fundamental that its happening by chance—by any mindless process—is inconceivable.

Howard's Law #19 is: If your philosophy says that intelligence came from unintelligent sources, your philosophy is probably wrong.

---

51. Bacote and Spencer, "What Are the Theological Implications for Natural Science?" 62.

52. Quoted Johnson, "Science and Religion: Bridging the Great Divide."

53. Quoted Geisler, *Baker's Encyclopedia of Christian Apologetics*, 446.

The Miracle of Man

> "A thousand monkeys sitting at typewriters for millions of years would never produce Hamlet... Shakespeare did it on the first try."
>
> —NORMAN GEISLER[54]

Only man discovered fire or invented the wheel. Only man has studied the galaxies or written the history of his own species. Only man can create art or music, invent light bulbs or computers. Christians can explain these facts—man is "a creator as well as a creature," because he is made in the image of *the* Creator.

On the other hand, if nature is all there is, "man," as we use the word, does not exist. *Rather, every human who ever lived, every thought he ever thought, every word he ever spoke, every whisper of conscience he ever heard, every choice he ever made, and every noble or sacrificial act he ever performed, was the result of nothing but the chance collision of atoms.* The dilemma facing modern man is not that he will die; it is that he, as man, never lived. Materialism, or "humanism," attempts to make man god, but in the end it reduces him to a mere animal. And in the process, it contradicts the experience of every member of *homo sapiens* who has ever walked upright on this planet.

So I would submit that undirected evolution, the idea that we are solely the result of chance and there is no higher answer, is not plausible. In fact, I would respectfully suggest that only one who has ruled out all other possibilities in advance would logically reach that conclusion. Our next piece of evidence for a Creator is intelligence, from the intelligent information in DNA to human intelligence. *Only a theist can say that intelligence comes from intelligence.*

---

54. Ibid., 278.

Chapter 13

"A Cosmos rather than a Chaos"
Why Is There Order in Nature?

"I'm not an atheist and I don't think I can call myself a pantheist. We are in the position of a little child entering a huge library filled with books in many languages. The child knows someone must have written those books. It does not know how. It does not understand the languages in which they are written. The child dimly suspects a mysterious order in the arrangement of the books but doesn't know what it is. That, it seems to me, is the attitude of even the most intelligent human being toward God. We see the universe marvelously arranged and obeying certain laws but only dimly understand those laws. Our limited minds grasp the mysterious force that moves the constellations."

—ALBERT EINSTEIN[1]

NASA FUNDS THE SETI (Search for Extraterrestrial Intelligence) Institute. Here scientists search the universe for signs of intelligent life. They do this by looking for patterns in the otherwise random, naturally-occurring radio waves spread throughout the universe, because they know that a complex, meaningful pattern would indicate it came from an intelligent source. This project was portrayed in the movie, "Contact,"[2] starring Jodie Foster. Her character discovers a repeating series of prime numbers in radio waves coming from the vicinity of the star Vega. She concludes, correctly, that they were sent by an intelligent species populating a planet orbiting that star.

1. Quoted Jammer, *Einstein and Religion*, 48.
2. "Contact," Warner Brothers, 1997.

I would like to consider in this chapter two facts about the universe which many men over the centuries have found to be significant. The first is that it exhibits many such complex, meaningful patterns. It is ordered rather than random, "a cosmos rather than a chaos."[3] The second is that it appears to be ordered to the exact specifications necessary to support life as we know it. I will argue that both of these facts point to a Creator.

From his earliest beginnings, man, with his innate common sense, has looked at the universe and said, "This didn't just happen; it must have been designed." And it is just common sense. If you or I were walking on a beach and saw a shape in the sand like the letter "J," we might say, "Look what the waves did." But if we saw "J (hearts) S," we would conclude that two young lovers had been there. We would never try to explain that shape and the message it contains as something the waves did. Yet from the laws of physics to the information encoded in our DNA, from the dance of the planets to the genius of a Beethoven or a Michelangelo, the order and intelligence in the universe is infinitely greater than this simple message.

Not only ordinary men, but many of the greatest thinkers in history have concluded that the universe is so ordered that it must have been designed by an intelligent being. Socrates taught that the universe "is governed by reason and by a wondrous regulating intelligence."[4] Sir Isaac Newton said, "This most beautiful system of the sun, planets and comets, could only proceed from the counsel and dominion of an intelligent and powerful being."[5] The eighteenth-century French philosopher Francois-Marie Voltaire, no friend of organized religion, wrote, "I shall always be of the opinion that a clock proves a clock-maker and that the universe proves a God."[6]

We take this order for granted. We rely on patterns which we see in nature to enable us predict future events—that day will always follow night, or that two hydrogen atoms and one of oxygen will always make water. Science could not exist without this assumption of order. If we could not rely on the same experiment, done the same way, under the same conditions, to get the same results, scientific experimentation would be meaningless. *Science assumes that the universe makes sense, and that we can make sense of the universe.*[7]

---

3. Dembski, *The End of Christianity*, 101.
4. Plato, "Philebus," §28d, 1106.
5. Newton, "General Scholium," 544.
6. Quoted Akerly, *Voltaire and Rousseau Against the Atheists*, 35.
7. Cook and O'Connor, "What Are the Philosophical Implications of Christianity for the Natural Sciences?" 48.

Nobel Prize-winning physicist Steven Weinberg is an atheist, but he wrote, "[T]here is a simplicity, a beauty, that we are finding in the rules that govern matter that mirrors something that is built into the logical structure of the universe at a very deep level;" and "My experience as a physicist leads me to believe that there is order in the universe."[8]

Physicist Paul Davies wrote:

> "The success of the scientific method at unlocking the secrets of nature is so dazzling it can blind us to the greatest scientific miracle of all: *science works* . . . [T]he fact that science works, and works so well, points to something profoundly significant about the organization of the cosmos."[9]

Flying with Isaac Newton

"Let's grant that there are laws of nature. We might verbally deny them, but we won't take the extraordinary step of proving our point by jumping off the fifth floor . . . The existence of the laws of nature is the single greatest mystery uncovered by science, one that baffles the most skeptical scientist as much as it does anyone else."

—ROY ABRAHAM VARGHESE[10]

This order is reflected in natural laws, such as the law of gravity, the laws of thermodynamics, or Newton's laws of motion. Albert Einstein said, "[The] universe is not ruled by wishful thinking, but by immutable laws."[11] Stephen Hawking said, "The more we discover about the universe, the more we find that it is governed by rational laws."[12] As Apollo 8 orbited the moon on the day after Christmas, 1968, NASA arranged for the astronauts to answer questions from the public through a radio hookup. Commander William Anders was asked by a young boy who was "driving" the spacecraft. Anders answered, "I think Isaac Newton is doing most of the driving right now!"[13]

---

8. Weinberg, *Facing Up: Science and its Cultural Adversaries*, 24, 45.

9. Davies, *The Mind of God*, 20–21.

10. Varghese, *The Wonder of the World*, 22, 24.

11. 1954 interview with William Hermanns; quoted Jammer, *Einstein and Religion*, 123.

12. Benford, "Leaping the Abyss: Stephen Hawking on Black Holes, Unified Field Theory and Marilyn Monroe," 29.

13. Woods and O'Brien, "Apollo Flight Journal."

Where do the laws of nature come from? How can inanimate objects follow laws? If we say these laws are just descriptions of what happens, why do they happen? Physicist Victor Stenger wrote, "[W]here did the laws of physics come from? They came from nothing."[14] That is the only possible answer for a materialist, but I would suggest that the more reasonable explanation was offered by Henry Margenau, long-time professor of physics at Yale: "What is the origin of the laws of nature? For this I can find only one convincing answer: they are created by God."[15]

Howard's Law #20 is: *If your philosophy says that natural laws came from nothing, your philosophy is probably wrong.*

Houses, Lutes, and Watches

"Some people read books in order to find God. Yet there is a great book, the very appearance of created things. Look above you; look below you! Note it; read it! . . . Can you ask for a louder voice than that? Why, heaven and earth cry out to you: 'God made me!'"

—ST. AUGUSTINE[16]

The ancient pagans believed that nature was eternal, but the gods brought order out of chaos. Theists have long argued that the order in the universe is evidence for a divine Creator. In the Psalms, King David wrote, *"The heavens declare the glory of God and the firmament shows His handiwork."*[17] The Apostle Paul wrote, *"For since the creation of the world, His invisible attributes are clearly seen, being understood by the things that are made."*[18]

The argument from order is the oldest argument in Christian apologetics. St. Ephram the Syrian, in the fourth century, reasoned that the obvious design in the universe required a Creator, just as a house requires a builder. He wrote, "I saw houses and knew that housebuilders were in residence."[19]

---

14. Stenger, *God, the Failed Hypothesis*, 131.

15. Margenau, "The Laws of Nature are Created by God," 61.

16. Augustine, "Sermon, Mai 126," 123. The belief that we can see evidence of God in nature has traditionally been known as "natural theology." St. Thomas Aquinas taught that from nature we can conclude God exists, that He is one, and something of His general nature. Aquinas did not believe that we could arrive at doctrines such as the Trinity, the incarnation, or salvation, without special revelation. Geisler, *Baker's Encyclopedia of Apologetics*, 521–522.

17. Psalm 19:1.

18. Romans 1:20.

19. Ephrem, "Self-examination," §1:123, quoted Oden, *Classic Christianity*, 86.

In the same century, St. Gregory of Nazienzus, the Bishop of Cappadocia, wrote:

> "[H]ow could this Universe have come into being or been put together, unless God had called it into existence and held it together? For everyone who sees a beautifully made lute [an ancient, stringed musical instrument], and considers the skill with which it has been fitted together and arranged, or who hears its melody, would think of none but the lutemaker."[20]

The eighteenth-century Christian philosopher William Paley wrote that if he walked across a heath and found a stone lying on the ground, he might conclude it just happened to be there, even that it had been there "forever." But if he found a watch, he would never consider that possibility. Given its complexity and the fact that it exists for a purpose, the watch was obviously designed by an intelligent being.[21]

Richard Dawkins wrote *The Blind Watchmaker*, responding to Paley's argument. He acknowledged the *appearance* of design—he defined biology as "the study of complicated things that have the appearance of having been designed for a purpose."[22] On another occasion, he said, "Living objects . . . look designed, they look overwhelmingly as though they're designed."[23] But Dawkins believes this appearance is only an illusion. (A materialist has to believe a lot of things are illusions!) He proposes a natural order which has produced life, including human life, by blind, natural processes. The problem with this idea is that the natural order must be so precisely tailored to produce life that it seems no less certain to have been designed than a man does. Is a watch factory more likely to have come about by chance than a watch?[24]

Of course, complexity by itself does not necessarily indicate design. The shape of the sand on a beach may be quite complex, with dunes large and small, but we would not assume it was intentionally shaped unless we saw a meaningful pattern in the complexity—"J (hearts) S" or a sand castle.

20. Gregory of Nazienzus, Oration XXVIII, "Orations," 277–278.
21. Paley, *Natural Theology*, 4.
22. Dawkins, *The Blind Watchmaker*, 4.
23. Dawkins, "Royal Institution Christmas Lectures," 1991; quoted Lennox, *God's Undertaker*, 79.
24. University of Delaware physicist Stephen Barr wrote, "What Dawkins does not seem to appreciate is that his Blind Watchmaker is something even more remarkable than Paley's watches. Paley finds a watch and asks how such a thing could have come to be there by chance. Dawkins finds an immense automated factory that blindly constructs watches, and feels that he has completely answered Paley's point. But that is absurd. How can a factory that makes watches be less in need of explanation than the watches themselves?" Barr, *Modern Physics and Ancient Faith*, 111.

Likewise, you can have order without design, if it is simple enough. Three dice rolled at the same time will occasionally come out 1, 2, 3, in order (statistically once every 216 rolls). *But sufficient complexity, together with sufficient order or meaning, always indicates design.* Mount Rushmore may have resulted from natural causes, but the carvings of the four presidents did not.[25]

In one sense, an artistic masterpiece such as Michelangelo's "Creation of Adam" is just a complex arrangement of matter, paint on plaster. Taken further, it is just the chemicals which make up the paint and the plaster. Further still, it is just molecules and atoms. But those atoms, molecules, and chemicals were arranged by an artistic genius to create a painting which has communicated meaning to millions of human minds.[26] The fact that, on a material level, it is "just atoms," does not make it any less meaningful or change the fact that an intelligent mind was necessary to create it. If we understand that an intelligent human mind is necessary to produce a work of art, does it make sense to say that no intelligence was necessary to create the human mind? Most men throughout history have concluded that both the cosmos and man himself are such masterpieces that they could not have come about by chance.

The Birth of Modern Science

"[I]t's a striking fact of history that Copernicus, Galileo and Kepler, Newton, Faraday and Maxwell, Einstein, Planck and Heisenberg, all believed in a divine Mind behind the world and Rationality at the foundation of reality."

—ROY ABRAHAM VARGHESE[27]

It is no coincidence that modern science was born and grew in that part of the world which believed in the Bible and its God. *The early scientists believed in an ordered universe because they believed in a God who ordered it.* This enabled them to do their experiments and expect consistent, meaningful results. Nicolaus Copernicus, the sixteenth-century astronomer who proposed that the earth was not the center of the universe, wrote that he was seeking to uncover "the mechanism of the universe, wrought for us by a supremely good and orderly creator."[28]

---

25. Geisler and Turek, *I Don't Have Enough Faith to Be an Atheist*, 118.
26. Varghese, *The Wonder of the World*, 50–51.
27. Ibid., 102.
28. Copernicus, *On the Revolutions of the Heavenly Spheres*, 1543; quoted Dembski and Witt, *Intelligent Design Uncensored*, 30.

"A COSMOS RATHER THAN A CHAOS"

Sir Francis Bacon, sometimes called the "father of the scientific method," wrote in 1605 that God gave us two "books" by which we could know Him, Scripture and nature. Bacon advised, "[L]et no man . . . think or maintain that a man can search too far, or be too well studied in the book of God's word, or in the book of God's works."[29] He also wrote:

> "[M]an by the Fall fell at the same time from his state of innocence and from his dominion over nature. Both of those losses however can even in this life be in some part repaired; the former by religion and faith, the latter by arts and sciences."[30]

Johannes Kepler, the seventeenth-century astronomer who first set out the laws of planetary motion, wrote, "Those laws are within the grasp of the human mind. God wanted us to recognize them by creating us after his own image so that we could share his own thoughts."[31]

In the nineteenth and twentieth centuries, even as materialism became dominant, many scientists continued to believe in God. In the 1850s, the great physicist James Clerk Maxwell had inscribed over the doors of the Cavendish Laboratory at Cambridge these words from Psalm 11: "Great are the works of the Lord; they are pondered by all who delight in them."[32]

Charles Darwin called himself an agnostic, but wrote:

> "Another sense of conviction in the existence of God, connected with reason, and not without feelings, impresses me as having much more weight. This follows from the extreme difficulty or rather impossibility of conceiving this immense and wonderful universe, including man with his capacity for looking far backwards and far into futurity, as the result of blind chance or necessity. When thus reflecting I feel compelled to look to a First Cause having an intelligent mind in some degree analogous to that of man; and I deserve to be called a theist."[33]

Albert Einstein rejected all established religions, but said:

> "[E]very one who is seriously engaged in the pursuit of science becomes convinced that the laws of nature manifest the

---

29. Bacon, *The Advancement of Learning*, Book 1, 42, 8.
30. Bacon, *Novum Organum Scientiarum*, 267.
31. Letter to Johannes George Herwart, April 9–10, 1599; quoted Plantinga, *Where the Conflict Really Lies*, 277.
32. Lennox, "Challenges from Science," 131. The quote is from Psalm 11:2.
33. *Life and Letters of Charles Darwin*, Vol. 1, 282.

existence of a spirit vastly superior to that of men, and one in the face of which we with our modest powers must feel humble."[34]

"I want to know how God created this world. I'm not interested in this or that phenomenon, in the spectrum of this or that element. I want to know His thoughts; the rest are details."[35]

Wernher von Braun, known as the "father of rocket science," wrote:

"It is as difficult for me to understand a scientist who does not acknowledge the presence of a superior rationality behind the existence of the universe as it is to comprehend a theologian who would deny the advances of science ...

Our outlook through this peephole [manned space flight] at the vast mysteries of the universe only confirms our belief in the certainty of its creator."[36]

Many scientists today believe in God. A 2009 survey by the Pew Research Center found that among American scientists, 33 percent said they believed in God, and an additional 18 percent believed in a "universal spirit or higher power."[37] Steven Jay Gould was not a theist, but he wrote:

"To say it for all my colleagues and for the umpteenth millionth time ... science simply cannot (by its legitimate methods) adjudicate the issue of God's possible superintendence of nature. We neither affirm nor deny it; we simply can't comment on it as scientists. If some of our crowd have made untoward statements claiming that Darwinism disproves God, then I will find Mrs. McInerney [Gould's third-grade teacher] and have their knuckles rapped for it ...

Either half my colleagues are enormously stupid, or else the science of Darwinism is fully compatible with conventional religious beliefs—and equally compatible with atheism."[38]

Science works on the assumption of order, even of design, regardless of the religious views of the scientist. University of California physicist and Nobel Prize-winner Charles Townes wrote:

---

34. Letter to P. Wright, January 24, 1936; quoted Jammer, *Einstein and Religion*, 55.
35. Salaman, "A Talk with Albert Einstein," quoted Jammer, *Einstein and Religion*, 123.
36. Von Braun, "My Faith."
37. Masci, "Scientists and Belief."
38. Gould, "Impeaching a Self-Appointed Judge," 118–119.

"Faith is necessary for the scientist to even get started ... Why? Because he must be personally committed to the belief that there is order in the universe and that the human mind—in fact his own mind—has a good chance of understanding this order."[39]

Francis Crick warned that biologists "must constantly keep in mind that what they see was not designed, but rather evolved."[40] Richard Dawkins wrote, "The illusion of purpose is so powerful that biologists themselves use the assumption of good design as a working tool."[41] Dawkins does not believe that the universe was designed, as the founders of modern science did. But in order to practice biology, he *assumes* that living organisms were designed, and designed well. *He acts as if something he believes to be false were true, and it works!*

Why does the universe make sense? Why are there natural laws, so as to make science possible? How can order come from chaos? This is the fourth great mystery for a materialist. The unmistakable order in the universe is our next piece of evidence for a Creator.

Did the Universe Know We Were Coming?

"[T]he earth's atmosphere, like the little bear's porridge, seems just right."
—OWEN GINGERICH[42]

Do you remember the story of Goldilocks and the Three Bears? After breaking into the bears' house, Goldilocks tries out their chairs, their bowls of porridge, and finally their beds. In each case, the little bear's things are "just right." In many odd ways, this is a "Goldilocks universe," just right for creatures like us. The universe is not only ordered; it appears to be precisely fine-tuned to support life as we know it. Princeton physicist Freeman Dyson wrote, "The more I examine the universe and study the details of its architecture, the more evidence I find that the universe in some sense knew we were coming."[43]

There are many examples of this fine-tuning, sometimes called the "anthropic principle." For example, physicists tell us that there are four basic forces in nature—gravity, electro-magnetism, the strong nuclear force,

---

39. Townes, *Making Waves*, 161.
40. Crick, *What Mad Pursuit*, 138.
41. Dawkins, *River Out of Eden*, 98.
42. Gingerich, *God's Universe*, 30.
43. Dyson, *Disturbing the Universe*, 250.

and the weak nuclear force. Scientists know of no reason why each of these forces is not either stronger or weaker. Each is independent of the others. But if any one of the four were even slightly different, life would be impossible anywhere in the universe.[44]

Another example has to do with the first fractions of a second after the big bang. Physicist John Polkinghorne, President of Queen's College, Cambridge, wrote:

> "For us to be possible requires a balance between the effects of expansion [explosion] and contraction [gravity] which at a very early epoch in the universe's history (the Planck time) has to differ from equality by not more than 1 in 10 to the 60th [power] ... [That] is the same as aiming at a target an inch wide on the other side of the observable universe, twenty thousand million light years away, and hitting the mark!"[45]

Again, we know of no reason why each of these forces should have been "just right." Yet if the force of the big bang had been any less, the universe would have collapsed back upon itself. Had it been any greater, the matter from the big bang would never have come together to form galaxies.[46] To put it another way, scientists have calculated that if the force of gravity varied in either direction by .0000000000000000000000000000 000001 percent, we would not exist.[47] Francis Collins wrote, "The existence of a universe as we know it rests upon a knife edge of improbability."[48]

Within the atom, a proton has 1836 times the mass of an electron, the exact ratio necessary for molecules to form. But they contain equal charges, the proton positive and the electron negative.[49]

Life can exist in only one to two percent of the range of possible temperatures, between absolute zero and the temperature of the stars. Were there even a slight change in the distance of the earth from the sun, the speed of its rotation, or its twenty-three-degree tilt on its axis, the earth would be either too hot or too cold for life as we know it.[50] To illustrate this point, we need only look at the two planets closest to us in the solar system.

---

44. Moreland, *Scaling the Secular City*, 47, 52.
45. Polkinghorne, *One World*, 57.
46. Jastrow, *God and the Astronomers*, 93; Townes, *Making Waves*, 182.
47. Geisler and Turek, *I Don't Have Enough Faith to Be an Atheist*, 102.
48. Collins, *The Language of God*, 73.
49. Varghese, *The Wonder of the World*, 398.
50. Denton, *Nature's Destiny*, 92; Geisler and Turek, *I Don't Have Enough Faith to Be an Atheist*, 105–106.

The average daily temperature on Venus would melt lead. The average temperature on Mars is minus eighty degrees, Fahrenheit.[51]

If Jupiter, a huge gaseous planet, were not just the right distance from both the sun and the earth, we would be bombarded with meteors and asteroids. Jupiter's gravitational pull acts as a shield, protecting us from such an assault. Geophysicist George Wetherill of the Carnegie Institute stated that if it were not for Jupiter, "there is a good chance we wouldn't be around to study the origin of the solar system."[52]

Examples from Chemistry and Biology

Examples of this fine-tuning are found not only in physics and astronomy, but also in chemistry and biology. For instance, oxygen releases tremendous amounts of energy when reacting with other elements, the most when reacting with hydrocarbons. This reaction, known as oxidation, provides the energy needed for all complex animal life. Oxidation also converts oxygen and hydrocarbons to water and carbon dioxide, which are necessary for plant life. Photosynthesis in plants does the opposite, taking in water and carbon dioxide, and producing the oxygen and hydrocarbons that animals need.[53]

The percentage of oxygen in the earth's atmosphere (approximately 21 percent), is just high enough to sustain fire, but not so high as to cause spontaneous combustion.[54] Similarly, if the percentage of carbon dioxide were higher, we would burn up from the greenhouse effect. If it were lower, the plants would be unable to maintain adequate photosynthesis.[55]

Carbon, in combination with other elements, makes up "all the machinery of the cell, and all the vital structures of living organisms,"[56] from amino acids or DNA to human flesh or the trunk of a redwood. This is not a coincidence. Carbon is unique in the number and diversity of compounds it can form, and it naturally forms these compounds within the temperature range necessary for life. Michael Denton wrote, "Carbon is so uniquely fit for its biological role, its various compounds so vital to the existence of life, that . . . 'If carbon did not exist, it would have to be invented.'"[57]

---

51. Behe, *The Edge of Evolution*, 211.
52. Quoted *Discover*, "Our Friend Jove," 15.
53. Denton, *Nature's Destiny*, 120–121, 137.
54. Gingerich, *God's Universe*, 30.
55. Geisler and Turek, *I Don't Have Enough Faith to Be an Atheist*, 101.
56. Denton, *Nature's Destiny*, 104–108.
57. Ibid., 116.

Water is uniquely suited to support life, in its ability to react with other chemicals, its transparency to light, its ability to conduct heat, and its viscosity (thickness)—the lowest of any known liquid at body temperature. Denton wrote, "There is indeed no other candidate fluid which is remotely competitive with water as the medium for carbon-based life."[58]

Water, like most substances, expands as it gets hotter and contracts as it gets colder, but unlike almost any other substance in nature, water expands when it freezes. This is why ice floats. If ice did not float, when lakes or rivers froze, it would sink to the bottom and kill most aquatic life.[59]

Sir Martin Rees, a Cambridge astronomer, wrote a book titled, *Just Six Numbers*, identifying six "constants" built into the cosmos, which he called a "recipe for a universe." He stated, "[I]f any one of them were to be 'untuned' [changed just slightly], there would be no stars and no life."[60] One of these numbers is the rate at which hydrogen converts to helium. It does so naturally, in a way that converts seven one-thousandths (0.007) of its mass to energy in the process. Our sun is fueled by this conversion. Scientists believe that the early universe, immediately after the big bang, was made up primarily of hydrogen, so this conversion was essential to its development. According to Rees, if this percentage were just one one-thousandth lower, 0.006, no transformation to helium could take place, and the universe would consist only of hydrogen. If it were one one-thousandth higher, 0.008, no hydrogen would have survived from the big bang. Either way, we would not be here.[61]

But Rees demonstrates how far some materialists will go to avoid the conclusion that there must be a Creator. Along with others, he has proposed that perhaps there are an infinite number of universes, so that it is not unlikely for one of them to be just right for life.[62] *There is absolutely no evidence for these other universes.* And since they would be undetectable by definition, there never could be. In scientific language, this suggestion could never be "falsified." John Polkinghorne called this idea "pseudo-science," and "a metaphysical guess."[63] Paul Davies wrote:

> "To postulate an infinity of unseen and unseeable universes just to explain the one we do see seems like a case of excess baggage carried to the extreme. It is simpler to postulate one unseen God."[64]

---

58. Ibid., 46.
59. Ibid., 26–28.
60. Rees, *Just Six Numbers: The Deep Forces that Shape the Universe*, 4.
61. Ibid., 54–55.
62. Ibid., 166–167.
63. Polkinghorne, *Serious Talk: Science and Religion in Dialogue*, 6.
64. Davies, *The Mind of God*, 190.

Howard's Law #21 is: If your philosophy requires you to believe in billions of undetectable universes, just to explain this one, your philosophy is probably wrong.

"A Put-up Job?"

These are just a few of over one hundred factors which have been identified, illustrating the anthropic principle.[65] Princeton physicist Donald Page calculated the odds for the universe randomly arriving at all these conditions to be one in ten to the 124th power.[66] That is like picking one particular atom at random, from all the atoms in the universe, one million trillion trillion trillion trillion times in a row!

Robert Jastrow said, "[T]he universe was constructed within very narrow limits, in such a way that man could dwell in it. It is the most theistic result ever to come out of science, in my view."[67]

Fred Hoyle described the universe as "a put-up job,"[68] and wrote:

> "A common sense interpretation of the facts suggests that a superintellect has monkeyed with physics, as well as with chemistry and biology, and that there are no blind forces worth speaking about in nature."[69]

James O'Keefe, a planetary scientist with NASA for almost 40 years, wrote:

> "We are, by astronomical standards, a pampered, cosseted, cherished group of creatures, our Darwinian claim to have done it all ourselves as ridiculous and as charming as a baby's brave efforts to stand on his own feet and refuse his mother's hand. If the universe had not been made with the most exacting precision we could never have come into existence. It is my view that these circumstances indicate that the Universe was created for man to live in."[70]

In all of human experience, finely tuned devices such as watches, smart phones, or spaceships are only produced by intelligent minds. We

---

65. Geisler and Turek, *I Don't Have Enough Faith to Be an Atheist*, 105.
66. Quoted Thomsen, "The Quantum Universe: A Zero Point Fluctuation?"
67. Jastrow, "The Astronomer and God," 22.
68. Quoted Gingerich, *God's Universe*, 58.
69. Hoyle, "The Universe: Past and Present Reflections," 8.
70. O'Keefe, "The Theological Impact of the New Cosmology;" Jastrow, *God and the Astronomers*, 118.

have never seen any of these devices develop on their own. Michael Denton wrote, "It is true . . . that 'wide-bodied jets evolved from small contraptions made in bicycle shops' . . . but they did not evolve by chance."[71] Suggesting a designer—God, the ultimate mind—as the explanation for the order and fine-tuning we see in the universe is not only logical; it is the only explanation which is consistent with our experience.[72] There are other arguments for the existence of God which we could discuss, but for the purposes of this book, this fine-tuning is our final piece of evidence. It does indeed look as if the universe, or its Creator, "knew we were coming."

---

71. Denton, *Evolution: A Theory in Crisis*, 317.
72. Collins, Robin; Strobel, *The Case for a Creator*, 145–146.

Chapter 14

Why, Lord?

Why do We Suffer? Part 1

"Man who is born of woman is of few days and full of trouble. He comes forth like a flower and fades away"

—JOB 14:1–2

THE STORY IS TOLD of Solon, one of the great sages of ancient Greece, who wept over the death of his son. A friend asked him, "Why do you weep, since weeping avails nothing?" Solon answered, "Precisely because it avails nothing."[1]

In 1977, Rabbi Harold Kushner's fourteen-year-old son, Aaron, died of progeria, a rare disease which causes premature aging, so that children grow feeble and die of "old age" in their teens. A few years later, Rabbi Kushner wrote of what he had learned from the experience:

> "I am a more sensitive person, a more effective pastor, a more sympathetic counsellor because of Aaron's life and death than I would ever have been without it. *And I would give up all of those gains in a second if I could have my son back.*"[2] (emphasis added)

In the small town where I live, there is a well-respected couple who had two teen-aged sons. One night, the older boy was out with some friends, and the driver took a foolish risk, as teenagers sometimes do, and caused a head-on collision. This couple's son was critically injured. They rushed to the hospital. When they got there, the younger boy jumped out to run in

---

1. Quoted Kreeft, *Love Is Stronger than Death*, 7–8.
2. Kushner, *When Bad Things Happen to Good People*, 133.

and check on his brother, while his parents parked the car. It was late at night, and the door where the boy got out was locked. As he ran around the hospital, looking for an entrance, he suffered a massive heart attack and fell to the ground, dead. His brother died a few hours later of his injuries from the accident. The joint funeral service was packed. It seemed the whole community came out to show their love and support for the parents. But no one could answer the question on every heart and mind—why?

The pollster George Barna once asked, if you could ask God one question, what would it be? The number one response, by an overwhelming margin, was, "Why is there so much suffering in the world?"[3] We have been considering arguments for the existence of the God of Scripture. We must now look at the primary argument—I would suggest it is the only good argument—against that God. It is the question of suffering or evil. Why would a good God allow suffering?

This is the question which caused Albert Einstein to reject the Jewish faith of his childhood. Similarly, Charles Darwin was raised a Christian and as a young man considered going into the ministry. He gradually lost his faith, the final straw being the death of his beloved ten-year old daughter of tuberculosis. Darwin wrote, "My theology is a simple muddle. I cannot look at the universe as the result of blind chance, yet I see no evidence of beneficent design in the details."[4]

"To Live Is To Suffer"

This is not a new question. It is the subject of the Book of Job, which many scholars believe is one of the oldest books in the Bible. Job pleaded with God:

> *"Why did I not die at birth?*
> *Why did I not perish when I came out of the womb?* . . .
> *For then I would have been asleep;*
> *Then I would have been at rest . . .*
>
> *For the thing I greatly feared has come upon me,*
> *And what I dreaded has happened to me.*
> *I am not at ease, nor am I quiet;*
> *I have no rest, for trouble comes."*[5]

---

3. Rhodes, "Tough Questions About Evil," 33.
4. Quoted Jastrow, *God and the Astronomers*, 9.
5. Job 3:11, 13, 25–26.

Make no mistake—trouble comes for all of us. Buddha's first noble truth is undeniable: "To live is to suffer." Every world-view must explain this fact. No philosophy which attempted to deny the reality of suffering would be worth a second look.

We not only suffer; we also die. The question is not so much why one person died, too young or under tragic circumstances, but why is there death at all? Why are we made of such stuff that our bodies wear out and die? Why has this always been the case, for every living creature on earth?

"Why would a good God allow evil?" is one of the most profound questions ever asked by man. The eighteenth-century philosopher David Hume put it this way: "Is [God] willing to prevent evil, but not able? Then he is impotent. Is he able, but not willing? Then he is malevolent. Is he both able and willing? Whence then is evil?"[6]

There are three basic answers to the question of evil, the same three answers we discussed earlier to the God question. The first is the atheist answer, which says there is no God. The second is the pantheist answer, which says there is no true evil. The third is the theist answer, which says that there is a good and loving God, and that He is all-powerful, but that evil is real. How can all three of these statements be true? So theism (again, we will consider primarily Christian teachings) has a challenge the other world-views do not have—it must explain the apparent contradiction.

Pantheism—"As the Snake I Bite; As the Healer I Cure"

Before we consider the Christian position in depth, let us look more closely at the other two answers. In pantheism, "God is everything and everything is god." Therefore, if good and evil exist, both must be part of god. So pantheists either say that good and evil are not real but illusions, or they say that god is both good and evil. In *Star Wars,* The Force had both a good and a "dark" side. The nineteenth-century Hindu teacher Ramakrishna said, "As the snake I bite; as the healer I cure."[7]

Pantheism is an old and respectable philosophy. I would suggest that it falls short because it fails to conform to the reality of human experience. If evil is an illusion, why do you lock your doors at night? If pain is an illusion, why do you go to the dentist? On the other hand, if god is everything and everything is god, are war, racism, and cancer part of god?[8] *Good and evil are real. Feeding hungry children is good and torturing them is evil, and*

---

6. Hume, *Dialogues Concerning Natural Religion,* 63.
7. Quoted Zacharias, *Jesus Among Other Gods,* 162.
8. Rhodes, "Tough Questions About Evil," 40.

I don't need a philosopher to tell me so! Nor am I inclined to listen to one who tries to tell me otherwise. Pantheism cannot explain true evil. But the human race has always known that *suffering is evil*.

Nor can pantheism offer any comfort for our suffering. Buddhism teaches that the cause of suffering is desire—if we had no desires, no entanglements, no loves, we could avoid pain. The night his son was born, Gautama Buddha left home, not to return for many years.[9] But is that the answer we are seeking?

Atheism—Judging Evil with No Reference Point

We discussed earlier the larger problem with atheism—it cannot explain man or the world we live in. As to the question of suffering, the problem is that when an atheist says suffering is "evil," he is saying that it is not what it should be. He is comparing it to some standard of what is good. But where does he get that standard? Christian philosopher Ronald Rhodes wrote:

> "The reality is that it is impossible to distinguish evil from good unless one has an infinite reference point that is absolutely good . . . if God does not exist, there is no ultimate basis to judge, for example, the crimes of Hitler."[10]

Referring to his days as a young atheist, C. S. Lewis wrote:

> "My argument against God was that the universe seemed cruel and unjust. But how had I got this idea of 'just' and 'unjust?'. . . I could have given up my idea of justice by saying it was nothing but a private idea of my own. But if I did that, then my argument against God collapsed too—for the argument depended on saying that the world was really unjust, not simply that it did not happen to please my private fancies."[11]

To be consistent, an atheist must agree with the pantheist that there is no true evil. Even "natural evils" such as earthquakes or cancers are just the normal workings of nature, and what is natural is right. In natural disasters, the weak and the poor usually suffer more than the strong and the rich. Is this not natural selection at work? A Christian can say that what is natural is not always right, because we are fallen creatures in a fallen world. Only one who believes in the fall can meaningfully say that suffering is evil.

---

9. Zacharias and Vitale, *Why Suffering?* 118.
10. Rhodes, "Tough Questions About Evil," 35.
11. Lewis, *Mere Christianity*, 31.

So here is Howard's Law # 22, and this one is not meant to be humorous: If your philosophy cannot say that suffering is truly evil, your philosophy is probably wrong.

It seems to me that most people who deny the existence of God on the basis of suffering are inconsistent. They do so on moral grounds, though they have no basis for true moral judgments. But one can say that the universe does not make sense, there is no God, no good or evil, and no meaning to anything. This view is called "nihilism," a belief in nothing. A nihilist cannot say that suffering is evil, but he can argue that because it is inconsistent with a good, loving, and all-powerful God, such a God must not exist. So we will attempt to answer this argument, even though it seems rare that it is consistently made.

But atheism can offer no meaning for our suffering, no consolation when we suffer, and no hope for the future. For an atheist, "Life is suffering; then you die."

Our post-Christian culture has no answer for the question of suffering. Neither pantheism nor atheism can provide a credible answer, because neither can say what we know to be true, that suffering is evil. *If the Bible has no answer, there is none.*

Christian Theism—The God Who Weeps

"God hates the sorrows of the world more than we do—even to the point of sending His Son to die so that eventually there might be healing."

—FRANCIS SCHAEFFER[12]

The Apostle John records that when Jesus confronted death at the tomb of Lazarus, he was "troubled," and He "wept."[13] The word translated here as "troubled" implies not only sorrow, but also anger.[14] Jesus knew that He was going to raise Lazarus from the dead, but He was sorrowful and angry over human suffering. So a Christian can be angry about suffering, as well. Francis Schaeffer wrote:

> "On [Christian beliefs] we can have an adequate ground for fighting evil, including social evil and social injustice. Modern man has no real basis for fighting evil, because he sees man as normal ... But the Christian has—he can fight evil without fighting God."[15]

12. Schaeffer, *Letters of Francis A. Schaeffer*, 156.
13. John 11:33, 35.
14. Burson and Walls, *C. S. Lewis and Francis Schaeffer*, 207.
15. Schaeffer, *He Is There and He Is Not Silent*, 301.

At the 1994 Mass for Sarajevo, after the genocide inflicted on the people of that city, Pope John Paul II said:

> "God is on the side of the oppressed. He is beside the parents who cry for their murdered children; He hears the impotent cry of the defenseless and downtrodden; He is in solidarity with women humiliatingly violated; He is near to refugees forced to leave their land and their homes. Do not forget the suffering of families, of the elderly, widows, and the young and children. It is His people who are dying."[16]

Christianity says that God shares our suffering and weeps for us. However, I believe we must reject one teaching which has become popular in recent years. This is the idea that God is good and loving, but He is not always able to help us in our suffering. Harold Kushner wrote a best-selling book, *When Bad Things Happen to Good People*, advocating this view. He affirmed God's love quite eloquently, but he questioned God's power. It is a well-written book, and Rabbi Kushner deserves our respect, for he wrote it out of his own suffering after the death of his son. But a God who is not all-powerful is not the God of Scripture, either the Old or New Testaments, and He is not the God we need. Like atheism and pantheism, this is not really an answer to the problem at all.

The old Christian teaching is that God is both absolutely good—"God has no dark side"[17]—and all-powerful. But then why is there evil? In the next chapter, we will look at some of the traditional Christian answers to this question.

Do You Mean that God Knows Better than I Do?

"What the caterpillar calls the end of the world, the master calls a butterfly."
—RICHARD BACH[18]

"If you have a God great and transcendent enough to be mad at because He hasn't stopped evil and suffering in the world, then you have . . . a God great and transcendent enough to have good reasons for allowing it to continue that you can't know."

—TIMOTHY KELLER[19]

16. John Paul II, *Pope John Paul II: His Essential Wisdom*, 74.
17. Kreeft, *The Philosophy of Jesus*, 16.
18. Bach, *Illusions: The Adventures of a Reluctant Messiah*, 134. Bach is a pantheist, but I believe Christians can rightly adopt this saying.
19. Keller, *The Reason for God*, 25.

Before we consider these answers, let me make two other brief points. First, we should not look at this question in a vacuum. We have spent thirteen chapters discussing some of the arguments for the existence of God. If our reasoning has been sound, these arguments are quite persuasive. Even if we found the answers to the question of suffering to be less than satisfactory, that would only be one point on the other side.

Second, we often forget another old teaching, that God is all-knowing, and He knows what is good for us far better than we do. Certainly there is much that we do not know. In the movie, "Hannah and Her Sisters," Woody Allen's character asked, "If there is a God, why are there Nazis?" His father answered, "How the . . . do I know why there are Nazis? I don't even know how the can opener works."[20]

We should acknowledge the obvious—*we are not God*. If there is a God, He knows more than we do. We see our little bit of the story; He sees all of it. Like a small child cannot understand why her parents allow a surgeon to hurt her, we cannot understand why God allows us to suffer. In fact, His knowledge exceeds ours infinitely more than our knowledge exceeds the child's.

This is the final answer of the Book of Job. When God appeared to Job in the final chapters, He did not give him an intellectual answer to why he suffered. He told him that he was not capable of understanding. He asked, *"Where were you when I laid the foundations of the world?"*[21] But Job was satisfied, because God was his answer. Meeting Him face-to-face, and knowing that God was with him in his suffering, was enough.

In "Five Sonnets," C. S. Lewis compared mankind to a bee:

> "That booms against the window-pane for hours
> Thinking that way to reach the laden flowers . . .
>
> We catch her in a handkerchief (who knows
> What rage she feels, what terror, what despair?)
> And shake her out and—gaily out she goes . . .
> But left to her own will
> She would have died upon the window sill."[22]

When we are suffering, are we not much like the bee caught in the handkerchief, in "terror" and "despair?" But God knows His plans for us; we do not. St. Augustine wrote that we could sooner hold the ocean in a

---

20. "Hannah and her Sisters," Orion, 1986.
21. Job 38:4.
22. Lewis, "Five Sonnets," IV, 13–14, V, 9–14, 141.

thimble than hold all of God in our minds.[23] *We cannot understand fully in this life why we suffer.* But I believe we can understand why we cannot understand—to fully understand God's ways, we would have to be His equals.

When I left the law firm with which I had worked for twenty-three years to begin what turned out to be a short career as a judge (I lost an election the following year), I thanked my long-time senior partner, telling him very sincerely that he had taught me all I knew about the practice of law. He responded, "That may be true, but just remember, I didn't teach you all I know!" God gave us our ability to perceive truth, but that ability is limited. He taught us all we know, but not all He knows.

The vast majority of men throughout history have suffered far more and died far younger than we do. In *The Problem of Pain*, Lewis asked his readers to "reflect for five minutes on the fact that all the great religions were first preached, and long practiced, in a world without chloroform [the first general anesthetic]."[24] And yet almost all men have believed in some kind of god. Are we the first people to recognize the problem? Or did they understand something we do not? The question is not new. The best answers are also very old. In the next chapter we will look at some of those answers.

---

23. Quoted Kreeft, *Catholic Christianity*, 27.
24. Lewis, *The Problem of Pain*, 5.

Chapter 15

Old Answers to an Old Question
Why do We Suffer? Part 2

"At the end of time, there will be a new heaven and a new earth, free of sin and suffering, where He will 'wipe every tear from their eyes.' Until that time, God uses the 'thorns and thistles' that have infested creation since the Fall to teach, chastise, sanctify and transform us, making us ready for that new heaven and earth."

—CHARLES COLSON AND NANCY PEARCEY[1]

WHY DO WE SUFFER? How can a loving God allow suffering and death? When a baby dies, is that "God's will?" These are profound questions, but they are not new ones. St. Augustine asked, "If there is no God, why is there good? If there is a God, why is there evil?"[2] This puts the question in balance. There is much love, joy, and beauty in the world, and creatures like us who can enjoy it. But we cannot ignore the opposite reality, and the Christian teachers have not ignored it. From the earliest days of the Church, many sermons have been preached and many books written[3] on the question of suffering, and a number of answers have been suggested. The question is certainly "above my pay grade," and I would not attempt to offer my own answers, but I can summarize some of what these wise men have said.

---

1. Colson and Pearcey, *How Now Shall We Live?* 207.
2. Quoted Kreeft, *Catholic Christianity*, 52.
3. Two of the best currently-available books on this subject are Lewis, *The Problem of Pain*, and Kreeft, *Making Sense Out of Suffering*.

Is It My Fault?

> "Do not then go beyond yourself to seek for evil . . . Each of us, let us acknowledge it, is the first author of his own vice."
>
> —ST BASIL THE GREAT, C370 AD[4]

The first traditional answer is human free will. Christians believe that God is all-powerful. He could directly control everything that happens. Instead, He has given us free will, and *He allows us to do things which He does not want us to do.* Those of us who are parents can understand, I think, how this might be. I want my daughter to do her homework and keep her room clean. I could see that she did so, if I monitored her actions every minute. But I do not do that, because I also want her to learn responsibility and self-discipline. So the good things which I want may not always happen, because I give her the freedom to do them, or not do them, on her own.[5]

Surely we can see the parallel to our Heavenly Father. Scripture teaches that God gives us free will, and much of our suffering occurs because we choose to do the wrong things. If the Bible is true, God made the world, made us, and gave us the moral law to tell us how to live in this world. We violate that law, hurt ourselves or others as a result, and then ask, "Why does God allow such suffering?" Francis Collins wrote:

> "It is humankind, not God, that has invented knives, arrows, guns, bombs, and all manner of other instruments of torture used through the ages . . . when we [use them] we shouldn't then blame God for the consequences."[6]

For a Christian, the entire Bible is the story of God's plan to save us from the mess we have made. But we made the mess. If God were going to eliminate evil from the world, He would have to start by eliminating us, because we are responsible for much of that evil.[7] Human free will is not the total answer to suffering, but it is an important part of the answer. I believe it is the answer to the question, "If there is a God, why are there Nazis?" Sheldon Vanauken wrote, "[T]he Nazis were men making choices."[8]

---

4. Basil the Great, "Hexaemeron," Homily II, 298.

5. This is an old illustration, and one to which I would think every parent can relate. However, I should add that it is unfair to my daughter. She is an excellent and very disciplined student. Now as to cleaning her room . . .

6. Collins, *The Language of God*, 43.

7. Poe, *The Inklings of Oxford*, 68.

8. Vanauken, "God's Will," 357.

Free will is the traditional explanation for the Christian doctrine of hell. C. S. Lewis called hell "the greatest monument to human freedom," and wrote, "I willingly believe that the damned are, in one sense, successful, rebels to the end; that the doors of hell are locked on the inside."[9] Timothy Keller wrote, "Hell, then, is the trajectory of a soul, living a self-absorbed, self-centered life, going on forever."[10] I believe the idea that God, in vengeance, "sends" people to hell is a misreading of Scripture. But if the essence of Heaven is the presence of God and our worship of him, and the essence of hell is absence from God and self-worship, it is our choice and He will honor that choice.

Why Did God Make Us Free?

"If you . . . say, 'God can give a creature free will and at the same time withhold free will from it,' you have not succeeded in saying anything about God; meaningless combinations of words do not suddenly acquire meaning simply because we prefix to them the two other words 'God can'. . .

[N]onsense remains nonsense even when we talk it about God."

—C. S. LEWIS[11]

I saw a cartoon a few years ago which showed God and one of His angels, looking down on the earth. The angel said, "If you give them free will, we'll need a lot more staff!"[12] But this raises a question—if God knew the mess we would make, why did He make us free? The traditional answer is that without true freedom, there could be no goodness, no relationships, and no love. God made "persons with whom to have fellowship, not just objects with which he could play."[13]

In the movie, "Bruce Almighty," Jim Carrey's character asks God how he can win back his girlfriend: "How do you make someone love you without affecting free will?" God, played by Morgan Freeman, replies, "Welcome to my world, son. If you come up with an answer to that one, you let me know."[14]

We ask, could God not have made us free, without the possibility of evil? But if we were only free to choose good, that would not be real

---

9. Lewis, *The Problem of Pain*, 116, 130.
10. Keller, *The Reason for God*, 79.
11. Lewis, *The Problem of Pain*, 18.
12. *National Review*, November 14, 2011, 27.
13. Poe, *See No Evil*, 34.
14. "Bruce Almighty," Universal, 2003.

freedom. It would be like an election in a totalitarian country, where only one candidate is on the ballot.

Likewise, if free will is to have any meaning, there must be a real world. There must be fixed natural laws, so that the consequences of our choices are real. But if there are fixed laws, we will not always like those consequences. Lewis wrote, "The permanent nature of wood which enables us to use it as a beam also enables us to use it for hitting our neighbor on the head."[15]

Could God protect us from our bad choices? Could life be like a movie set, where if we mess up, we can do another take? Could wood be strong when we need it to hold up a roof, but turn to foam when we hit someone with it? That would not be a real world. *If we have real freedom in a real world, there will be real consequences for bad choices.*

Part of my legal practice is in family courts. I am continually impressed—and depressed—by how many damaged people I see. Much of that damage we do to ourselves, or others do to us, by breaking God's laws. *Much of our suffering is self-inflicted.*

"The Devil Made Me Do It!"

> "For still our ancient foe
> Doth seek to work us woe;
> His craft and power are great,
> And armed with cruel hate;
> On earth is not his equal."
>
> —MARTIN LUTHER[16]

The second traditional answer is very unpopular, but we will never answer any deep or profound question if we limit ourselves to popular answers. And this answer comes directly from Scripture. It is that some of our suffering is caused by Satan. In the book of Job, Satan comes before God twice and asks permission to torment Job. God allows him to do so, but only within certain limits.[17] Job is an ancient book, but here we get a sophisticated picture of the relationship between God's goodness, His sovereignty, and evil. God is never the source of evil. He is not the source of Job's suffering—Satan is. But God is sovereign, and Satan can do nothing beyond what God allows.

---

15. Lewis, *The Problem of Pain*, 22–23.

16. Luther, Martin, "A Mighty Fortress is Our God," 1531, translated Hedge, Frederick, 1853.

17. Job 1:12, 2:6.

In the twenty-first century, you can get "laughed out of school," for seriously mentioning the devil. But both the Old and New Testaments teach that God created angels before He created men, that some of those angels used their free will to rebel against Him,[18] and that they cause much of the suffering in the world.[19] C. S. Lewis called our world "enemy-occupied territory."[20] In his space novel, *Out of the Silent Planet,* he described Earth as being cut off from the rest of the solar system because our "dark eldil," or ruler, had rebelled and taken the planet with him.[21] This is only fiction, but it may help us understand the teaching that this world is presently under Satan's power, and he is the cause of much of our suffering.

St. Augustine, responding to the hope among Christians that their persecution was over after the Emperor Constantine converted to Christianity, warned, "The Emperor has become a Christian—the Devil has not."[22]

Satan is also the tempter, who inspires human evil, all the way back to the Garden of Eden. We should not apologize for this teaching, both because it is Biblical and because it makes sense of our shared experience. *Much of our suffering is brought about by the evil "ruler of this world."*[23]

That Medicine Tastes Terrible!

"What do people mean when they say, 'I am not afraid of God because I know He is good?' Have they never even been to a dentist?"

—C. S. LEWIS[24]

In one sense, these two answers probably explain most of our suffering. But in another sense, they do not answer the question at all. Why does God even *allow* us to suffer, if He could prevent it? If I could prevent my daughter

---

18. Isaiah 14:12–15; Revelation 12:7–9.

19. Job chapters 1 and 2; Ephesians 6:11–12. After the effects of the fall, this is the most common traditional Christian explanation for "natural evils" such as earthquakes or hurricanes—this world is temporarily under Satan's control. Eastern Orthodox theology, in particular, has traditionally attributed natural evils to Satan and his angels, all the way back to his original rebellion (even before man). Moshier, "What is God's Purpose for Natural Disasters?" 145. C. S. Lewis seems to have shared this view. Lewis, *The Problem of Pain,* 137–138.

20. Lewis, *Mere Christianity,* 36.

21. Lewis, *Out of the Silent Planet,* 120–121.

22. Quoted Short, "Saint From Hippo," 35.

23. John 12:31; 14:30.

24. Lewis, *A Grief Observed,* 43.

from suffering and did not do so, what kind of father would I be? David Hume said that if God is able to prevent evil but not willing, He is "malevolent." The French writer, Charles Baudelaire, said, "If there is a God, he is the devil."[25] But Christians say that "God is love." So we are back to our original question—why does a good and loving God allow suffering?

In short, the Biblical answer is that our suffering is for our good. This answer is hard for us to understand, and even harder to accept. But we must remember another unpopular teaching at this point, that of the fall. In fact, I am convinced we can never begin to understand suffering apart from this doctrine. *God did not make me the way I am.* He made mankind perfect. I am the way I am because of the fall.

We do not take our sin very seriously, but God does—so seriously that He went to the cross for that sin. If our sin caused Him such suffering, might it not cause us some as well? If God is going to cure us of our sin while respecting our free will, might that process not require suffering?

Harry Lee Poe wrote that God had three choices: "[D]estroy people, enslave people so that they cannot do evil, or change people so that they desire not to do evil."[26] God chose to change us, but that process involves pain, both for Him and for us.

Now that I think about it, there are times when I may allow my daughter to suffer. I take her to the dentist! Once when she was little, she was sick and the doctors thought she might have meningitis. The only way to find out was to test her spinal fluid. So her mother and I stood by her hospital bed, holding her hand and stroking her head, while the doctor stuck a huge needle into her back. As it turned out, she did not have meningitis, and she got better within a few days. But love is more than kindness. We are kind to our pets—if they are suffering, we have them "put to sleep." But we put our family members through painful surgery and rehabilitation.

True love does what is good for the beloved, not what is easy or painless. Peter Kreeft wrote, "I believe that suffering is compatible with God's love if it is medicinal, remedial and necessary; that is, if we are desperately sick and need a cure. And that's our situation."[27]

"A Great Gymnasium"

According to Scripture, all of nature was corrupted by the fall. Many things are wonderful, but nothing is perfect. Fruits and vegetables spoil. Animals,

---

25. Quoted Schaeffer, *The God Who is There*, 110.
26. Poe, *The Inklings of Oxford*, 68.
27. Kreeft, Peter; Strobel, *The Case for Faith*, 44.

including humans, die. There are earthquakes and tornados, cancers and dementia. *Nature contains a fatal flaw.* The old teachers said that even this general "fallenness" is for our good. It keeps us from being satisfied in this world, in our sin and without God. Lewis wrote:

> "The Christian doctrine of suffering explains, I believe, a very curious fact about the world we live in. The settled happiness and security which we all desire, God withholds from us by the very nature of the world; but joy, pleasure and merriment, He has scattered broadcast . . . The security we crave would teach us to rest our hearts in this world and oppose an obstacle to our return to God; a few moments of happy love, a landscape, a symphony, a merry meeting with our friends, a bathe or a football match, have no such tendency. Our Father refreshes us on the journey with some pleasant inns, but will not encourage us to mistake them for home."[28]

Norman Geisler and Frank Turek wrote, "This earth is an uncomfortable home; but it's a great gymnasium for the hereafter."[29]

This is the traditional Christian explanation for death—it is for our good. We are meant to live forever, but as we were created, not as we are now. This sinful, corrupted life must end. In the fourth century, St. Gregory of Nazianzus wrote:

> "[H]ere too [God] makes a gain, namely death, and the cutting off of sin, in order that evil may not be immortal. Thus his punishment is changed into a mercy; for it is in mercy, I am persuaded, that God inflicts punishment."[30]

Some of our suffering may be for the good of others. As Christ suffered for us, so we may be called upon to suffer for one another. This is a hard teaching, but if I truly love you, my neighbor, as myself, will I not be willing to suffer for you? Christian philosopher William Dembski wrote, "In a fallen world, the only currency of love is suffering."[31]

Christianity teaches that we are "desperately sick"—we are sinners, and our sin separates us from God, for He is holy. But He is our only source for joy, peace, meaning, or life itself. This spiritual sickness is worse than any physical sickness. Spiritual death is worse than physical death, and we are

---

28. Lewis, *The Problem of Pain*, 116.
29. Geisler and Turek, *I Don't Have Enough Faith to Be an Atheist*, 392.
30. Gregory of Nazianzus, Oration XXVIII, "Orations," 282.
31. Dembski, *The End of Christianity*, 23.

dying spiritually. So although the healing process may be painful, it is for our eternal good. *Some of our suffering is medicinal.*

I Hate School!

"Our fathers disciplined us for a little while as they thought best; but God disciplines us for our good, that we may share in His holiness. No discipline seems pleasant at the time, but painful. Later on, however, it produces a harvest of righteousness and peace for those who have been trained by it."

—HEBREWS 12:10-11

To illustrate the next traditional answer, closely related to the last, let me ask you again to think as a parent. If your child is playing in the road, will you just call out and ask her if she is having fun? Of course not. It is an act of love to teach her the things she needs to know, even if the lessons are painful. Sometimes, because I love my child, I may have to discipline her. We call God our Heavenly Father. Do we think He would do any less for (or to) us? But we are like children, and discipline is not what we want. As Lewis wrote:

> "We want, in fact, not so much a Father in Heaven as a grandfather in heaven—a senile benevolence who, as they say, 'liked to see young people enjoying themselves,' and whose plan for the universe was simply that it might be truly said at the end of each day, 'a good time was had by all.'"[32]

But God is not an indulgent grandfather. He is a righteous and loving father. Because He is righteous, He cannot ignore our sin. Because He loves us, He went to the cross to save us from that sin. And because God loves us, He may discipline us—for our good. When I was a boy, and my mother punished me, she would sometimes say, "This hurts me more than it hurts you." I thought that was the silliest thing I had ever heard! Now, as a parent, I understand it. I discipline my child *because* I love her, even though it hurts both of us at the time.

The idea of "growth through suffering" is taught by every one of the world's major religions. Suffering builds character; a life of ease does not. We do not develop courage unless we confront danger, patience unless we face obstacles, compassion unless we experience need. *In a fallen world, some good things only come through suffering.* In the movie, "The Third Man," Orson Welles' character said:

32. Lewis, *The Problem of Pain*, 31.

"In Italy for thirty years, under the Borgias, they had warfare, terror, murder and bloodshed, but they produced Michelangelo, Leonardo da Vinci, and the Renaissance. In Switzerland they had brotherly love. They had five hundred years of democracy and peace, and what did that produce? The Cuckoo clock."[33]

We ask, what kind of God would cause us pain? But perhaps we should ask, what kind of God would not hate the sin that is destroying us? Julian of Norwich, a 14th century mystic, wrote, "So pain endures for a time. Its role is to purge us, make us know ourselves, and it drives us to the Lord to plead for mercy."[34] George MacDonald said, "To make a man happy as a lark, might be to do him grievous wrong; to make a man wake, rise, look up, turn, is worth the life and death of the Son of the Eternal."[35] Lewis called pain God's "megaphone, to rouse a deaf world."[36]

As usual, Lewis provides the perfect illustration. In one of The Chronicles of Narnia, *The Silver Chair*, the children and their Marsh-wiggle guide, Puddleglum, are captured by a wicked witch and trapped in her underworld kingdom. She places them under an enchantment and tells them that there is no world above the ground; they only imagined it. They are almost convinced. Finally Puddleglum, with great effort, attempts to stomp out the magical fire which is causing the enchantment. The pain in his feet clears his mind—"There is nothing like a good shock of pain for dissolving certain kinds of magic"—and the smell of his burning feet does the same for the others. Able again to think clearly, the children defeat the witch and escape.[37] It is pain that brings them to their senses. If we are in mortal danger and only pain will rescue us, could love do anything else?

For a Christian, one of the primary purposes of this life is our sanctification, or purification. God uses our experiences, good and bad, to make us into the kind of people He wants us to be. The Old Testament Israelites repeatedly turned away from God. Only when they suffered did they repent. Do we think we do not need to repent? That we will do so without suffering? Has human nature changed?

In the Biblical story, Joseph was a proud, arrogant young man who was sold into slavery by his jealous brothers. He spent time in an Egyptian prison. Eventually, by God's providence, he overcame all that and rose to a

---

33. "The Third Man," British Lion Films, 1949.

34. Julian of Norwich, *Revelations of Divine Love*, 1396; quoted Bell and Dawson, *From the Library of C. S. Lewis*, 130.

35. MacDonald, "The Hardness of the Way," *Unspoken Sermons*, 105..

36. Lewis, *The Problem of Pain*, 91.

37. Lewis, *The Silver Chair*, 158–159.

position of power from which he could save his family from famine. But he had to go through the suffering first, in order to become the kind of person God could use. The next traditional answer is that God frequently uses our suffering to teach us lessons we could not learn any other way. *Some of our suffering is educational.*

"I Go to Prepare a Place for You"

"I've read the last chapter in the book, and we win!"

—WALTER MARTIN[38]

Another part of the answer is, "wait." Christians believe that Christ defeated evil on the cross. He defeated suffering by suffering and death by dying[39]— and by rising again. We do not fully experience that victory, *yet*. We are promised that God will make everything right, but He has not done so, *yet*. We do not understand why He delays. But does the one who argues that suffering proves there is no God, know there can be no good reason? Is the critic himself all-knowing?[40]

Scripture says that our story did not begin with suffering, in Eden, and it will not end that way, in Heaven. Jesus said:

> "Let not your heart be troubled . . . In my Father's house are many mansions; if it were not so I would have told you. I go to prepare a place for you; and . . . I will come again and receive you to myself, that where I am, there you may be also."[41]

The Apostle Paul wrote, *"For I reckon that the sufferings of this present time are not worthy to be compared with the glory which shall be revealed in us."*[42] In Revelation, we are promised that *"God will wipe away every tear from their eyes."*[43] This world, with all its technological achievements, cannot dry our tears, but He will.

At the end of J.R.R. Tolkien's *The Lord of the Rings* trilogy, Sam Gamgee discovers that the wizard, Gandalf, is not dead, but alive. He says, "Gandalf, I thought you were dead! But then I thought I was dead myself. Is everything

---

38. Quoted Rhodes, "Tough Questions About Evil," 38.
39. Kreeft, *Making Sense Out of Suffering*, 127.
40. Geisler, "The Collapse if Modern Atheism," 132–133.
41. John 14:1–3.
42. Romans 8:18.
43. Revelation 21:4.

sad going to become untrue?"⁴⁴ The Christian answer is that indeed, one day everything sad is going to become untrue. *All our suffering is temporary.*

"You Understand Sleep When You Are Awake"

These are some of the traditional Christian answers to the question of suffering. I would suggest that they are more intellectually sound (if I remember the doctrine of the fall) and more true to human experience than any other answers. Do they always satisfy me emotionally? No—and especially not when I am suffering. But I know that I should not base my beliefs on my emotions.

C. S. Lewis wrote one of the classic Christian books on the question of suffering, *The Problem of Pain*. Then he watched his wife, Joy Davidman, die of cancer, and he wrote another book, *A Grief Observed*. It was a journal of his thoughts and feelings over the months following his wife's death, originally published under an assumed name. In that book, he expressed his questions, his doubts, even his anger toward God, much like Job:

> "When you are happy . . . if you . . . turn to Him with gratitude and praise, you will be—or so it feels—welcomed with open arms. But go to Him when your need is desperate, when all other help is vain, and what do you find? A door slammed in your face, and a sound of bolting and double bolting on the inside. After that, silence. . . .
>
> Not that I am (I think) in much danger of ceasing to believe in God. The real danger is in coming to believe such dreadful things about Him."⁴⁵

> "What reason have we, except our own desperate wishes, to believe that God is, by any standard we can conceive, 'good'? Doesn't all the *prima facie* evidence suggest exactly the opposite?"⁴⁶

But later in the same journal, he wrote:

> "Feelings, feelings, and feelings. Let me try thinking instead. From the rational point of view, what new factor has [Joy]'s death introduced into the problem of the universe? What grounds has it given me for doubting all that I believe? I already knew that these things, and worse, happened daily . . . We were

---

44. Tolkien, *The Return of the King*, 951.
45. Lewis, *A Grief Observed*, 6–7.
46. Ibid., 29.

even told, 'Blessed are they that mourn' . . . If my house has collapsed at one blow, that is because it was a house of cards . . . If I had really cared, as I thought I did, about the sorrows of the world, I should not have been so overwhelmed when my own sorrow came."[47]

Lewis ultimately reaffirmed his Christian beliefs and wrote, "You can't see anything properly while your eyes are blurred with tears."[48] Years earlier he had written, "You understand sleep when you are awake, not when you are sleeping . . . You can understand . . . drunkenness when you are sober, not when you are drunk."[49] When we are suffering, any intellectual answer will seem very unreal. So let me say again, with the utmost respect, that we must not rely on our feelings as a guide to truth.

The Ultimate Answer—"Our God Has Gone Deeper Still"

Christianity offers another answer, one that we are invited not only to understand, but to experience. That answer is Jesus. He is the living and loving God, who became man and took our sufferings onto Himself on the cross. Now He promises, *"Blessed are those who mourn, for they will be comforted;"*[50] *"Come unto me, all ye who labor and are heavy-laden, and I will give you rest."*[51]

British theologian John R.W. Stott wrote:

> "I could never believe in God, if it were not for the cross . . . In the real world of pain, how could we worship a God who was immune to it? . . . [I]n imagination I have turned . . . to that lonely, twisted, tortured figure on the cross, nails through hands and feet, back lacerated, limbs wrenched, brow bleeding from thorn-pricks, mouth dry and intolerably thirsty, plunged in God-forsaken darkness. That is the God for me! . . . He suffered for us. Our sufferings become more manageable in light of His."[52]

Christian novelist Dorothy Sayers wrote:

> "[F]or whatever reason God chose to make man as he is—limited and suffering and subject to sorrows and death—He had the

47. Ibid., 36–37.
48. Ibid., 45.
49. Lewis, *Mere Christianity*, 75.
50. Matthew 5:4.
51. Matthew 11:28.
52. Stott, *The Cross of Christ*, 335–336.

honesty and the courage to take His own medicine. Whatever game He is playing with His creation, He has kept His own rules and played fair."[53]

Peter Kreeft suggested:

> "The next time something bad happens to you through no fault of your own, and you are about to complain to God, 'I didn't deserve that,' look at a crucifix and say those same words to Him ... It gives you a sense of perspective."[54]

Corrie Ten Boom's Christian family hid Jews from the Nazis in Holland during World War II. Finally they were caught. Her entire family spent time in concentration camps. Her father and one sister died in those camps. Corrie was sent to the notorious women's concentration camp at Ravensbruck. She was freed shortly before the end of the war, the result of a "clerical error." One week after she was freed, all the women prisoners of her age were sent to the gas chambers.[55] Corrie Ten Boom later wrote of the concentration camp, "This darkness is very deep, but our God has gone deeper still. When you have been to Calvary, even Ravensbruck looks small."[56]

God's ways are not our ways, and we cannot understand why He allows us to suffer. But the cross says that He loves us enough to bear our suffering with us, and therefore we can trust Him. Alister McGrath wrote, "[T]here is no suffering on earth that is not also borne by God."[57]

The early church fathers were determined to make clear that Jesus is both fully God and fully man. Because He is fully man, He understands our pain and suffering, loneliness and despair, grief and fear, even death. Because He is fully God, He can do something about it. He is *Immanuel*, "God with us," even in our suffering.

Bringing Good from Evil

God also can and will bring real good from our suffering. Scripture never promises that nothing bad will happen to us, but it does promise, *"All things work together for good to those who love God."*[58] For a materialist, suffering is

---

53. Sayers, *Creed or Chaos*, 6.
54. Kreeft, *Before I Go*, 168.
55. Ten Boom, *The Hiding Place*, 250.
56. Quoted Kreeft, *The Philosophy of Tolkien*, 186.
57. McGrath, *The Twilight of Atheism*, 184.
58. Romans 8:28.

pointless, but for a Christian, it has a purpose. God will redeem our suffering and bring good from it.

My idea of how this might work is not that God says, "I am going to let that Howard fellow suffer for a while, until he finally learns to control his temper" (although that would not be inconsistent with God's love, if it were the only way I could learn that lesson). Rather, I believe that God allowed Satan to corrupt the earth after the fall, with all the suffering that results, because this would be for our ultimate good, in ways we cannot understand. St. Augustine wrote, "God judged it better to bring good out of evil than not to permit any evil to exist."[59] *Suffering is evil.* Much of what happens in this world is evil. But as Christians, we are promised that God will take every evil thing which happens to us and bring good from it, either in this life or the next.

We are given several examples of this in Scripture. We mentioned earlier the Old Testament story of Joseph. Many years after his brothers sold him into slavery, they came to Egypt for food in a time of famine. Joseph was in charge of the food supply, but they did not recognize him. When he disclosed to them who he was, they were afraid, because of what they had done to him. He said, *"You meant it for evil, but God meant it for good."*[60] In the end, Joseph's suffering led both to the rescue of his family from famine and to the establishment of the ancient nation of Israel.

In the New Testament, God took the greatest evil ever committed, the murder of the man who was also God, and brought from it the greatest good that ever happened, the salvation of mankind. This is why we call the day that Jesus died, "Good Friday."[61] Christianity says that suffering is truly evil, but evil will not have the final word. On the cross, good overcame evil.

---

59. Augustine, "Enchiridon," §27, 355.
60. Genesis 50:20.
61. Kreeft, *Catholic Christianity*, 134.

Chapter 16

Don't All Roads Lead to God?
Two Other Objections

"If I did not believe in God, I should still want my doctor, my lawyer and my banker to do so."

—G. K. CHESTERTON[1]

TWO OTHER QUESTIONS ARE frequently raised by opponents of the theistic religions. First, why are these religions so exclusive? Why do they insist their God is the only one, or that theirs is the only way to God? Second, if they are true, why has so much evil been done in the name of these religions?

Are All Religions Equally True?

"It is rather ridiculous to ask a man just about to be boiled in a pot and eaten . . . why he does not regard all religions as equally friendly and fraternal."

—G. K. CHESTERTON[2]

There is something in the modern mind which finds the idea that all religious beliefs are equally true, that "all roads lead to God," very appealing. But this idea refutes itself. If all religious beliefs are equally true, this must include the belief, held by most religions, that all such beliefs are *not* equally true. And do we really mean *all* religions? What about those which required infant sacrifice or enslaved women as temple prostitutes? What about Jim

---

1. Quoted Kreeft, *Back to Virtue*, 194.
2. Chesterton, *The Everlasting Man*, 232.

Jones' teachings, which led over 900 people to commit mass suicide at Jonestown, Guyana in 1978? Rationally, the idea that all religions are equally true is impossible. But we want to believe it—it fits the spirit of our age.

It has been said that in ancient Greece the common folk believed all the various religions to be true, the philosophers believed them all to be false, and the politicians believed them all to be useful![3] Human nature never changes, and neither do politicians! But ultimately, there must be a right answer—God either exists or He does not. The law of non-contradiction says that if two statements disagree, both cannot be true. We accept this law in every area of life except religion. Peter Kreeft explains why we make this one exception:

> "Whenever you're dealing with anything real, you always believe in the ... law of non-contradiction ...
>
> So if you believe that different religions can be true even when they contradict each other, you're really saying that religions aren't real but fictions, like elves. When you say that all religions are true, you're really saying that they're all false!"[4]

Christianity is exclusive in the sense that if you disagree with it, Christians believe you are mistaken. But all religions are exclusive in this sense. Even those branches of Hinduism which say that all religions are true, disagree with any religion which claims that only it has the truth. Atheism is equally exclusive, if not more so. C. S. Lewis wrote:

> "If you are an atheist you ... have to believe that the main point in all the religions of the whole world is simply one huge mistake. If you are a Christian, you are free to think that all ... religions, even the queerest ones, contain some hint of the truth."[5]

Howard's Law #23 is: If your philosophy says that the teachings of Jesus and the teachings of Jim Jones are equally true, your philosophy is probably wrong.

---

3. Zacharias, *Jesus among Other Gods*, 142. This is a paraphrase of Edward Gibbon, *The History of the Decline and Fall of the Roman Empire*, written in 1776.
4. Kreeft, *Because God Is Real*, 94.
5. Lewis, *Mere Christianity*, 29.

A Religion Based in History

"In the first century, a tiny group of Jewish dissidents spread a preposterous message about a condemned felon who rose from the dead. From such ignoble beginnings, Christianity grew into a force that dominated Western culture and eventually the world."

—CHARLES COLSON AND NANCY PEARCEY[6]

Christianity is based, more than any other religion, in history. The Bible continually refers to real historical people, places, and events. Therefore, it is easier to verify or refute. If Christianity is true, God became man—the man Jesus of Nazareth—and he came as a baby, born in Bethlehem, a real town, on a particular night on the calendar, during the reign of King Herod in Judea. Thirty-some years later, He was executed on a cross just outside of Jerusalem, on a particular day, on orders of Pontius Pilate, the local governor. Three days after that, He bodily rose from the dead. He was then seen by His disciples on multiple occasions and by over five hundred people all together.[7]

Christianity says that these are not myths, but historical facts. So they must be either true or false. St. Ignatius, Bishop of Antioch in the late first century, said that Jesus "was truly born, truly lived, truly died, and truly rose."[8] Francis Schaeffer wrote that if Christianity is true, it was true "in space and time."[9]

So there is a connection to history which makes Christianity different from other religions. But if Christianity is true, other religions, to the extent that they disagree, must be false. If Christianity is false, one of the other religions may be true, or the atheist may be right. But the law of non-contradiction applies to religious truth just as it does to any other truth. All religions cannot be true anymore than all answers to a math problem can be correct.

---

6. Colson and Pearcey, *How Now Shall We Live?* 287.
7. I Corinthians 15:6.
8. Quoted Dockery and George, *The Great Tradition of Christian Thinking*, 63.
9. Schaeffer, *The God Who Is There*, 116, 180.

"The Only Unanswerable Argument against Christianity"

> "There are five Gospels, Matthew, Mark, Luke, John, and the Christian, and some people will never read the first four."
>
> —EARLY 20TH CENTURY EVANGELIST GYPSY SMITH[10]

The second accusation made against theists—and here I will speak only of Christians—is more troublesome. It is that we do not practice what we preach. G. K. Chesterton once said, "The only unanswerable argument against Christianity is Christians."[11] Many non-believers have made similar statements. Mahatma Ghandi said, "I like their Christ; I don't like their Christians."[12] Friedrich Nietzsche said, "I will believe in the redeemer when the Christian looks a little more redeemed."[13] Albert Einstein wrote, "[W]hile religion prescribes brotherly love . . . the actual spectacle more resembles a battlefield than an orchestra."[14]

There is much truth in these statements, and this fact should cause us, as Christians, great shame. Jesus told His disciples, *"By this shall all men know that you are my disciples, if you love one another."*[15] Later, he prayed for future believers—for us—*"that they also may be one in Us, that the world may believe that You sent Me."*[16] Our "oneness" is supposed to persuade the world to believe in Him! The Apostle Paul called the church the "body of Christ."[17] But as Martin Luther King, Jr. said, "Yes, I see the Church as the body of Christ. But oh! How we have blemished and scarred that body!"[18]

Two historical events in particular are often argued as evidence against Christianity, the crusades and the inquisition. In the seventh century, Muslim armies from Arabia conquered Palestine, most of the Middle East, much of North Africa, and even invaded Spain and France, all in the name of Allah. In the eleventh century, Pope Urban II sent his armies to take this territory back for Christianity. Thus began the crusades, attempted military conquests pursued in the name of Christ. Even today, the Muslim world has

---

10. Quoted Zacharias, "The Church's Role in Apologetics and the Development of the Mind," 304.
11. Quoted Kreeft, *Fundamentals of the Faith: Essays in Christian Apologetics*, 46.
12. Quoted Zacharias, Ravi; Strobel, *The Case for Faith*, 150.
13. Ibid.
14. Einstein, "Religion and Science: Irreconcilable?" 19.
15. John 13:35.
16. John 17:21.
17. I Corinthians 12:12–27.
18. Quoted White, "Tough Questions about Black Islam," 185.

not forgotten. In 1981, after Mehmet Ali Agka attempted to kill Pope John Paul II, a letter was found among his papers, saying, "I have decided to kill John Paul II, supreme commander of the Crusades."[19] I am not a Muslim. I cannot say whether the Islamic conquest of these lands was contrary to their teachings. Mohammed was a military commander. But the crusades were clearly contrary to the teachings of Christ.

In 1163, Pope Alexander III began an effort to root out heresy in the church. This grew into what we know as the inquisition. A second, similar event occurred in Spain in the 1400s. The inquisitions used the power of the state to kill and imprison those whose religious beliefs were contrary to church teachings. Christians long ago concluded that this was a tragic error.

Today there are no crusades or inquisitions, but as Christians, we still fail, again and again, to live up to Christ's teachings. Some of these failures make the headlines, such as the "troubles" in Northern Ireland in the late twentieth century—terrorist actions committed by both sides in a dispute between Protestants and Catholics. *But our most basic failure is that we have lost the love we were commanded to have, for Christ, for one another, and for the world.* People saw the first-century church and said, "Look how they love one another!"[20] When they look at us, they do not see that love, and they are not attracted to us or to Christ.

We are told that there are hypocrites in the church. It is true. Historian Hilaire Belloc once commented that the church must be in God's hands, because given the people who have been in charge of it on earth, it could not have survived until now without divine help![21] But the fact that we as Christians do not practice perfectly what our Master taught does not prove that He was wrong. Francis Collins asked, "Would you judge Mozart's "The Magic Flute" on the basis of a poorly rehearsed performance by fifth graders?"[22] The question is whether Jesus was who He said He was, the Son of God, and whether His teachings were true. Those teachings have attracted millions of people over the centuries, despite our failure to live up to them. Mexican novelist Carlos Fuentes was not a Christian, but he wrote:

> "One can only imagine the astonishment of the ... thousands of Indians who asked for baptism as they came to realize that they were being asked to adore a god who sacrificed himself for men instead of asking men to sacrifice themselves to gods."[23]

19. Wilkin, "Gregory VII and the Politics of Spirit," 2.
20. Tertulian, *Apology*, §39:7, 178.
21. Quoted Muggeridge, *Confessions of a Twentieth Century Pilgrim*, 139.
22. Collins, *The Language of God*, 42.
23. Quoted Royal, "Columbus and the Beginning of the World," 63–64.

Abolishing Slavery and Building Hospitals

It is also true that great good has been done by Christians, following, though imperfectly, the teachings of Christ. The idea of human equality came from Christian beliefs. The atheist philosopher Friedrich Nietzsche wrote that the Christian concept of the equality of souls "furnishes the prototype of all theories of equal rights."[24]

The concept of governmental leaders as servants of the people first arose in Christian cultures, as did the practice of religious freedom. America, predominantly Christian, has granted more freedom to more different religions than any other nation in history. Ravi Zacharias, who was born in India and has seen many different cultures, wrote:

> "Isn't it ironic that when Islam is in a position of power, Islamic beliefs are forced on everyone, and that when atheism has the upper hand, atheistic beliefs are enforced on everyone? Only in Christianity is the privilege given both to believe and to disbelieve without any enforcement."[25]

I am convinced that if America continues to become less Christian and more secular, minority religions will soon find that they have less religious freedom.

It is well-documented that Americans give more to charity than any other people. And American church-goers not only give to their own churches; they give more to secular charities than do non-church-goers.[26] Eastern cultures do not share this tradition. One Chinese proverb says, "The tears of strangers are only water."[27]

The earliest hospitals were built by Christians, the first by St. Basil the Great in Caesaria, Capadocia (now Turkey), in 369, AD.[28] The earliest universities, in Bologna and Paris in the twelfth century, then Oxford and Cambridge in the thirteenth century, were all founded by Christians.[29] The same was true in America. Harvard was established in 1636 by the Puritans, and for its first one hundred years, every member of its faculty was a clergyman. Its first charter said, "Everyone shall consider the main end of his life and studies to know Jesus Christ which is eternal life."[30]

---

24. Nietzsche, *The Will to Power*, 401.
25. Zacharias, *The End of Reason*, 63.
26. Myerson, "The Generosity of America," 3.
27. Quoted D'Souza, *What's So Great about Christianity?* 66.
28. Schmidt, *How Christianity Changed the World*, 151–152.
29. D'Souza, *What's So Great about Christianity?* 97.
30. Oakes, "The Last Hope for the University," xxii. It is said that in the eighteenth

William Wilberforce came from a wealthy eighteenth-century British family and was elected to Parliament when he was still in his twenties. Shortly thereafter, he underwent what he called a "great change" and became a fervent Christian. He became interested in the plight of slaves through his acquaintance with John Newton, a former slave trader who had also become a devout Christian (and who wrote the hymn, "Amazing Grace"). Wilberforce made it his life's work to abolish slavery, filing his first bill to that effect in 1787. It went nowhere, but he re-filed the same bill every year for thirty-eight years. Finally in 1833, after Wilberforce had retired and just three days before his death, Parliament passed his bill, abolishing slavery in the British Empire.[31]

In America as well, the abolitionist movement began in Christian churches, led first by the Quakers and then by such men as Presbyterian evangelist Charles Finney.[32] The American civil rights movement was rooted in Christian theology and led by Christian ministers such as Martin Luther King, Jr. This was not a coincidence. *These men opposed slavery because their religion told them it was wrong. They fought for civil rights because their religion told them it was right.*

Most advances in the status of women have occurred first in Christian cultures. There were more women than men in the early church, and the Romans scorned Christianity as a "religion for women."[33] From its earliest days, Christianity opposed the killing of female babies, which was common in Greek and Roman cultures.[34] The early Church taught that marriage should be a matter of mutual choice, that adultery was as sinful for a man as for a woman, and that divorce laws should apply equally to both sexes.[35] *These teachings grew out of the radical Judeo-Christian idea that all human beings, male and female, were equally created in the image of God.*[36]

The belief in a God who is Love and Truth, and who commands the same from us, has had a great impact on the morals and ethics of individuals throughout history. Jewish radio talk-show host Dennis Prager once asked a caller who denied that religion influences morals, suppose you are driving at night through a bad section of a major city, and your car breaks down. You have to get out and walk. As you round a corner, you see a group of

---

century, when Harvard's faculty began to lose their zeal for the Christian faith, Yale was founded to fill the void! Ibid.

31. Belmonte, "William Wilberforce: A Man for All Seasons," 32–34.
32. D'Souza, *What's So Great about Christianity?* 73–75.
33. D'Souza, "Created Equal: How Christianity Shaped the West," 2–3.
34. D'Souza, *What's So Great about Christianity?* 71.
35. Ibid., 62, 71.
36. Colson, *My Final Word,* 88.

tough-looking young men coming toward you. Would you or would you not feel better to learn they had just come from a Bible study?[37]

From the Judeo-Christian moral code to art and architecture, Western culture grew out of Christianity. Can you imagine Western civilization without Gothic cathedrals or the Sistine Chapel? Without Dante's *Divine Comedy* or Milton's *Paradise Lost*? Michelangelo's *Pieta* or da Vinci's *The Last Supper*? Handel's *Messiah* or Beethoven's *Ode to Joy*? Without Christianity, our civilization as we know it would not exist.[38]

"One Death Is a Tragedy. Ten Million Is Just a Statistic."

"Once in power, the Bolsheviks made Utopia an extremely bloody business."
—FRENCH HISTORIAN STEPHANE COURTOIS[39]

Some of the "new atheist" writers have blamed religion in general, and Christianity in particular, for much of the evil in the world. Journalist Christopher Hitchens wrote, "Religion poisons everything."[40] Richard Dawkins called religion "The root of all evil."[41] Steven Weinberg said, "With or without religion, you would have good people doing good things and evil people doing evil things. But for good people to do evil things, that takes religion."[42]

While evil has certainly been done in the name of religion, I believe these men are guilty of gross exaggeration. But what about the other side of the coin? Nazi Germany, the Soviet Union, and Communist China were or are all atheist regimes, and that short list makes up a "Hall of Fame" of murderers and oppressors of the twentieth century. Hitler oversaw the killing of approximately eleven million people,[43] Stalin an estimated twenty million,[44] and Mao some sixty-five million.[45] Stalin is reported to have

---

37. Quoted Colson and Pearcey, *How Now Shall We Live?* 193.
38. D'Sousa, *What's So Great about Christianity?* 46.
39. Courtois, *The Black Book of Communism*, 738.
40. Hitchens, *God is Not Great: How Religion Poisons Everything*.
41. "The Root of All Evil," BBC Documentary, 2006; quoted Dembski, *The End of Christianity*, 4.
42. "Why We Are Here: The Great Debate," *International Herald Tribune*, April 26, 1999; quoted Strobel, *The Case for Faith*, 198.
43. *World Book Encyclopedia*, 1991, Vol. 9, 254n.
44. D'Sousa, *What's So Great about Christianity?* 218.
45. Courtois, *The Black Book of Communism*, 4. Historians Jung Chang and Jon Halliday estimate the number killed under Mao at seventy million. Chang and Halliday, *Mao: The Unknown Story*, 613.

said, about the famine he engineered in the Ukraine, "One death is a tragedy. Ten million is just a statistic."[46]

I am not arguing that these men killed because they were atheists—I believe they killed because they were fallen sinners, like the rest of us. But I would suggest that atheism provides no restraint against such evil, for at least three reasons. First, atheistic ideologies invariably seek to create a paradise on earth. In the absence of any absolute moral standards, this end will justify any means, including killing those who oppose it. Second, if man is only an accidental arrangement of atoms, his life is meaningless and so is his death. It is only logical to sacrifice one man—or a million—for the greater good. Third, when an atheist oppresses those weaker than himself, he is acting consistently with his belief that the ultimate reality is the survival of the fittest. When a Christian is guilty of oppression, he is acting contrary to what he believes to be the ultimate reality, an ethical and loving God.

Howard's Law #24 is: *If your philosophy was shared by the greatest mass-murderers in history, your philosophy is probably wrong.*

Building a Society on the Survival of the Fittest

"If nature does not wish that weaker individuals should mate with the stronger, she wishes even less that a superior race should intermingle with an inferior one; because in such case all her efforts, throughout hundreds of thousands of years, to establish an evolutionary higher stage of being, may thus be rendered futile."

—ADOLPH HITLER, *MEIN KAMPF*[47]

There are many good moral and ethical atheists. My grandfather, if not an atheist, was certainly an unbeliever, who almost never darkened the door of a church. But my father called him one of the most honest men he ever knew. Such men live better than their philosophy, and this inconsistency is their greatest virtue.

But what happens if a society is built on an atheistic philosophy? Until the twentieth century, this had never been tried. Now it has been, and the results were tragic. Nazi Germany, the Soviet Union, and Communist China were all expressly based on atheistic teachings. The Nazis first organized in 1920 and came to power in Germany in 1933. By 1945, they had started World War II and slaughtered millions in the holocaust.

46. Quoted Kreeft, *How to Win the Culture War*, 43.
47. Hitler, *Mein Kampf*, 162.

Please do not misunderstand me—World War II and the holocaust had many causes. And I love Germany. I took my wife there on our honeymoon. I love the history (walled villages, castles, and cathedrals), the scenery (the mountain lakes of Bavaria or the Mosel River valley), and the people (even the maid in the little inn who ordered us "Out, out, out!" because it was five minutes past checkout time, and she was ready to clean!).

But which culture is more likely to start a war of conquest or attempt to eliminate an "inferior" race, one whose philosophy is based on the survival of the fittest, or one built on a religion whose founder said, *"Inasmuch as you did it to one of the least of these my brethren, you did it to me?"*[48] Not only Jews were killed in the holocaust; so were the mentally handicapped, homosexuals, and anyone else regarded as inferior or "unfit." The Nazis referred to these people with the phrase, "life unworthy of life."[49] The holocaust had many causes, but it is not a coincidence that it occurred in a society built on such a philosophy. Friedrich Nietzsche wrote:

> "Equality is a lie concocted by inferior people who arrange themselves in herds to overpower those who are naturally superior to them. The morality of 'equal rights' is herd morality, and because it opposes the cultivation of superior individuals, it leads to the corruption of the human species."[50]

> "Through Christianity, the individual was made so important . . . that he could no longer be sacrificed. But the species endures only through human sacrifice."[51]

Adolph Hitler held that the elimination of the weak was beneficial for the survival of the rest of society, that "nature intended it that way."[52] *Hitler personally presented the writings of Nietzsche to both Mussolini and Stalin.*[53]

The Nazis also practiced "eugenics," an attempt to scientifically improve the human race through forced sterilization, abortion, and even infanticide (the killing of live babies) of those deemed unfit. They referred to this policy as "social Darwinism," and they were not misusing the term. In Darwin's second best-selling book, *The Descent of Man*, he wrote:

---

48. Matthew 25:40.
49. Colson, *My Final Word*, 47; Kreeft, *Catholic Christianity*, 226–227.
50. Quoted Zacharias, *The End of Reason*, 98.
51. Nietzsche, *The Will to Power*, 142.
52. Quoted Zacharias, *The End of Reason*, 51.
53. Ibid.

"No one who has attended to the breeding of domestic animals will doubt that this [allowing the inferior to breed] must be highly injurious to the race of man. It is surprising how soon a want of care, or care wrongly directed, leads to the degeneration of a domestic race; but excepting in the case of man himself, hardly anyone is so ignorant as to allow his worst animals to breed . . .

At some future period, not very distant as measured by centuries, the civilized races of man will almost certainly exterminate and replace the savage races throughout the world."[54]

Before World War II, these ideas were gaining popularity in other Western countries, including America. The Darwinist biology textbook which was the subject of the famous "Scopes Trial" in 1925, taught that there are five races of men, culminating in "the highest type of all, the Caucasians, represented by the civilized white inhabitants of Europe and America."[55] It was this racism and other aspects of social Darwinism which inspired William Jennings Bryan, a political liberal, to champion the creationist cause in the Scopes case.[56]

United States Supreme Court Justice Oliver Wendell Holmes, an outspoken Darwinist, once suggested "restricting propagation by the undesirables and putting to death infants that didn't pass the examination."[57] This was not just idle talk. Justice Holmes wrote the majority opinion in a 1927 case, *Buck v. Bell*, which must rank as one of the Supreme Court's all-time lowest points. The Court ordered the forced sterilization of Carrie Buck, a poor girl from Virginia who had become pregnant while in a foster home (probably from rape), and whom the courts deemed "feeble-minded." Holmes wrote:

---

54. Darwin, *The Descent of Man*, 151–152, 178. Darwin continued, "The break between man and his nearest allies will then be wider, for it will intervene between man in a more civilized state, as we may hope, even than the Caucasian, and some ape as low as a baboon, instead of as now between the negro or Australian and the gorilla." Ibid., 178.

55. The full quote read, "The Races of Man—At the present time there exist upon the earth five races or varieties of man, each very different from the other in instincts, social customs, and, to an extent, in structure. There are the Ethiopian or negro type, originating in Africa; the Malay or brown race, from the islands of the Pacific; the American Indian; the Mongolian or yellow race, including the natives of China, Japan, and the Eskimos; and, finally, *the highest type of all, the Caucasians, represented by the civilized white inhabitants of Europe and America.*" (emphasis added) Hunter, George William, *Essentials of Biology: Presented in Problems*, 320; quoted Geisler and Turek, *I Don't Have Enough Faith to Be an Atheist*, 421, n20.

56. D'Sousa, *What's So Great about Christianity?* 145.

57. Letter to Justice Felix Frankfurter, September 3, 1921; quoted Alschuler, *Law without Values: The Life, Work and Legacy of Justice Holmes*, 28.

> "We have seen more than once that the public welfare may call upon the best citizens for their lives. It would be strange if it could not call upon those who already sap the strength of the State for these lesser sacrifices... It is better for all the world if, instead of waiting to execute degenerate offspring for crime or to let them starve for their imbecility, society can prevent those who are manifestly unfit from continuing their kind... Three generations of imbeciles are enough."[58]

This language is shocking to us, but Justice Holmes was merely following the logic of his Darwinist philosophy. If the guiding principle of nature is the survival of the fittest, why should those who "sap the strength of the State" not be sacrificed for the greater good?

Ideas Have Consequences

"Christians have two boundary conditions: (1) what men can do, and (2) what men should do. Modern man does not have the latter boundary. Only technology limits him. Modern man does what he can do."

—FRANCIS SCHAEFFER[59]

In America and other Western cultures today, we are teaching our children these same ideas—that they are only animals, the ultimate law is the survival of the fittest, and moral rules are all man-made. What are the likely consequences this time? C. S. Lewis prophetically wrote, more than 60 years ago:

> "We make men without chests [proper sentiments about right and wrong] and expect of them virtue and enterprise. We laugh at honor and are surprised to find traitors in our midst. We castrate and bid the geldings be fruitful."[60]

Harry Lewis, the former Dean of Harvard College, wrote in 2010:

> "I am not among those who regret the departure of God from the academy... Yet I regret the extent to which God took with him, when he left the classroom, questions of values and morals and purposes with which young people struggle today as they

---

58. *Buck v. Bell*, 274 U.S.200, 1927.
59. Schaeffer, *Back to Freedom and Dignity*, 369.
60. Lewis, *The Abolition of Man*, 35.

always have. As much as ever, a good education owes students guidance on examining their own lives"[61]

When we teach our children that moral standards are man-made, can we complain if they make their own? If we tell our youth they are nothing more than animals, can we be surprised when they act that way?

Francis Schaeffer suggested that even science will not remain unaffected by the loss of its Judeo-Christian foundation in truth and morals:

> "I also think science as we have known it is going to die. I think it is going to be reduced to two things: mere technology, and another form of sociological manipulation. I do not believe for a moment that science is going to be able to continue with its objectivity once the base that brought forth science has been totally destroyed."[62]

The efforts toward eugenics in America and other Western countries in the 1920s and 30s were rejected after the world saw the evils of Nazism, but they are beginning to return. In 2012, two "medical ethicists," Alberto Giubilina and Francesca Minerva, published an article in the *Journal of Medical Ethics* titled, "After-birth Abortion: Why Should the Baby Live?" They discussed the "ethics" of killing a healthy baby after it is born, writing, "[H]aving a child can itself be an unbearable burden for the psychological health of the woman or for her already existing children," and "[T]o bring up such children might be an unbearable burden . . . on society as a whole, when the state economically provides for their care." They concluded, "Merely being human is not in itself a reason for ascribing someone a right to life," and "[K]illing a newborn could be ethically permissible in all the circumstances where abortion would be."[63]

Peter Singer, a bioethics professor at Princeton and a leading proponent of animal rights, argues that we should measure the value of any life only by its utility, by what good it is to the rest of society. Since "[T]he life of a newborn baby is of less value than the life of a pig, a dog or a chimpanzee," Singer has also proposed that parents be allowed to have their newborn infants killed, at least until they become self-aware.[64]

You can say that these men are extremists. *But ideas have consequences, and ideas which deny the God-given dignity and value of human life have devastating consequences for societies which adopt them.* Has evil been done

---

61. Lewis, "Forward," Willard, *A Place for Truth*, 9.
62. Schaeffer, *He is There and He is Not Silent*, 328.
63. Giubilina and Minerva, "After-birth Abortion: Why Should the Baby Live?"
64. Singer, *Practical Ethics*, 122–126.

in the name of religion, even in the name of Christ? Sadly, yes—many times. But it is because we have not lived up to our beliefs. Even greater evil has been done, in just the last century, by societies built on atheistic philosophies, and it is a logical result of those beliefs. The God of Scripture is not the cause of evil in the world. He is our only hope to overcome that evil.

Chapter 17

"How Should We Then Live?"
The Practical Conclusion

"Christianity is a statement, which if false, is of no importance, and if true, of infinite importance. The one thing it cannot be is moderately important."
—C. S. LEWIS[1]

"Life offers only one tragedy in the end: not to have been a saint."
—LEON BLOY[2]

IN THE OLD TESTAMENT book of Ezekiel, the prophet repeatedly tells the people of Israel that they have sinned, and warns them of coming judgment. In chapter 33, he urges them to repent and to ask God, *"How should we then live?"*[3] We will turn in this chapter from the intellectual question of whether God exists to the practical question: If God is real, *"How should we then live?"*

The ancient Greek philosophers such as Aristotle believed that the greatest good in human life, what they called the *"summum bonum,"* was

---

1. Lewis, "Christian Apologetics," 101.

2. As quoted Kreeft, *How to Win the Culture War*, 108. This is the last line of Bloy's novel, *The Woman Who Was Poor*. In the I. J. Collins translation, it reads, "'There is only one misery,' she said, the last time she saw him, 'and that is—NOT TO BE SAINTS.'" Bloy, *The Woman Who Was Poor*, 312.

3. Ezekiel 33:10. At least two books have taken this verse for their titles: Schaeffer, *How Should We Then Live?* and Colson and Pearcey, *How Now Shall We Live?*

found through being in right relation with the ultimate reality. Aristotle said that the goal of human life is happiness, but he taught that both meaning and happiness are found through virtue,[4] and he was right. "It is a good soul, not a good bank account, that makes you happy."[5] The early Christians adopted these ideas, and Western civilization was built on this tradition. But in twenty-first-century America, our most popular beliefs are based on materialistic assumptions, and so are our life-styles. We agree that our goal is happiness, but we define happiness not as a good soul, but merely a good feeling. We seek it not in virtue, but in pleasure.

Again, it all comes back to the God question. *If there is a God, He is the summum bonum.* I must look at the world the way He does, and pleasing Him must be the chief purpose of my life. If there is no God, and we humans are the highest beings (the highest stage of evolution so far), my reasonable purpose is to manipulate the material universe through technology, to satisfy my own desires.[6] So my belief about God determines how I look at life. Am I trying to change myself to please the ultimate reality, or trying to change reality to please myself?

But as Christians, do we live as though pleasing God were our highest purpose? Do we seek His will in the important decisions of our lives? Do we give Him the largest part of our time, thought, or money? How can we tell God that we are too busy for Him?

What do we want most for our children? Most of us will say that we want them to be healthy, happy, well-educated, and successful. There is nothing wrong with any of these things, but do we think they are God's priorities? What about our children's relationship with Him? What about learning virtue and developing character? According to the old saying, "A father's number-one job is to get his kids to Heaven." I am not holding myself out as a perfect parent by any means, but my wife and I have sent our daughter to Christian schools from kindergarten on (she is now at a Christian college), for this reason—*the most important thing about her education is that it be a Christian education.*

Do we share the Gospel with our neighbors? Jesus commanded us to "*make disciples of all the nations.*"[7] Our culture says that trying to convert someone from one religion to another shows intolerance of other faiths. If "all roads lead to God," this makes sense. But if Christianity is *true* and I love my neighbor, how can I not share the Good News of Christ with him?

---

4. Kreeft, *Making Sense Out of Suffering*, 63–64.
5. Kreeft and Tacelli, *Handbook of Christian Apologetics*, 141.
6. Lewis, *The Abolition of Man*, 77.
7. Matthew 28:19.

Does our faith influence our politics? Many excellent books have been written on what a Christian world-view would mean to our culture and politics.[8] I am going to resist the temptation to tell you what positions I think a Christian should take on the issues of our day—that is not the purpose of this book. But I am convinced that we must take our positions on those issues not from our culture but from God's character, not from *USA Today* but from God's Word.

If We Are Only Atoms

Our world-views will determine how we look at the eight human characteristics we have discussed. If materialism is true, we are only collections of atoms. We are not really "persons" or "selves" in any meaningful sense. Our consciousness is "a riddle wrapped in a mystery inside an enigma." Our reasoning is just the random result of natural causes, and there is no real truth, only "my truth" and "your truth." Free will is an illusion. Our actions are all determined by natural causes, and I am no more responsible for injuring you than a wild animal would be.

On materialistic assumptions, our moral notions are merely the accidental results of nature. There is no true right or wrong. We are "free" (whatever freedom means to a determined being) to do whatever we want, unless someone else can stop us. Of course, that other person is also unrestricted by any real right or wrong, so if what he wants is to kill us, we had better be able to defend ourselves. But we cannot say that he is wrong.

If man is not fallen, the cause of crime is not inside the criminal; it must come from society. So we constantly try to change our political, economic, or educational systems, seeking to solve our social problems. Individually, my highest goal is to "be myself," to do whatever seems natural for me, and I will very much resent anyone telling me not to do so. Is this not an almost perfect picture of twenty-first-century American culture?

If true joy does not exist, in this life or the next, I might as well "eat, drink, and be merry," for "that's all there is." If "you only live once," as the saying goes, your only rational goal is to seek as much pleasure as you can, for as long as you can.

If we are only atoms, our existence is a fluke, and life has no meaning. Our ideas of human dignity, equality, and rights; of freedom, love, and beauty, are like our notions of morality—only the accidental results of

---

8. See, for example: Colson and Pearcey, *A Dance with Deception*; Kreeft, *How to Win the Culture War*; Neuhaus, *Doing Well and Doing Good*; and Schaeffer, *How Should We Then Live?*

evolution. So we must "make our own meaning." These are the dominant beliefs of our twenty-first-century culture, and they are the basis for our rules for living. Sadly, the dysfunction in our society tells us that these rules do not work very well.

If We Are Made in the Image of God

On the other hand, if my consciousness reflects an eternal soul created by God, I can speak meaningfully of my "human dignity." But you also have that same dignity, and this changes how I must treat you. Our personhood gives us a basis for inter-personal morality. If God has given me the ability to perceive truth, I must pursue it to the best of my ability. "God is no fonder of intellectual slackers than of any other slackers." If I make real choices, I am responsible for those choices.

If there is a righteous God who "loves love and hates hatred," who loves justice and hates oppression, I had better obey His laws. I have no right to argue, compromise, or make my own rules. If God did not make me the way I am, if my "natural" tendencies are not really natural, but I am fallen and corrupted by sin, I cannot trust my own thoughts or desires, but must seek His will.

If I can find real joy through a right relationship with God, I will make that relationship my chief priority. If I am going to live forever, that will change how I look at this life. Pastor and author David Platt says that as Christians, we are not living for twenty years from now, but for twenty billion years from now![9] Missionary Jim Elliott and two co-workers were murdered in Ecuador in 1956 by a remote tribe which they were trying to reach with the Gospel. After his death, his wife found these words written in his journal: "He is no fool who gives what he cannot keep to gain that which he cannot lose."[10]

If I was created by God for a purpose, my life has meaning. I know where I came from and where I am going. I have real dignity and rights. You and I are truly equal. Love and beauty are real. These are the Judeo-Christian beliefs on which Western civilization was built. They work because they are true, and they give meaning and hope to my life.

So there are two world-views, and how a person thinks will determine how he lives. The Apostle Paul wrote, "*Let this mind be in you which was also in Christ Jesus.*"[11] If we think like Christ, surely we will not live like

---

9. Platt, *Counter Culture*, 54.
10. Elliott, *The Journals of Jim Elliott*, 174.
11. Philippians 2:5.

the world. But as Christians, we often seem to do exactly that. Do we not believe what we say we do? I am convinced that most often, our beliefs are sincere—on Sunday mornings. But on Monday through Saturday, we fail to apply those beliefs to our lives. We think like the world does, and therefore we live like the world does.

Pascal's Wager

"May God, if there is one, save my soul, if I have one."

—FRANCOIS-MARIE VOLTAIRE[12]

If the God of Scripture is real, how should we respond? Speaking first to non-believers, Christianity talks of what it calls "salvation." This is God's incredible offer to forgive our sins, restore the relationship we were meant to have with Him, and give us eternal life. Our part is repentance—true sorrow for our sins and a desire to live according to His will; and faith—believing that Christ died for our sins, and trusting God enough to obey Him.

But what if you have examined the evidence and are still unsure? What is called "Pascal's wager" was first proposed in the eleventh century by Muslim theologian Al-Ghazali[13] and was popularized by Blaise Pascal in the seventeenth century. Pascal described someone, "seeing too much to deny [God] and too little to be sure."[14] He wrote:

> "Yes; but you must wager. It is not optional. You are embarked [just by living] . . . Let us weigh the gain and the loss in wagering that God is. Let us estimate these two chances. If you gain you gain all; if you lose you lose nothing. Wager, then, without hesitation, that He is . . .
>
> Now, what harm will befall you in taking this side? You will be faithful, honest, humble, grateful, generous, a sincere friend, truthful. Certainly you will not have those poisonous pleasures, glory and luxury, but will you not have others? I will tell you that you will thereby gain in this life, and that, at every step you take on this road, you will see so great certainty of gain, so much nothingness in what you risk, that you will at last recognize that

---

12. Quoted Geisler, *Baker Encyclopedia of Christian Apologetics*, 765.

13. Al-Ghazali wrote, "But should he say that a future life is possible but that the doctrine is so involved in doubt and mystery that it is impossible to decide whether it be true or not, then one may say to him: 'Then you had better give it the benefit of the doubt!'" Al-Ghazali, *The Alchemy of Happiness*, 71.

14. Pascal, *Pensees*, #229, 64.

you have wagered for something certain and infinite, for which you have given nothing."[15]

I had a friend in high school who was a nonbeliever. I am sure he never heard of Pascal's wager, but he commented to me once that he was risking more than I was—after we both died, if I was wrong I would never know it, but if he was wrong he would! Peter Kreeft wrote, "Faith is a 'no-lose' bet and atheism is a 'no-win' bet."[16]

Wishful Thinking

"The Christian ideal has not been tried and found wanting. It has been found difficult and left untried."

—G. K. CHESTERTON[17]

"This God... has always been, to say the least, hard to live with. Human beings have always preferred gods for whom they can write the job description."

—LESLIE ZEIGLER[18]

Christians are often accused of "wishful thinking." In a sense, it is true. We want to believe that we are more than just accidents, that our lives have meaning, and that we will live forever. But if we were going to invent a God, who would invent the God of the Old Testament? He is *righteous*. He said, *"Thou shalt not,"* and He will be our Judge. Rabbi Abraham Heschel said, "God is not nice. He is not an uncle. God is an earthquake."[19]

I am convinced that wishful thinking more often works the other way, that we choose not to believe in God because we do not want him to exist. This may be to avoid the traditional moral rules, or just to be "autonomous," in charge of our own lives. We prefer tame gods, vague "spirits" who do not try to tell us how to live. The popular twentieth-century writer Julian Huxley once said that for him and his contemporaries, "The reason we accepted Darwinism even without proof is because we didn't want God to interfere with our sexual mores."[20]

15. Pascal, *Pensees*, #233, 66–68.
16. Kreeft, "The Choice of a Lifetime," 289–290.
17. Chesterton, *What's Wrong with the World?* 37.
18. Zeigler, "Christianity or Feminism," 181.
19. Quoted Needleman, *The New Religions*, 6.
20. TV interview with Merv Griffin; quoted Kennedy, *Skeptics Answered*, 154.

We have quoted the philosopher Thomas Nagle several times. He understands very well the intellectual problems with Darwinian materialism, but he remains an atheist. Why? In *The Last Word*, he wrote:

> "I want atheism to be true and I am made uneasy by the fact that some of the most intelligent and well-informed people I know are religious believers. It isn't just that I don't believe in God and naturally hope that I'm right in my belief. It's that I hope there is no God! I don't want there to be a God; I don't want the universe to be like that."[21]

Autonomy is very tempting. We want to say, "It's my life. How I live it is up to me." But autonomy is a fraud. How many of our choices are really ours? How many are influenced by our genes, our culture, or our peers? If materialism is true, all our actions are brought about solely by natural causes. *If you choose materialism in order to be free, remember that materialism says freedom is an illusion.* Sheldon Vanauken wrote that if we live as materialists, "We shall not have achieved autonomy. We shall have become automatons."[22] Only if there is a God can we have real, though limited, freedom. But it is a gift from Him. Surely it would be foolish to use that freedom to reject Him?

I believe that for most of us, this is the crux of the matter. If I acknowledge that God exists, I must submit my will to His. My relationship with God can never be a relationship of equals! So I have a choice. *I can choose God, eternal life, meaning, and joy; or I can choose the illusion of autonomy. But I cannot have both.*

I would suggest that we should believe in God—and submit our lives to him—for at least two reasons. The most important is that He is real. *I believe Christianity is true.* It seems to me that the evidence strongly supports this conclusion, and "the only honest reason anyone ever has for believing anything is that they think it is true."[23] But I would also submit that for a rational person, meaning for life and hope for the future surely outweigh personal autonomy and moral "freedom," and the short-term pleasures they can bring.

---

21. Nagle, *The Last Word*, 130.
22. Vanauken, "God's Will," 362.
23. Kreeft, *Between Heaven and Hell*, 68.

Do Not Look Out for Number One

"[F]rom a Christian point of view, love is the works of love."
—SOREN KIERKEGAARD[24]

What about believers? *"How should we then live?"* Let me propose three rules for a meaningful and fulfilling life. All three run contrary to the accepted wisdom of our culture, but there is nothing wrong with being counter-cultural if the culture is going the wrong way!

First, do not look out for number one. Self-centeredness is our "natural" attitude, in our fallen state, but it is not the way we were made, and it will not bring us joy, only misery and harm. The comedian Rodney Dangerfield said, "While you're looking out for number one, you're going to step in a lot of number two!"[25]

Our culture says that doing what we want is the way we will find happiness. We make self-centeredness (we call it "self-expression") a virtue, rather than a fault. Harry Lee Poe said, "People no longer go off in search of glory. Instead, they go off in search of themselves."[26] But all the misery in our wealthy, pleasure-seeking world screams that happiness does not lie down this road.

University of Pennsylvania psychologist Martin Seligman writes that Americans since 1960 have more money, more education, and more access to entertainment than any people in history. Yet we suffer from ten times more depression than ever before. He notes that this epidemic is found only in wealthy countries, and that even in America, groups such as the Amish are unaffected. Why is this? Dr. Seligman concludes that it is because we are focused on self—we have "produced a generation of narcissists."[27]

Stephen Covey, in his best-selling book, *The 7 Habits of Highly Effective People*, wrote that until about fifty years ago, self-help books in America all emphasized how to become better people. In the last fifty years, they have emphasized how to achieve wealth, power, or success.[28] But despite a multitude of such books, we are not happy.

Often we "look out for number one" not from selfishness but from fear, to avoid being hurt. But what others do to us does not really hurt us, in our

---

24. Kierkegard, Soren, *Journals and Papers*, 1849; quoted Ferreira, *Love's Grateful Striving*, 23.
25. Quoted Kreeft, *Before I Go*, 67.
26. Poe, *See No Evil*, 77.
27. Seligman, *Authentic Happiness*, 117–118.
28. Covey, *The 7 Habits of Highly Effective People*, 26–27.

souls. What we do to others does. "It does you no harm to be Charlie Brown trying to kick the football, but it does do you harm to be Lucy holding it [and pulling it away]."²⁹

Our culture not only encourages us to "look out for number one;" it tells us to seek the things of this world. None of these things will satisfy us, nor last. But there is another way. Kreeft wrote:

> "The three most popular idols are money, sex and power. The three deadliest of the seven deadly sins are greed, lust and pride. These are the three main sources of evil, 'the world, the flesh and the devil.' That's why monks take three vows: poverty, chastity and obedience."³⁰

We are not all called to be monks, but we are all called to let God's love change our lives. A man once saw Mother Teresa embrace a leper. He told her that he "wouldn't do that for all the money in the world." She responded that she wouldn't either—she did it for the love of Christ.³¹

The true rule is illustrated by the children's acrostic for the word joy— to find true J.O.Y., put Jesus first, others second, and yourself last. *Do not look out for number one. Only a life lived for something bigger than yourself can bring real joy.*

Do Not Be Yourself

Second, do not be yourself. "Be yourself" may be the most popular motto of our culture. Like most false ideas, it contains a small bit of truth—we should not be hypocrites, pretending to be something we are not, in order to deceive. But failing to live up to our beliefs does not prove we are hypocrites; it only proves we are fallen sinners.

Scripture never talks about being ourselves. Instead, it tells us to be like Christ. Jesus said, *"[Y]ou shall be perfect, just as your Father in heaven is perfect."*³² The Apostle Paul wrote that he *"imitate[ed] Christ,"* and we should to do the same.³³ The Apostle Peter wrote that we should *"follow in His steps."*³⁴ The young people had the right idea a few years ago when they

---

29. Kreeft, *Before I Go*, 102.
30. Ibid, 62.
31. D'Sousa, *What's So Great about Christianity?* 307.
32. Matthew 5:48.
33. I Corinthians 11:1.
34. I Peter 2:21.

asked, "What would Jesus do?" I am invited to come to God, "Just as I Am." But I must come to Him for the purpose of being changed, to be like Him.

Our society glorifies self-indulgence, especially if it has anything to do with sex. *We define our desires as the essence of who we are, and then say, "Be yourself."* But this philosophy of life has not made us happy, nor has it made us better people.

Until recent times, most all men have understood that the essence of a human being is not his desires, but the "self" which chooses whether to follow those desires or to resist them. The ability to control our desires, as much as any characteristic, is what distinguishes us from other animals. Plato wrote that the head (reason) rules the belly (natural appetites) through the chest (proper moral sentiments).[35] Sigmund Freud talked of the *id*, which represents our desires, and the *ego*, which represents "reason and common sense," and attempts to control those desires. He used the analogy of a horse (the *id*) and rider (the *ego*).[36]

Christianity says that God gave us our desires and He wants to fulfill them. But because we are fallen, our desires in this life are corrupted. So we must often resist them, because they will lead to harm, either to ourselves or to others. *On the other hand, if we choose to act better than we are, that effort will begin to make us truly better. Every time we resist temptation, we become stronger. Every time we yield, we become weaker.*

Sadly, we have chosen to become less than human—less than what God intended us to be. We have said that there is no such thing as free will, and have chosen slavery to our animal passions over human freedom and responsibility. We have said that there is nothing more to life than pleasure, and have made ourselves miserable seeking it. We have said that we are only animals, and have begun to devolve back into apes.[37]

"Look out for number one" and "be yourself" are among our society's most popular mottos for living, but they are only expressions of what the Bible calls sin. In fact, sin is why they are such shallow, naive philosophies. "Be yourself" assumes that "yourself" is entirely good, rather than a good thing gone bad. *Do not be yourself. Be like Christ.*

---

35. Lewis, *The Abolition of Man*, 34. This is a paraphrase of Plato's teaching, both in *The Republic* and *Timaeus*.

36. Freud, "The Ego and the Id," 25.

37. Kreeft, *C. S. Lewis for the Third Millennium*, 140.

Do Not Pursue Happiness

> "If humanism were right in declaring that man was born to be happy, he would not be born to die. Since his body is doomed to die, his task on earth evidently must be of a more spiritual nature."
>
> —ALEKSANDR SOLZHENITSYN[38]

Third, do not pursue happiness. Thomas Jefferson listed "the pursuit of happiness" among our God-given rights. But I would suggest that happiness, at least as our culture defines it, is an unworthy pursuit for beings made in the image of God. Scripture never tells us to pursue happiness. Rather, it says, *"Pursue . . . holiness, without which no one will see the LORD."*[39] The answer the Israelites received in Ezekiel to their question, *"How should we then live?"* was, *"Turn, turn from your evil ways."*[40] The command to be holy should not surprise us, if we believe in a holy God. Francis Schaeffer asked, "How could a perfect God say, 'Just sin a little bit?'"[41]

The pursuit of happiness never succeeds. But if we pursue God and His holiness, we will find true joy, substantially in this life and fully in the life to come. The way to be truly happy is not to pursue happiness! But this illustrates a universal principle. Jesus said, *"[W]hoever desires to save his life will lose it, but whoever loses his life for My sake will find it."*[42]

What would it mean, in practice, to be holy? First, our hearts and wills must be totally committed to God. C. S. Lewis wrote, "In the end, there are only two kinds of people—those who say 'Thy will be done' to God and those to whom God in the end says, 'Thy will be done.'"[43]

Second, God's holiness is defined in the Old Testament, again and again, in terms of two characteristics. They are first mentioned together in Exodus 34, when God, on Mt. Sinai, described Himself to Moses: *"The LORD, the LORD God . . . abounding in goodness and truth."*[44] These two words are sometimes translated as *"love and faithfulness."*[45] But the Hebrew words, *hessed* and *emeth*, represent the two main parts of morality—the morality we all know—love, mercy, or kindness; and truth, justice, or integrity.

38. 1978 graduation address at Harvard; quoted Noebel, *Understanding the Times*, 7.
39. Hebrews 12:14.
40. Ezekiel 33:11.
41. Schaeffer, *The God Who Is There*, 167.
42. Matthew 16:25.
43. Lewis, *The Great Divorce*, 69.
44. Exodus 34:6. See also II Samuel 2:6, Psalm 40:11, and Psalm 61:7.
45. Exodus 34:6, NIV.

This is what God is like. He is Love and He is Truth. So if I am to be like him, I must *"love my neighbor as myself,"* and practice integrity in all my dealings. That is basic, but it is not easy. Lewis wrote:

> "Sometimes, Lord, one is tempted to say that if you wanted us to behave like the lilies of the field you might have given us an organization more like theirs. But that, I suppose, is . . . your grand enterprise . . . to make that terrible oxymoron, a 'spiritual animal.' To take a poor primate, a beast with nerve endings all over it, a creature with a stomach that wants to be filled, a breeding animal that wants its mate, and say, 'Now get on with it. Become a god.'"[46]

We are "spiritual animals," and the unbelievably high goal to which we are called is to be like God! We are supposed to be holy! We cannot make ourselves holy; He must do it. But He will not do it against our wills.

So while our performance in this life will not be perfect, our commitment to God must be absolute and our lives must show it. The popular saying goes, "The only difference between sinner and saint is one's forgiven and the other ain't." But this must not be so! Our destiny is to be *"perfect as [our] Father in Heaven is perfect."* Even in this life, we must *"pursue holiness,"* and never be satisfied with anything less. The great saints have always been those most grieved by their own sin.

Do not pursue happiness. Pursue holiness. We were made in the image of God, the height of His creation. To seek mere earthly happiness—to seek anything less than to be like Him—is to aim much too low.

---

46. Lewis, *A Grief Observed*, 72.

Chapter 18

Cross Examination

> "The first thing we do, let's kill all the lawyers."
> —WILLIAM SHAKESPEARE.[1]

SINCE I AM A trial lawyer by trade, I thought it would be fun to conclude this book with an imaginary cross-examination of a fictional scientist and materialist on some of the questions we have discussed. The scene is a typical courtroom in Kentucky (where else?) where Dr. Arnold Einstein, a renowned scholar with the highest possible degrees in physics, biology, chemistry, astronomy, cosmology, geology, paleontology, physiology, and anthropology (!) has just testified that not only evolution, but undirected evolution, with no plan, no purpose, and most of all, no God, has been firmly established by science. It is time for his cross-examination. All the substantive answers which follow are based on actual statements by prominent scholars in the relevant fields.

Q—Dr. Einstein?

A—Yes. Dr. *Arnold* Einstein.

Q—Are you related to *Albert* Einstein?

A—Of course. The Einstein family has produced many great scientists.

Q—What is your relationship?

A—Ah... between myself and Albert? I can't tell you *exactly*.

Q—Just the best you can?

---

1. William Shakespeare, "Henry the Sixth," Act 4, Scene 2, 83.

A—Well... I don't know... We're all related, through our evolutionary predecessors, aren't we? Are you related to Perry Mason?

Q—Not at all. But let's get on to our subject. I want to talk with you first about why anything exists. Do you agree that the big bang was the beginning of the universe?

A—Of course, counselor. You're wasting my time here.

Q—Then let me ask you a tougher question. What caused the big bang?

A—Ah... that is tougher. No one knows the answer to that question.

Q—Are you familiar with Robert Jastrow and Paul Davies?

A—Of course. They are both highly respected physicists. Not as highly regarded as myself, but...

Q—Both of them have said that nothing existed before the big bang, not even scientific laws, so those laws could not explain the big bang.[2] Do you agree?

A—Well... yes, I suppose so.

Q—And neither did matter, energy, space, or time exist before the big bang?

A—That is the currently-accepted scientific view.[3]

Q—So did the universe evolve from *nothing*?

A—We don't have an answer to that question yet. There are still a lot of mysteries in science.

Q—It would seem that there are only two options. Either something has always existed or something came from nothing. But science says both that nature has not always existed—the universe had a beginning— and that something cannot come from nothing...

JUDGE ITIS—Is there a question in there somewhere, counselor?

Q—I apologize, Your Honor. Dr. Einstein, if nature has not always existed and if something cannot come from nothing, isn't the only remaining possibility that something *outside of nature* has always existed? If there doesn't appear to be a natural answer, shouldn't we consider a supernatural one?

A—No! I am a scientist! We do not resort to the supernatural, just because we don't understand something!

2. Jastrow, *God and the Astronomers*, 105; Davies, *The Mind of God*, 57.
3. Barrow and Tippler, *The Anthropic Cosmological Principle*, 442.

Q—Can science explain an uncaused universe any more than it can explain an uncaused God?

A—Well, perhaps not, but the whole idea of God is *unscientific* . . . no highly respected scientist believes in the supernatural.

Q—Are you familiar with Francis Collins, the geneticist who was head of the human genome project and is also a devout Christian?

A—Ok, *almost* no respected scientist. You can always find one exception.

Q—Or Theodosius Dobzhansky, the renowned evolutionary biologist from Columbia University, who was a devout Eastern Orthodox Christian?

A—I said almost.

Q—Or Charles Townes, the Nobel Prize-winning physicist from Cal-Berkeley? Or Owen Gingerich, the astronomer from Harvard?

A—Ok, counselor. There are a few.

Q—You are familiar with Steven Jay Gould, the late paleontologist from Harvard?

A—He wasn't a theist!

Q—No, but do you remember what he said?

> "Science simply cannot by its legitimate methods adjudicate the issue of God's possible superintendence of nature . . . Either half my colleagues are enormously stupid, or else the science of Darwinism is fully compatible with conventional religious beliefs—and equally compatible with atheism."[4]

A—Ok, some scientists are religious. But many of them are not that highly respected in the scientific community.

Q—How do you define who is or is not "highly respected?"

A—Well, someone who resorts to supernatural explanations generally is not.

Q—Here's to circular reasoning!

JUDGE ITIS—Counselor . . .

Q—I apologize, Your Honor. Isn't the bottom line, Dr. Einstein, that materialistic science has no explanation for why anything exists and the

---

4. Gould, "Impeaching a Self-Appointed Judge," 118–121.

only explanation on the market is the Christian answer, that an eternal God created the universe?

A—That answer is not "on the market," where I shop. It's unscientific.

Q—Let's go on to our next issue. The big bang has occurred. We have a universe, but it is a lifeless universe. Where did the first life come from?

A—There are scientists working on that. It's called "abiogenesis."

Q—Have they been successful?

A—Not yet, but I believe they will be. It's just going to take some time.

Q—A leap of faith, Doctor?

A—No! I am a highly respected scientist! We don't know how life began, but we are here, so it must have happened.[5]

Q—You do like circular reasoning, don't you? But let's put aside what scientists can accomplish in the laboratory. Have scientists ever *observed* life coming from non-life? In nature?

A—Well . . . no.

Q—In Darwin's time, they believed in "spontaneous generation," the idea that maggots, for instance, could develop from rotting meat. But Louis Pasteur proved that flies only come from eggs laid by other flies, correct?

A—Of course.

Q—In all of human experience, life only comes from life?

A—In all of *human* experience. We weren't around when the first life developed.

Q—If materialism is true, the first life had to develop from some non-living bit of matter?

A—Yes, but you're just arguing for a "God-of-the-gaps." Anything that science can't yet explain, you attribute to God.

Q—And you attribute everything to natural causes, even when science can't explain it?

A—Of course. I am a scientist!

Q—John Eccles, the Nobel prize-winning physiologist, called the idea that science will eventually find all the answers, "simply a religious belief,

---

5. Dawkins, *The God Delusion*, 137.

not even a religious belief; it is a superstition based upon no evidence worth considering at all."[6] Wasn't he right?

A—He was a Roman Catholic!

Q—I thought no respected scientist believed in God?

JUDGE ITIS—Alright, counselor. I believe you've made that point. Let's move on.

Q—Yes, Your Honor. Doctor, non-living matter is not organized in cells. Can you explain how hundreds of amino acids arranged themselves in just the right sequence to make a protein, or how thousands of proteins arranged themselves just right to make a living cell?

A—Not in detail, no.

Q—I understand that they do not order themselves spontaneously?

A—That appears to be the case.

Q—How did DNA come about? Non-living things do not have DNA, but it is absolutely essential for life. Yet it is incredibly complex.

A—Probably from RNA, or some other less complex predecessor.

Q—RNA is still very complex, with thousands of nucleotide bases, all precisely arranged. Jeffrey Bada, the chemist with the Scripps Institute, said, "We know that RNA is too complex to have arisen out of the simple molecules of the primordial soup."[7] Don't you have to agree?

A—Probably.

Q—How did RNA develop, then, in a bit of non-living matter?

A—We don't know. Probably through something analogous to natural selection, operating on the organic chemicals. It is called "chemical evolution."

Q—Natural selection functions through reproduction, in living things. Chemicals don't generally reproduce. What is the "analogous" mechanism? And which chemicals?

A—We don't know, counselor. Again, there are scientists working on that.

Q—Are you familiar with the French biologist Jacques Monod's chicken-or-egg question about DNA? He pointed out that for DNA to develop, the proteins from which it is made must already exist, but the amino acids are arranged, so as to form the right proteins, based on

---

6. Eccles, "Modern Biology and the Turn to Belief in God," 50.
7. Dreifus, "A Marine Chemist Studies How Life Began."

instructions contained in the DNA. He called it a "veritable enigma."[8] Wasn't he right? Aren't the DNA and the proteins mutually dependent on one another?

A—I'm familiar with that dilemma. You're very good at asking the unanswered questions.

Q—Doesn't this go beyond an unanswered question? Isn't it unanswerable?

A—Well, George Wald said life arising spontaneously is "impossible," but he believed it to be true.[9]

Q—Is that your position?

A—Well, it seems impossible, in a practical sense, but there is no other explanation, so I accept it.

Q—No other *natural* explanation?

A—Yes. I'm only interested in natural explanations. I don't believe in miracles.

Q—Are you sure? Hundreds of amino acids develop spontaneously from the primordial soup, then arrange themselves in just the right order to form each of thousands of different proteins; then all those proteins arrange themselves just right to form a cell capable of life; and DNA, containing millions of bits of intelligent information, arranges itself spontaneously, to direct that process. You don't call that a miracle? I think you are a true man of faith!

A—No! I am a highly respected scientist!

Q—There is no one generally-accepted materialistic explanation for the origin of life, is there?

A—Not at this time.[10]

Q—Let's talk about how man got here.

A—Darwin answered that question. Even your theistic scientists believe in evolution.

Q—Many of them do, but they believe that the evolutionary process must have been divinely directed, or it couldn't have happened, right?

A—If they are theists, I suppose so, but that is religion, not science.

---

8. Quoted Bedau and Cleland, *The Nature of Life*, 141.
9. Wald, "The Origin of Life," 46.
10. National Academy of Sciences, *Science, Evolution and Creationism*, 18.

Q—You believe evolution happened by chance, without any plan or purpose. Isn't that also religion or philosophy? Can science prove the absence of plan or purpose?

A—Well, no, but that belief is based on my scientific . . . outlook.

Q—Among your many areas of expertise, you are a paleontologist?

A—Yes. And the fossil record proves Darwin was correct. The oldest fossils represent the simplest organisms, and they get more complex as you move forward in time.

Q—Ok, but Darwin also acknowledged that in his day the "gravest objection"[11] that could be raised against his theory was the lack of transitional forms in the fossil record. He predicted that those transitional forms would be found, but that hasn't happened, has it?

A—Well . . . there have been some.

Q—We mentioned Steven Jay Gould earlier. Would you disagree with his statement that "The extreme rarity of transitional forms in the fossil record persists as the trade secret of paleontology?"[12]

A—No. We have not found as many transitional forms as we might have hoped.

Q—In fact, aren't there actually fewer transitional forms now than were believed to exist in Darwin's time, because so many have been disproved since then?[13]

A—That has happened.

Q—Isn't the fossil record pretty complete by now, in the sense that most all the basic types of fossils which will ever be found have been found?[14]

A—Probably.

Q—Then isn't it strange, if all those millions of transitional organisms lived, that almost all of the fossils which have been found correspond to known phyla, basic types of plants or animals that we know about, and not to transitional forms between those basic types?

11. Darwin, *On the Origin of Species*, 325.

12. Gould wrote, "The extreme rarity of transitional forms in the fossil record persists as the trade secret of paleontology. The evolutionary trees that adorn our textbooks have data only at the tips and nodes of their branches; the rest is inference, however reasonable, not the evidence of fossils." Gould, "Evolution's Erratic Pace."

13. Raup, "Conflicts between Darwin and Paleontology," 25.

14. Nilsson, *Synthetische Artbilddung*; quoted Simmons, *What Darwin Didn't Know*, 304.

A—Well, strange, perhaps, but not impossible.

Q—Darwin proposed random mutations, with the few that were advantageous being adopted by natural selection, as the mechanism for evolution. And he said it would take "numerous, successive, slight modifications,"[15] for this process to work, right?

A—Of course.

Q—Natural selection couldn't explain a big jump all at once, such as a whole new body part?

A—That is correct. Although, you mentioned Steven Jay Gould. He and some other paleontologists once proposed what they called "punctuated equilibrium,"[16] which involved larger jumps, but that theory was never widely accepted.

Q—The reason they proposed this was that they could not explain the gaps in the fossil record?

A—I suppose so. But as I said, that hypothesis has been largely rejected.

Q—And the reason it has been rejected is that no one can come up with a natural mechanism which would explain those large jumps?

A—That is correct.

Q—Wouldn't an intelligence guiding the process provide that mechanism?

A—No! I am a highly respected scientist! I believe we will find a *natural* explanation, if we look long enough. And only a small percentage of the organisms which ever lived left fossils. So I would say that there are no real gaps, just gaps in the evidence we have.

Q—Can you give us even a theoretical explanation of how these major transitions might have occurred, without an intelligence directing the process? How did entirely new body parts develop? How did the transition take place from cold-blooded to warm-blooded animals, or from egg-bearing species to those that give live birth? How did birds develop a one-way breathing mechanism which circulates air, when every other animal, before or after, uses two-way bronchial tubes, breathing in and out?[17]

---

15. Darwin, *On the Origin of Species*, 210.

16. Eldredge and Gould, "Punctuated Equilibria: an Alternative to Phyletic Gradualism," 193–223.

17. Denton, *Evolution: A Theory in Crisis*, 211–212.

A—Well, I can't give you a step-by-step explanation, but in general, by natural selection.

Q—Natural selection only adopts mutations that are immediately advantageous to the organism. How could each of the thousands of intermediate steps have been advantageous? How could the bird have even survived to reproduce, when its lungs were partly of one kind and partly of another?

A—I can't explain the chain of evolution fully, but there are theories. For instance, scientists believe that fish evolved into amphibians because one odd group of fish had a peculiar fin anatomy that could transform into legs ... over many generations, of course.[18] That's just one example.

Q—I ask for a bird and you give me a fish! Can you explain how each intermediate stage between a fin and a leg would be advantageous? Wouldn't you get a bad fin before you got a good leg?

A—I can't explain it in detail, but it is possible.

Q—You are familiar with Michael Behe, the microbiologist from Lehigh University?

A—Yes ... He is way out of the mainstream. I mean, He has the credentials, but ...

Q—He argues that many biological systems are "irreducibly complex," that is, they have many interrelated parts, all working together, and they could not have evolved gradually, without guidance, because they would not have worked at all at the many intermediate stages, without all the parts.[19]

A—Very few highly-respected scientists agree with him.

Q—One of Dr. Behe's examples is the bacterial flagellum. Amazing little organs, aren't they?

A—They are truly amazing. The most efficient machines in the universe, for their size.[20]

Q—It is my understanding that these are microscopic, acid-powered, rotary "motors" which propel bacteria through the bloodstream. They

---

18. Gould, *The Meaning of Life: Reflections in Words and Pictures of Why We Are Here*, 33.

19. Behe, *Darwin's Black Box*, 53–73.

20. Harvard biologist Howard Berg, quoted Dembski and Wells, *The Design of Life*, 149.

are made of numerous parts, some thirty different types of proteins, and they would not work at all without any one of them?

A—That appears to be correct.[21]

Q—Can you explain how the bacterial flagellum could have evolved by Darwin's "numerous, successive, slight modifications," without any guidance? How each step could have been useful, so that it would have been preserved by natural selection?

A—Not in detail, I can't. One theory is that something which may not have been useful for one purpose may have served some other purpose, especially at the microscopic level. But you are arguing for a "God-of-the-gaps" again. We just don't have all the answers yet.

Q—And you are arguing for "science-of-the-gaps," are you not?

A—I am a scientist.

Q—Let's talk about the *order* in the universe. You couldn't do scientific experiments without the assumption that the universe is ordered, could you?

A—That is true, counselor. I agree that there is order in the universe.[22] But I assume you are going to argue that this order indicates design and I disagree with that conclusion.

Q—Richard Dawkins said, "The illusion of purpose is so powerful that biologists themselves use the assumption of good design as a working tool."[23] Don't you as a scientist have to *assume* the existence of purpose or design, in order to practice your science?

A—We don't assume that the universe *was* designed. We just act *as if* it were.

Q—I'm going to let that one go. But are you telling me that *you act as if something were true which isn't true, and it works*?

A—Well . . . it seems so.

Q—Do you believe in natural laws? The law of gravity? The laws of thermodynamics?

---

21. Behe, *Darwin's Black Box*, 70–73. Michael Denton writes that the bacterial flagellum is "the only structure in the entire living kingdom which exhibits a true rotary motion," and "[I]t is very hard to envisage a hypothetical evolutionary sequence of simpler rotors through which it might have evolved gradually." Denton, *Evolution: A Theory in Crisis*, 224–225.
22. Weinberg, *Facing Up: Science and its Cultural Adversaries*, 45.
23. Dawkins, *River Out of Eden*, 98.

A—Of course.

Q—Albert Einstein said that these laws reflect an order in the universe and that this order "manifest[s] the existence of a spirit vastly superior to that of men."[24] He said this represented his "conception of God."[25] Isn't that a very reasonable conclusion?

A—Albert's ideas on religion are hard to understand. But I don't agree that order proves there was a designer. The universe could have just happened that way.

Q—Can you estimate the odds of that?

A—No. I'm not a mathematician.

Q—Donald Page, the physicist from Princeton, estimated the odds for the universe randomly arriving at all the conditions necessary for life at one in ten to the 124th power.[26] In other words, far less likely than picking one particular atom, at random, from all the atoms in the universe. Can you disagree?

A—As I said, I'm not a mathematician. Sometimes you get lucky.[27]

Q—With all due respect, Doctor, is that the best you can do? We got "lucky?"

A—One possible explanation is that there might be billions of universes, so the odds would be pretty good that one would turn out to be just right for life.[28]

Q—Isn't it true that there is no evidence for those other universes, and it is impossible, by definition, that they could ever be detected?

A—So it seems.

Q—Don't scientific theories generally have to be "falsifiable" to be accepted?

A—Generally, yes.

Q—But this hypothesis is not falsifiable?

A—No.

24. Letter to P. Wright, January 24, 1936; quoted Jammer, *Einstein and Religion*, 93.
25. Einstein, "On Scientific Truth," 262.
26. Quoted Craig, "In Defense of Rational Theism," 143.
27. Dawkins, *The Blind Watchmaker*, 207–208.
28. Rees, *Just Six Numbers: The Deep Forces that Shape the Universe*, 166–167.

Q—John Polkinghorne, the physicist who was President of Queens College, Cambridge, called this idea "pseudo-science" and "a metaphysical guess."[29] Can you disagree with him?

A—He's also an Anglican Priest!

Q—Another respected scientist who believes in God?

JUDGE ITIS—Counselor . . .

A—Look, I'm not saying these other universes definitely exist, but it has been suggested.

Q—Let's talk about human beings. Can you explain human consciousness, from natural causes?

A—No. No one can. Consciousness, or the "self," is one of the greatest mysteries in nature.[30]

Q—If materialism is true, the self is just a product of natural causes, within the physical body?

A—Yes.

Q—How can unconscious, impersonal causes produce conscious, personal selves?

A—As I said, it is a mystery.

Q—What about human reason? How does the physical brain produce valid reasoning?

A—I can't give you a complete explanation, but I don't see that as a serious problem. Many animals have considerable intelligence. We just have more. Our brains are just more developed than theirs. Natural selection preserves what works.

Q—Do you believe we have the ability to perceive real *truth*, about something beyond our senses?

A—There is a lot of debate about what "truth" means, but in laymen's terms, it appears so.

Q—And everything is the result of non-rational natural causes, including your thoughts and mine?

A—Especially yours, counselor!

Q—What about the thoughts that led you to conclude materialism is true? Were they just the result of non-rational natural causes?

---

29. Polkinghorne, *Serious Talk: Science and Religion in Dialogue*, 6.
30. Pinker, *How the Mind Works*, 60.

A—Well . . . apparently.

Q—Then how can you trust those thoughts to be true?

A—Again, I am not sure what truth is. I would just say that we seem to be able to reach conclusions which fit with our experience.

Q—Human reasoning works, doesn't it?

A—It appears to.

Q—But how? How can electro-chemical reactions inside your brain be true about something on the other side of the universe? How can one bit of matter be true about another bit of matter?

A—I can't tell you, counselor. Again, it is a mystery.

Q—Do you believe in free will?

A—(Hesitates) Well . . . we seem to experience it . . . but theoretically, no. I don't see how there could be real free will.

Q—If everything has a natural cause, that precludes free will, doesn't it?

A—It would seem so.

Q—Or to put it another way, if we do make real, free choices, materialism is simply false?

A—Well . . .

Q—Doctor, you seem to be *choosing your words* very carefully right now. Are you really choosing them, or were your answers programmed by an impersonal nature billions of years ago?

A—Honestly, counselor, I don't know.

Q—I appreciate your honesty. But that leads us to another question—why be honest? Do you believe in a real, objective law of right and wrong?

A—Objective? No. I believe that our notions of right and wrong have developed over many centuries, as we have learned what helps us get along. They are relative, not absolute. They may have a basis in evolution. Many scientists believe that we developed these notions because they helped the human race survive, and so were preserved by natural selection.[31] Either way, I am telling you the truth now because I am under oath and we have learned that society functions better if people tell the truth in court. How would the courts function if people regularly came to court and lied?

---

31. Ruse and Wilson, "The Evolution of Ethics," 310.

Q—Doctor, you might be surprised how often that happens. But are you saying that if you were not in court, you would lie to me? I get the impression you are generally an honest man. Why?

A—Yes, I try to be. Why? I don't know. Probably because I was raised that way.

Q—Is honesty better than dishonesty?

A—It works better for society, but in an absolute sense, I couldn't say that.

Q—If I am in a situation where honesty doesn't work better for me—if I have a chance to win a case and get a lot of money—why shouldn't I lie under oath? Why should I care what works best for society? Why shouldn't I just look out for myself?

A—Logically, there is no reason.[32] Fortunately, not many people look at things that way.

Q—Again, Doctor, you might be surprised. Nature itself is not moral, is it?

A—Oh no. You only have to look at the tiger or the shark to see that.

Q—So if our moral notions come from nature, your idea that we should tell the truth is just an arbitrary result of evolution, like our having two eyes rather than three?

A—Yes, I suppose so.

Q—But you don't live that way, do you, Doctor? As if morality is just something we made up or an accident of nature?

A—We seem to believe very strongly in certain moral notions, even though we can see intellectually that they must be relative, or have natural causes.

Q—On both of these last two points, free will and morality, you as a materialist live as if you were a theist, don't you? You don't believe in free will or morals, but you practice both?

A—I believe in morals. I just don't believe they are absolute. As to free will, I don't know what I believe. It certainly seems that I am making free choices, but . . .

---

32. Jean Paul Sartre wrote, "Suppose someone says to me, 'What if I want to be dishonest?' I'll answer, 'There's no reason for you not to be.'" "The Humanism of Existentialism," 57. See also Nielson, "Why Should I Be Moral?" 90.

Q—Doctor, will you agree with me that there are some questions, such as whether God exists, which are "metaphysical," that is, beyond physics or science?

A—I believe that nature is all there is, so theoretically, if we knew enough, science should be able to provide all the answers. But there may be questions that are beyond science. I agree that the question of whether God exists is not a scientific question.

Q—Earlier, you rejected the idea of God as "unscientific." What is wrong with giving an unscientific answer to a non-scientific question?

A—Probably nothing. But I am a scientist. I look at things from a scientific viewpoint. The idea of a God is outside science.[33]

Q—Can science say that there is nothing outside of science?

A—Well, no. I don't believe there is anything outside of nature, but I can't say it is impossible.

Q—One last question, Doctor. Hypothetically, if there were a supernatural Creator like the Christian God, wouldn't that explain a lot more about both the universe and about how we all live—consciousness, reason, free will, and why you feel the need to be honest, for example—than materialism can?

A—That's an interesting argument, counselor . . . I'm not ready to agree with you, but it does seem that it would explain some of those things, yes.

Q—Thank you, Dr. Einstein. I have no further questions.

---

33. Wald, "The Origin of Life," 45.

Bibliography

Akerly, J., *Voltaire and Rousseau Against the Atheists*, New York, Wiley and Putnam, 1845.
Alschuler, Albert, *Law Without Values: The Life, Work and Legacy of Justice Holmes*, Chicago, University of Chicago Press, 2000.
Aquinas, Thomas, *Summa Theologica*, c1274, translated Fathers of the English Dominican Provence, New York, Benziger Brothers, 1947.
———, "The Work of the Six Days of Creation," c1254, *Thomas Aquinas, Selected Writings*, translated and edited McInerny, Ralph, New York, Penguin, 1998.
Aristotle, *Metaphysics*, c350 B.C., translated Apostle, Hippocrates, Bloomington, IN, Indiana University Press, 1966.
Asimov, Isaac, "In the Game of Energy and Thermodynamics, You Can't Even Break Even," *Smithsonian*, August 1970.
Augustine, *The City of God*, 426 AD, Book XI, translated Walsh, Gerald, et al, New York, Image, 1958.
———, *Confessions*, 401 AD, translated Boulding, Maria, New York, Vintage, 1997.
———, *Confessions*, 401 AD, translated Pilkington, J. G., Garden City, NY, International Collectors Library, 1962.
———, "Enchiridon," 420 AD, *Library of Christian Classics*, Vol. VI, London, Westminster, 1955.
———, "The Literal Meaning of Genesis," 416 AD, translated Hill, Edmund, *On Genesis*, edited Rotelle, John, Hyde Park, NY, New City, 2006.
———, "Sermon, Mai 126," c425 AD, *The Essential Augustine*, edited Bourke, Vernon, Indianapolis, Hackett, 1974.
———, "Unfinished Literal Commentary on Genesis," 390 AD, translated Hill, Edmund, *On Genesis*, edited Rotelle, John, Hyde Park, NY, New City, 2006.
Bach, Richard, *Illusions: The Adventures of a Reluctant Messiah*, New York, Delacorte, 1977.
Bacon, Francis, *The Advancement of Learning*, 1605, London, J. M. Dent, 1954.
———, *Novum Organum Scientarium*, 1620, *The New Organon*, translated Spalding, James, Ellis, Robert, and Heath, Douglas, edited Anderson, Fulton, Indianapolis, Bobbs Merrill, 1960.
Bacote, Vincent, and Spencer, Stephen, "What Are the Theological Implications for Natural Science?" *Not Just Science*, edited Chappell, Dorothy, and Cook, E. David, Grand Rapids, Zondervan, 2005.

Bailey, David, *Do Scientists Understand the Origin of Life?* http://www.sciencemeetsreligion.org/evolution/origin.php

Barash, David, "Dennett and the Darwinizing of Free Will," *Human Nature Review*, Vol. 3, March 22, 2003, http://human-nature.com/nibbs/03/dcdennett.html

Barr, Stephen, *Modern Physics and Ancient Faith*, Notre Dame, IN, Notre Dame University Press, 2003.

Barrow, John and Tippler, Frank, *The Anthropic Cosmological Principle*, Oxford, Clarenden, 1986.

Basil, "Hexaemeron," c370 A.D., *The Patristic Understanding of Creation*, edited Dembski, William, Downs Wayne, and Frederick, Fr. Justin, South Bend, Erasmus, 2008.

Basker, James, *Abraham Lincoln in His Own Words*, New York, Gilderman Lehrman, 2009.

Becket, Samuel, *Waiting for Godot*, 1956, London, Faber and Faber, 1988.

Bedau, Mark and Cleland, Carol, *The Nature of Life: Classical and Contemporary Perspectives from Philosophy and Science*, Cambridge, Cambridge University Press, 2010.

Begley, Sharon, "Francis Collins Talks about Science and Faith," *Newsweek*, Dec. 27, 2010.

———, "Science Finds God," *Newsweek*, July 20, 1998.

Behe, Michael, *Darwin's Black Box*, New York, Free Press, 1996.

———, *The Edge of Evolution*, New York, Free Press, 2007.

Bell, James Stuart and Dawson, Anthony, *From the Library of C. S. Lewis: Selections from Writers Who Influenced His Spiritual Journey*, New York, Doubleday, 2009.

Belmonte, Kevin, "William Wilberforce: A Man for All Seasons," Wilberforce, William, *A Practical View of the Prevailing Religious System of Professed Christians in the Higher and Middle Classes in this Country, Contrasted with Real Christianity*, 1797, *Real Christianity*, Ventura, CA, Regal, 2006.

Benardete, Doris, *Mark Twain's Wit and Wisecracks*, White Plains, NY, Peter Pauper, 1998.

Benford, Gregory, "Leaping the Abyss: Stephen Hawking on Black Holes, Unified Field Theory and Marilyn Monroe," *Reason*, Vol. 4.02, April, 2002, http://www.thefreelibrary.com/Leaping+the+Abyss%3a+Stephen+Hawking+on+black+holes%2c+unified+field...-a084246681

Bernstein, Leonard, *The Joy of Music*, New York, Simon and Schuster, 1959.

Berra, Yogi, *When You Come to a Fork in the Road, Take It*, New York, Hyperion, 2001.

Blake, William, "The Gray Monk," c1805, *Blake's Poetry and Designs*, edited Johnson, Mary Lynn and Grant, John, New York, W. W. Norton, 1979.

Bloy, Leon, *The Woman Who Was Poor*, translated Collins, I.J., New York, Sheed and Ward, 1947.

Bright, Bill, *Jesus and the Intellectual*, Wayne, NJ, New Life, 2002.

Brooks, Rodney, "Living Machines," *A Place for Truth*, edited Willard, Dallas, Downers Grove, IL, InterVarsity, 2010.

Bryson, Bill, *A Short History of Nearly Everything*, New York, Broadway, 2003.

Burson, Scott and Walls, Jerry, *C.S. Lewis and Francis Schaeffer*, Downers Grove, IL, InterVarsity, 1998.

Chalke, Steve and Watkis, Anthony, *Intelligent Church*, Grand Rapids, Zondervan, 2006.

Chang, Jung and Halliday, Jon, *Mao: The Unknown Story*, New York, Alfred A. Knopf, 2005.
Chesterton, G.K, *The Everlasting Man*, 1925, San Francisco, Ignatius, 1993.
———, *Heretics*, 1905, New York, Barnes & Noble, 2007.
———, *Orthodoxy*, 1908, New York, Barnes and Noble, 2007.
———, *Saint Francis of Assisi*, 1933, San Francisco, Ignatius, 2002.
———, *Saint Thomas Aquinas*, 1923, San Francisco, Ignatius, 1986.
———, *What's Wrong with the World?* 1910, San Francisco, Ignatius, 1994.
Chomsky, Noam, "Form and Meaning in Natural Languages," *Language and Mind*, Orlando, Harcourt, Brace, Jovanovich, 1972.
———, *Language and the Problems of Knowledge*, Cambridge, MA, MIT Press, 1988.
Cicero, "Laws," *The Patristic Understanding of Creation*, edited Dembski, William, Downs, Wayne, and Frederick, Fr. Justin, Riesel, TX, Erasmus, 2008.
Cockerill, Gareth, *Christian Faith in the Old Testament*, Nashville, Thomas Nelson, 2014.
Collins, Francis, "Faith and the Human Genome," *Perspectives on Science and Christian Faith*, Vol. 55(3), 2003.
———, *The Language of God*, New York, Free Press, 2007.
Colson, Charles, "The Common Cultural Task: The Culture War from a Protestant Perspective," *Evangelicals and Catholics Together*, edited Colson, Charles and Neuhaus, Richard John, Dallas, Word, 1995.
———, *My Final Word*, Grand Rapids, Zondervan, 2015.
———, *Who Speaks for God?* Westchester, IL, Crossway, 1985.
Colson, Charles and Pearcey, Nancy, *A Dance with Deception*, Dallas, Word, 1993.
———, *How Now Shall We Live?* Wheaton, IL, Tyndale House, 1999.
Conway, David, *The Rediscovery of Wisdom*, New York, Macmillan, 2000.
Cook, E. David and O'Connor, Robert, "What Are the Philosophical Implications of Christianity for the Natural Sciences?" *Not Just Science*, edited Chappell, Dorothy and Cook, E. David, Grand Rapids, Zondervan, 2005.
Coonradt, Dean, "Religion and Governor Ventura," *Los Angeles Times*, October 17, 1999, http://articles.latimes.com/1999/oct/17/local/me-23334
Courtois, Stephane, *The Black Book of Communism*, Cambridge, MA, Harvard University, 1999.
Covey, Stephen, *The 7 Habits of Highly Effective People*, New York, Simon and Schuster, 2013.
Craig, William Lane, *The Existence of God and the Beginning of the Universe*, Arrowhead Springs, CA, Here's Life, 1979.
———, "In Defense of Rational Theism," Moreland, J.P. and Nelson, Kai, *Does God Exist?* Amherst, NY, Prometheus, 1993.
———, "Tough Questions about Science," *Who Made God?* edited Zacharias, Ravi and Geisler, Norman, Grand Rapids, Zondervan, 2003.
———, *Reasonable Faith*, Wheaton, IL, Crossway, 1984, 2008.
Crick, Francis, *The Astonishing Hypothesis: the Scientific Search for the Soul*, New York, Scribner, 1995.
———, *Life Itself*, New York, Simon and Schuster, 1981.
———, *What Mad Pursuit*, New York, Basic Books, 1988.
Darrow, Clarence, "Living," *The Best of Humanism*, edited Greeley, Roger, Amherst, NY, Prometheus, 1988.

BIBLIOGRAPHY

Darwin, Charles, *The Descent of Man*, 2d ed., New York, A.L. Burt, 1874.
———, *Life and Letters of Charles Darwin*, edited Darwin, Francis, 1887, New York and London, D. Appleton, 1925.
———, *On the Origin of Species*, 1859, New York, Barnes and Noble, 2004.
Davidman, Joy, *Smoke on the Mountain*, London, Westminster, 1953.
Davies, Paul, *The Mind of God*, New York, Simon and Schuster, 2005.
Dawkins, Richard, *The Blind Watchmaker*, New York, Norton, 1986, 2006.
———, *The God Delusion*, Boston, Houghton-Mifflin, 2006.
———, "Religion's Misguided Missiles," *The Guardian*, September 15, 2001, http://www.theguardian.com/world/2001/sep/15/september11.politicsphilosophyandsociety1
———, *River Out of Eden*, New York, Basic Books, 1995.
———, *The Selfish Gene*, Oxford, Oxford University Press, 1976.
———, *Unweaving the Rainbow*, Boston, Houghton Mifflin, 1998.
Dawkins, Richard and Pinker, Steven, "Is Science Killing the Soul?" The Guardian-Dillons Debate, *Edge*, Vol. 53, April 8, 1999, http://edge.org/conversation/is-science-killing-the-soul
Dembski, William, *The End of Christianity*, Nashville, B and H, 2009.
Dembski, William and Wells, Jonathon, *The Design of Life*, Dallas, Foundation for Thought and Ethics, 2008.
Dembski, William and Witt, Jonathon, *Intelligent Design Uncensored*, Downers Grove, IL, InterVarsity, 2010.
Denton, Michael, *Evolution: A Theory in Crisis*, Bethesda, MD, Adler and Adler, 1985.
———, *Nature's Destiny*, New York, Free Press, 1998.
Descartes, Rene, *Discourse on Method*, 1637, translated Clarke, Desmond, London, Penguin, 1999.
Dewey, John, "My Pedagogic Creed," 1929, *The Essential Dewey*, edited Hickman, Larry and Alexander, Thomas, Bloomington, Indiana University Press, 1991.
Dickens, Charles, *A Christmas Carol*, 1843, New York, Barnes and Noble, 2004.
———, *Tale of Two Cities*, 1877, Woodstock, GA, American Book, 1911.
Dillard, Annie, *Pilgrim at Tinker Creek*, New York, Harper and Row, 1974.
Discover, "Our Friend Jove," July, 1993, Vol. 14, No. 7.
Dockery, David and George, Timothy, *The Great Tradition of Christian Thinking*, Westchester, IL, Crossway, 2012.
Dostoevsky, Fyodor, *The Brothers Karamazov*, 1880, translated Garnett, Constance, New York, W. W. Norton, 1976.
Doyle, Arthur Conan, "The Sign of Four," 1890, *The Complete Sherlock Holmes*, Vol. I, New York, Barnes and Noble, 2003.
———, "A Study in Scarlet," 1887, *The Complete Sherlock Holmes*, Vol. 1, New York, Barnes and Noble, 2003.
Dreifus, Claudia, "A Marine Chemist Studies How Life Began," *The New York Times*, May 18, 2010, http://www.nytimes.com/2010/05/18/science/18conv.html?ref=science&_r=0
D'Souza, Dinesh, "Created Equal: How Christianity Shaped the West," *Imprimis*, November, 2008.
———, *What's So Great about Christianity?* Carol Stream, IL, Tyndale House, 2007.
Dyson, Freeman, *Disturbing the Universe*, New York, Basic Books, 1979.
Eccles, John, "A Divine Design: Some Questions on Origins," *Cosmos, Bios, Theos*, edited Marganou, Henry and Varghese, Roy, Chicago, Open Court, 1997.

———, "Modern Biology and the Turn to Belief in God," *The Intellectuals Speak Out about God*, edited Varghese, Roy, Dallas, Lewis and Stanley, 1984.

Eddington, Arthur, "The End of the World from the Standpoint of Mathematical Physics," *Nature*, Vol. 127, March 21, 1931; www.nature.com/nature/journal/v127/n3203/pdf/127447a0.pdf

———, *The Expanding Universe*, Cambridge, Cambridge University Press, 1952.

———, *The Nature of the Physical World*, Cambridge, Cambridge University Press, 1929.

Einstein, Albert, "On Scientific Truth," 1930, *Ideas and Opinions*, Woodinville, WA, Bonanza, 1954.

———, "Religion and Science: Irreconcilable?" *Christian Unitarian Register*, Vol. 127, June 1948, http://www.einsteinandreligion.com/irrec2.html

Eldredge, Niles and Gould, S.J., "Punctuated Equilibria: an Alternative to Phyletic Gradualism," 1972, reprinted Eldredge, Niles, *Time Frames*, Princeton, Princeton University Press, 1985.

Elford, R. John, "Christianity and War," *The Cambridge Companion to Christian Ethics*, edited Gill, Robin, Cambridge, Cambridge University Press, 2001.

Elliott, Jim, *The Journals of Jim Elliott*, edited Elliott, Elizabeth, Glasgow, Pickering and Inglis, 1978.

Encyclopedia Jrank, "The Life-Lie," http://encyclopedia.jrank.org/articles/pages/3546/The-Life-Lie.html

Ferguson, Andrew, "The Heretic," *The Weekly Standard*, March 25, 2013.

Ferreira, M. Jamie, *Love's Grateful Striving*, Oxford, Oxford University Press, 2001.

Flew, Antony, *There Is a God*, New York, Harper Collins, 2007.

Fox, S.W., *The Origins of Pre-Biological Systems and of their Molecular Matrices*, Cambridge, MA, Academic, 1965.

Franklin, Benjamin, *Poor Richard's Almanac*, reprinted in *Benjamin Franklin Wit and Wisdom*, White Plains, NY, Peter Pauper, 1998.

Freud, Sigmund, *Civilization and its Discontents*, 1930, translated Strachey, James, London, Hogarth, 1973.

———, "The Ego and the Id," 1923, *The Standard Edition of the Complete Psychological Works of Sigmund Freud*, Vol. XIX, London, Hogarth, 1964.

———, *The Future of an Illusion*, 1928, translated Robson-Scott, W.D., London, Hogarth, 1973.

———, "Reflections on War and Death," 1918, translated Brill, A.A. and Kuttner, Alfred, New York, Bartleby.com, 2010, http://www.bartleby.com/282/2.html

Gates, Bill, *The Road Ahead*, New York, Viking Penguin, 1995.

Geisler, Norman, *Baker Encyclopedia of Christian Apologetics*, Grand Rapids, Baker Academic, 2005.

———, "The Collapse of Modern Atheism," *The Intellectuals Speak Out about God*, edited Varghese, Roy, Dallas, Lewis and Stanley, 1984.

Geisler, Norman and Turek, Frank, *I Don't have Enough Faith to Be an Atheist*, Westchester, IL, Crossway, 2004.

Ghandi, Mahatma, "Introduction to Varnavyavastha," 1934, *The Penguin Ghandi Reader*, edited Mukherjee, Rudrangshu, London, Penguin, 1996.

Al-Ghazali, Abu Hamed, *The Alchemy of Happiness*, c1100, translated Field, Claud, London, Ashrof, 1971.

Gingerich, Owen, *God's Universe*, Cambridge, MA, Harvard University Press, 2006.

Giubilina, Alberto and Minerva, Francesca, "After-birth Abortion: Why Should the Baby Live?" *Journal of Medical Ethics*, February 23, 2012, http://jme.bmj.com/content/early/2012/03/01/medethics-2011-100411.full

Gleiser, Marcelo, *A Tear at the Edge of Creation*, New York, Free Press, 2010.

Gould, Stephen Jay, "Evolution's Erratic Pace," *Natural History*, Vol. 86, #5, May, 1977, http://community.compuserve.com/n/docs/docDownload.aspx?webtag=ws-religion&guid=878883eb-b629-4e63-8a0a-283f7812b64f

———, "Impeaching a Self-Appointed Judge," *Scientific American*, July, 1992.

———, *The Meaning of Life: Reflections in Words and Pictures of Why We Are Here*, edited Friend, David, New York, Time, 1991.

———, *Wonderful Life*, New York, Norton, 1989

Gregory of Nazianzus, "Orations," *The Patristic Understanding of Creation*, edited Dembski, William, Downs, Wayne, and Frederick, Fr. Justin, South Bend, Erasmus, 2008.

Haeckel, Ernst, *The Wonders of Life*, New York, Harper and Brothers, 1905.

Harold, Franklin, *The Way of the Cell*, Oxford, Oxford University Press, 2001.

Harris, Sam, *The End of Faith*, New York, W.W. Norton, 2004.

Hawking, Stephen, *A Brief History of Time*, 1978, New York, Bantam, 2005.

Hawking Stephen, and Penrose, Roger, *The Nature of Space and Time*, Princeton, Princeton University Press, 1996.

Heeren, Fred, *Show Me God*, Dallas, Searchlight, 1995.

Heidegger, Martin, *An Introduction to Metaphysics*, 1953, translated Fried, Gregory and Polt, Richard, New Haven, Yale University Press, 2000.

Hitchens, Christopher, *God is Not Great: How Religion Poisons Everything*, Indianapolis, Hatchett, 2007.

Hitler, Adolph, *Mein Kampf*, London, Hurst and Blackett, 1942.

Hocutt, Max, "Toward an Ethic of Mutual Accommodation," *Humanistic Ethics*, edited Storer, Morris, Amherst, NY, Prometheus, 1980.

Horn, Miriam, "America's Old Master," *U. S. News and World Report*, March 31, 1997.

Hoyle, Fred, *The Intelligent Universe*, New York, Holt, Reinhart & Winston, 1983.

———, "The Universe: Past and Present Reflections," *Engineering and Science*, Nov. 1981, http://calteches.library.caltech.edu/3312/1/Hoyle.pdf

Hoyle, Fred and Wickramasinghe, Chandra, *Evolution from Space*, New York, Simon and Schuster, 1981.

Hume, David, *Dialogues Concerning Natural Religion*, 1779, edited Popkin, Richard, Indianapolis, Hackett, 1980.

———, "An Enquiry Concerning Human Understanding," 1777, edited Beauchamp, Tom, Oxford, Oxford University Press, 1999.

Huxley, Julian, *The Uniqueness of Man*, London, Chatto and Windus, 1941.

James, William, *Some Problems of Philosophy*, 1911, Westport, CT, Greenwood, 1968.

Jammer, Max, *Einstein and Religion*, Princeton, Princeton University Press, 1999.

Jastrow, Robert, "The Astronomer and God," *The Intellectuals Speak Out about God*, edited Varghese, Roy, Dallas, Lewis and Stanley, 1984.

———, *God and the Astronomers*, 1st edition, New York, Warner, 1980.

———, *God and the Astronomers*, 2d edition, New York, W. W. Norton, 1992.

———, "What Forces Filled the Universe with Energy Fifteen Billion Years Ago?" *Cosmos, Bios, Theos*, edited Marganou, Henry and Varghese, Roy, Chicago, Open Court, 1997.

Jeyachandran, L.T., "Tough Questions about Hinduism and Transcendental Meditation," *Who Made God?* edited Zacharias, Ravi and Geisler, Norman, Grand Rapids, Zondervan, 2003.

John Paul II, "Message to the Pontifical Academy of Sciences: Magisterium Is Concerned With the Question of Evolution for It Involves Conception of Man," October. 22, 1996, http://www.ewtn.com/library/papaldoc/jp961022.htm

———, *Pope John Paul II: His Essential Wisdom*, edited Kelly-Gangi, Carol, New York, Fall River, 2005.

Johnson, George, "Science and Religion: Bridging the Great Divide," *The New York Times*, June 30, 1998, http://www.nytimes.com/1998/06/30/science/essay-science-and-religion-bridging-the-great-divide.html?src=pm&pagewanted=2

Kant, Immanuel, *The Critique of Pure Reason*, 1787, translated Norman Kemp Smith, New York, Macmillan, 1958.

Kaufmann, Walter, *Critique of Religion and Philosophy*, New York, Harper and Row, 1972.

Keller, Timothy, *The Reason for God*, New York, Riverhead, 2008.

Kennedy, James, *Skeptics Answered*, Colorado Springs, Multnomah, 1997.

Kenny, Anthony, *The Five Ways: St. Thomas Aquinas' Proofs of God's Existence*, New York, Schocken, 1969.

———, *From Empedacles to Wittgenstein*, Oxford, Oxford University, 2008.

King, Martin Luther Jr., "Letter From a Birmingham Jail," 1963, http://www.africa.upenn.edu/Articles_Gen/Letter_Birmingham.html

Kinlaw, Dennis, *Let's Start with Jesus*, Grand Rapids, Zondervan, 2005.

———, *This Day with the Master*, Wilmore, KY, Frances Asbury, 2002.

———, *We Live as Christ*, Greenwood, IN, OMS International, 2001.

Kreeft, Peter, *Back to Virtue*, San Francisco, Ignatius, 1986.

———, *Because God Is Real*, San Francisco, Ignatius, 2008.

———, *Before I Go*, New York, Sheed and Ward, 2007.

———, *Between Heaven and Hell*, Downers Grove, IL, InterVarsity, 1982.

———, *Catholic Christianity*, San Francisco, Ignatius, 2001.

———, "The Choice of a Lifetime," Moreland, J. P. and Nielson, Kai, *Does God Exist?* Amherst, NY, Prometheus, 1993.

———, *Christianity for Modern Pagans*, San Francisco, Ignatius, 1993.

———, *Ecumenical Jihad*, San Francisco, Ignatius, 1996.

———, *Everything You Always Wanted to Know about Heaven*, San Francisco, Ignatius, 1990.

———, *Fundamentals of the Faith: Essays in Christian Apologetics*, San Francisco, Ignatius, 1988.

———, *Heaven: The Heart's Deepest Longing*, San Francisco, Ignatius, 1989.

———, *How to Win the Culture War*, Downers Grove, IL, InterVarsity, 2002.

———, *Jesus Shock*, South Bend, St. Augustine's, 2008.

———, *Love Is Stronger than Death*, San Francisco, Ignatius, 1992.

———, *Making Sense Out of Suffering*, Cincinnati, St. Anthony Messenger, 1986.

———, *Philosophy 101 by Socrates*, San Francisco, Ignatius, 2002.

———, *The Philosophy of Jesus*, South Bend, St. Augustine's, 2007.

———, *The Philosophy of Tolkien*, San Francisco, Ignatius, 2005.

———, *A Refutation of Moral Relativism*, San Francisco, Ignatius, 1999.

———, *Socrates Meets Descartes*, San Francisco, Ignatius, 2007.

———, *Socrates Meets Kant*, San Francisco, Ignatius, 2009.
———, *Three Philosophies of Life*, San Francisco, Ignatius, 1989.
———, *You Can Understand the Bible*, San Francisco, Ignatius Press, 2005.
Kreeft, Peter and Tacelli, Ronald, *Handbook of Christian Apologetics*, Downers Grove, IL, InterVarsity, 2004.
Kurtz, Paul, "Humanist Manifesto II," *Humanist Manifesto I and II*, Amherst, NY, Prometheus, 1984.
Kushner, Harold, *When Bad Things Happen to Good People*, New York, Avon, 1981.
Leibniz, Gottfried, *Leibniz Selections*, edited Wiener, Phillip, New York, Charles Scribner's Sons, 1951.
Lennox, John, "Challenges from Science," *Beyond Opinion*, edited Zacharias, Ravi, Nashville, Thomas Nelson, 2007.
———, *God's Undertaker: Has Science Buried God?* Oxford, Lion Hudson, 2009.
Lewis, C.S., *The Abolition of Man*, 1947, New York, Macmillan, 1978.
———, "Christian Apologetics," *God in the Dock: Essays on Theology and Ethics*, edited Hooper, Walter, Grand Rapids, Eerdmans, 1970.
———, "De Futilitate," *Christian Reflections*, edited Walter Hooper, Grand Rapids, Eerdmans, 1978
———, *The Discarded Image*, Cambridge, Cambridge University Press, 1964.
———, "Dogma and the Universe," 1943, *God in the Dock: Essays on Theology and Ethics*, edited Hooper, Walter, Grand Rapids, Eerdmans, 1970.
———, "The Efficacy of Prayer," 1959, *The World's Last Night and other Essays*, Orlando, Harcourt, 1987.
———, "Five Sonnets," *C. S. Lewis, Poems*, edited Hooper, Walter, London, Geoffey Bles, 1964.
———, *The Four Loves*, 1960, Orlando, Harcourt, 1988.
———, "The Funeral of a Great Myth," *Christian Reflections*, edited Hooper, Walter, Grand Rapids, Eerdmans, 1978.
———, *The Great Divorce*, 1946, New York, HarperCollins, 2001.
———, *A Grief Observed*, 1961, New York, Harper Collins, 1996.
———, "Is Theology Poetry?" 1946, *The Weight of Glory and other Addresses*, edited by Walter Hooper, New York, Harper Collins, 1980
———, *The Last Battle*, 1956, New York, Macmillan, 1980.
———, "Learning in War-Time," 1949, *The Weight of Glory and other Addresses*, New York, Harper Collins, 1980.
———, *Letters to Malcolm: Chiefly on Prayer*, Orlando, Harcourt, Brace, Jovanovich, 1964.
———, "On Living in an Atomic Age," 1948, *Present Concerns*, edited Hooper, Walter, Orlando, Harcourt, 1986.
———, "Membership," 1945, *The Weight of Glory and other Addresses*, edited Hooper, Walter, New York, Harper Collins, 2001.
———, *Mere Christianity*, 1943, New York, Macmillan, 1984.
———, *Miracles*, 1947, New York, Harper Collins, 2001.
———, *Out of the Silent Planet*, New York, Macmillan, 1965.
———, *Prince Caspian*, 1951, New York, Macmillan, 1980.
———, *The Problem of Pain*, 1940, New York, Harper Collins, 1996.
———, "Religion Without Dogma?" 1946, *God in the Dock: Essays on Theology and Ethics*, edited Hooper, Walter, Grand Rapids, Eerdmans, 1970.

———, *The Silver Chair*, 1953, New York, Macmillan, 1980.
———, *Surprised by Joy*, 1955, Orlando, Harcourt, 1988.
———, "Transposition," 1949, *The Weight of Glory and other Addresses*, New York, Harper Collins, 2001.
———, *The Voyage of the Dawn Treader*, 1952, New York, Macmillan, 1980.
———, "The Weight of Glory," 1942, *The Weight of Glory and other Addresses*, New York, Harper Collins, 2001.
———, "The World's Last Night," 1952, *The World's Last Night and other Essays*, Orlando, Harcourt, 1987.
Lewontin, Richard, "Billions and Billions of Demons," New York Review of Books, January 9, 1997, http://www.drjbloom.com/Public%20files/Lewontin_Review.htm
Little, Paul, *Know Why You Believe*, Wheaton, IL, Victor, 1973.
Locke, John, *Essays Concerning Human Understanding*, 1690, edited Pringle-Pattison, A.S., Oxford, Oxford University Press, 1964.
Longfellow, Henry Wadsworth, "A Psalm of Life," 1863, *Favorite Poems of Henry Wadsworth Longfellow*, Garden City, NY, International Collectors Library, 1947.
Lopatin, Peter, "Indestructible Dream," *The Weekly Standard*, December 3, 2012.
MacDonald, George, *Unspoken Sermons: Series I, II, and III*, Radford, VA, Wilder, 2008.
Macklin, Ruth, "Dignity is a Useless Concept," *British Medical Journal*, December 20, 2003, http://www.ncbi.nlm.nih.gov/pmc/articles/PMC300789/
Madison, James, *The Federalist Papers*, New York, New American Library of World Literature, 1961.
Maimonides, Moses, *Guide for the Perplexed*, 1190, translated Friedlander, M., New York, Pardes, 1904.
Margenau Henry, "The Laws of Nature are Created by God," *Cosmos, Bios, Theos*, edited Margenau, Henry and Varghese, Roy, Chicago, Open Court, 1992.
Marx, Karl, *Critique of Hegal's Philosophy of Right*, translated Jolin, Annette and O'Malley, Joseph, Cambridge, Cambridge University Press, 1970.
Masci, David, "Scientists and Belief," http://www.pewforum.org/2009/11/05/scientists-and-belief/
Mayr, Ernst, *What Evolution Is*, New York, Basic Books, 2001.
McDowell, Josh and McDowell, Sean, *The Unshakable Truth*, Eugene, OR, Harvest House, 2010.
McGrath, Alister, *Mere Apologetics*, Grand Rapids, Baker, 2012.
———, *The Twilight of Atheism*, Colorado Springs, Waterbrook, 2004.
Meyer, Stephen, *Darwin's Doubt*, New York, Harper One, 2013.
———, *Signature in the Cell*, New York, Harper One, 2009.
Michelangelo Gallery, "The Last Judgment," http://www.michelangelo-gallery.com/the-last-judgment.aspx
Mills, David, "To See through a Glass Darkly: C.S. Lewis, George Orwell and the Corruption of Language," *The Pilgrim's Guide*, edited Mills, David, Grand Rapids, Eerdmans, 1998.
Milton, John, *Paradise Lost*, 1667, New York, W.W. Norton, 2005.
Mitchell, C. Ben, *Ethics and Moral Reasoning: A Student's Guide*, Wheaton, IL, Crossway, 2013.
Monod, Jacques, *Chance and Necessity*, translated Weinhouse, Austryn, New York, Alfred A. Knopf, 1971.

Montgomery, John Warwick, "Why Human Rights Are Impossible without Religion," *A Place for Truth*, edited Willard, Dallas, Downers Grove, IL, InterVarsity, 2010.

Montville, Leigh, *Ted Williams: The Biography of an American Hero*, New York, Doubleday, 2004.

Moreland, J.P., *The God Question*, Eugene, OR, Harvest House, 2009.

———, *Scaling the Secular City*, Grand Rapids, Baker, 1987.

Morris, Henry M., "Evolution Ex Nihilo," *Acts and Facts*, September, 2011.

Mortenson, Terry, and Ury, Thane, *Coming to Grips with Genesis*, Green Forrest, AZ, Master Books, 2012.

Moshier, Stephen, "What is God's Purpose for Natural Disasters?" *Not Just Science*, edited Chappell, Dorothy and Cook, E. David, Grand Rapids, Zondervan, 2005.

Mott, Nevill, "Science Will Never Give Us the Answers to All Our Questions," *Cosmos, Bios, Theos*, edited Marganou, Henry and Varghese, Roy, Chicago, Open Court, 1997.

Muggeridge, Malcolm, *Confessions of a Twentieth Century Pilgrim*, New York, Harper and Row, 1988.

Murphree, Jon Tal, *A Loving God and a Suffering World*, Downers Grove, IL, InterVarsity, 1981.

Myerson, Adam, "The Generosity of America," *Imprimis*, January, 2010.

Nagle, Thomas, *The Last Word*, Oxford, Oxford University Press, 1997.

———, *Mind and Cosmos*, Oxford, Oxford University Press, 2012.

National Academy of Sciences, *Science, Evolution and Creationism*, Washington, DC, National Academies, 2008.

Needleman, Joseph, *The New Religions*, New York, Doubleday, 1970.

Neuhaus, Richard John, *Doing Well and Doing Good*, New York, Doubleday, 1992.

Newton, Isaac, "General Scholium," 1687, *Principia: Mathematical Principles of Natural Philosophy*, translated Motte, Andrew, Berkeley, University of California Press, 1947.

Nielson, Kai, "Why Should I Be Moral?" *American Philosophical Quarterly*, Vol. 21, 1984.

Nietzsche, Friedrich, *The Will to Power*, 1885, translated Kaufmann, Walter and Hollingdale, R. J., New York, Random House, 1967.

Noebel, David, *Understanding the Times*, Manitou Springs, CO, Summit, 2006.

Novak, David, "The Mind of Maimonides," *The Second One Thousand Years*, edited Neuhaus, Richard John, Grand Rapids, Eerdmans, 2001.

Oakes, Edward, "Pascal: The First Modern Christian," *The Second One Thousand Years*, edited Neuhaus, Richard John, Grand Rapids, Eerdmans, 2001.

Oakes, J. Stanley, Jr., "The Last Hope for the University," *The Intellectuals Speak Out about God*, edited Varghese, Roy, Dallas, Lewis and Stanley, 1984.

Obama, Barack, "Remarks by the President at the Acceptance of the Nobel Peace Prize," December 10, 2009, http://www.whitehouse.gov/the-press-office/remarks-president-acceptance-nobel-peace-prize

———, "Remarks by the President to the Nation on the BP Oil Spill," June 15, 2010, https://www.whitehouse.gov/briefing-room/legislation

Oden, Thomas, *Classic Christianity*, New York, Harper Collins, 1992.

———, *The Living God*, New York, Harper Collins, 1987.

Ordway, Holly, *Not God's Type*, San Francisco, Ignatius, 2010.

Origen, "Contra Celsum," *The Patristic Understanding of Creation*, edited Dembski, William, Downs Wayne, and Frederick, Fr. Justin, South Bend, Erasmus, 2008.
Orwell, George, *Animal Farm*, 1946, New York, Signet, 1962.
Ovid, *Metamorpheses*, 8 AD, translated Melville, A.D., Oxford, Oxford University Press, 1986.
Paley, William, *Natural Theology*, 1809, Sunnyvale, CA, Loki's, 2014.
Pascal, Blaise, *Pensees*, 1670, translated Trotter, William, New York, E. F. Dutton, 1958.
Payne, Albert, *Mark Twain, A Biography*, New York, Harper and Brothers, 1912.
Pearcey, Nancy and Claxton, Charles, *The Soul of Science*, Westchester, IL, Crossway, 1994.
Penfield, Wilder, *The Mystery of the Mind*, Princeton, Princeton University Press, 1975.
Penzias, Arno, "Creation Is Supported by All the Data So Far," *Cosmos, Bios, Theos*, edited Marganou, Henry and Varghese, Roy, Chicago, Open Court, 1997.
Pine, Joslyn, *Wit and Wisdom of the American Presidents*, New York, Dover, 2001.
Pinker, Stephen, *How the Mind Works*, New York, W.W. Norton, 1997.
———, "The Stupidity of Dignity," *The New Republic*, May 27, 2008, https://newrepublic.com/article/64674/the-stupidity-dignity
Plantinga, Alvin, *Where the Conflict Really Lies*, Oxford, Oxford University Press, 2011.
Plato, "The Apology of Socrates," c399 BC, translated Jowett, Benjamin, *The Dialogues of Plato*, New York, Bantom, 1986.
———, "Laws," c360 BC, translated Bury, R.G., *Plato XI: The Laws II*, Cambridge, MA, Harvard University Press, 1984.
———, "Philebus," c347 BC, *The Collected Dialogues of Plato*, edited Hamilton, Edith and Cairns, Huntington, New York, Pantheon, 1961.
———, *The Republic*, c380 BC, translated Reeve, C.D.C., Indianapolis, Hackett, 2004.
Platt, David, *Counter Culture*, Carol Stream, IL, Tyndale House, 2015.
Poe, Harry Lee, *The Inklings of Oxford*, Grand Rapids, Zondervan, 2009.
———, *See No Evil*, Grand Rapids, Kregel, 2004.
Polkinghorne, John, *One World*, Princeton, Princeton University Press, 1986.
———, *Serious Talk: Science and Religion in Dialogue*, London, Trinity International, 1995.
Popper, K.R., "Scientific Reduction and the Essential Incompleteness of all Science," *Studies in the Philosophy of Biology*, edited Ayala, Francisco and Dobzhansky, Theodosius, Berkeley, University of California Press, 1974.
Prothero, Stephen, "A Buddhist Moment in America," *U. S. Today*, February 22, 2010.
Raup, David, "Conflicts between Darwin and Paleontology," *Field Museum of Natural History Bulletin*, Vol. 50, January 1979, https://archive.org/details/cbarchive_121465_conflictsbetweendarwinandpaleo1930
Rees, Martin, *Just Six Numbers: The Deep Forces that Shape the Universe*, New York, Basic Books, 2000.
Reynolds, John Mark, *When Athens Met Jerusalem*, Downers Grove, IL, InterVarsity, 2009.
Rhodes, Ronald, "Tough Questions about Evil," *Who Made God?* edited Zacharias, Ravi and Geisler, Norman, Grand Rapids, Zondervan, 2003.
Richter, Sandra, *The Epic of Eden*, Downers Grove, IL, InterVarsity, 2008.
Robertson, James D., *Handbook of Preaching Resources from Literature*, Grand Rapids, Baker, 1972.
Ross, Hugh, *The Creator and the Cosmos*, Colorado Springs, NavPress, 1993.

———, *A Matter of Days*, Colorado Springs, NavPress, 2004.

Rousseau, Jean-Jacques, *The Social Contract*, 1762, *The Social Contract and Discourses*, translated Cole, G.D.H., London, E.F. Dutton, 1950.

Royal, Robert, "Columbus and the Beginning of the World," *The Second One Thousand Years*, edited Neuhaus, Richard John, Grand Rapids, Eerdmans, 2001.

Ruse, Michael, "Is Rape Wrong on Andromeda?" *Extraterrestrials: Science and Alien Intelligence*, edited Regis, Edward, Jr., Oxford, Oxford University Press, 1985.

Ruse, Michael and Wilson, E.O., "The Evolution of Ethics," *Religion and the Natural Sciences: The Range of Engagement*, edited Hutchingson, James, New York, Holt, Rinehart & Winston, 1993.

Russell, Bertrand, *Why I Am Not a Christian*, New York, Simon and Schuster, 1957.

Russell Bertrand, and Copleston, Frederick, "A Debate on the Existence of God," *The Existence of God*, edited Hick, John, New York, Macmillan, 1964.

Ryle, Gilbert, *The Concept of Mind*, 1949, Chicago, University of Chicago Press, 2000.

Sagan, Carl, *Cosmos*, New York, Random House, 1980.

Salaman, Esther, "A Talk with Albert Einstein," *The Listener*, Vol. 54, 1955.

Sanders, N. K. "The Epic of Gilgamesh," http://www.aina.org/books/eog/eog.pdf.

Sartre, Jean-Paul, *Being and Nothingness*, translated Brown, Hazel, New York, Philosophical Library, 1956.

———, "The Humanism of Existentialism," *Essays in Existentialism*, New York, Citadel, 1965.

———, "No Exit," *No Exit and Three Other Plays*, New York, Vintage, 1946.

Sayers, Dorothy L., *Creed or Chaos*, 1949, Bedford, NH, Sofia Institute, 1974.

Schaeffer, Francis, *Back to Freedom and Dignity*, 1972, *The Complete Works of Francis A. Schaeffer*, Vol. 1, Westchester, IL, Crossway, 1982.

———, *Death in the City*, 1969, *The Complete Works of Francis A. Schaeffer*, Vol. 4, Westchester, IL, Crossway, 1982.

———, *Escape from Reason*, 1968, *The Complete Works of Francis A. Schaeffer*, Vol.1, Westchester, IL, Crossway, 1982.

———, *The God Who Is There*, 1968, *The Complete Works of Francis A. Schaeffer*, Vol.1, Westchester, IL, Crossway, 1982.

———, *He Is There and He Is Not Silent*, 1972, *The Complete Works of Francis A. Schaeffer*, Vol. 1, Westchester, IL, Crossway, 1982.

———, *How Should We then Live?* 1976, *The Complete Works of Francis A. Schaeffer*, Vol 5, Westchester, IL, Crossway, 1982.

———, *Letters of Francis A. Schaeffer*, edited Dennis, Lane, Westchester, IL, Crossway, 1985.

Schmidt, Alvin, *How Christianity Changed the World*, Grand Rapids, Zondervan, 2004.

Scientific American, "Profile: Francis Crick—The Mephistopheles of Neurobiology," February, 1992, Vol. 266, No. 2.

Scotus, John Duns, *Philosophical Writings*, translated Wolter, Allan, Indianapolis, Hackett, 1987.

Seligman, Martin, *Authentic Happiness*, New York, Free Press, 2002.

Shakespeare, William, "Henry the Sixth," 1594, *The Second Part of King Henry the Sixth*, edited Brooks, Tucker, New Haven, Yale University Press, 1923.

———, "Macbeth," 1611, *William Shakespeare's Macbeth: A Source Book*, edited Leggatt, Alexander, New York, Routledge, 2006.

———, "The Merchant of Venice," 1605, *The Merchant of Venice: Text and Context*, edited M. Lindsey Kaplan, New York, Ballard / St. Martins, 2002.

———, *The Tragedy of Hamlet, Prince of Denmark*, 1603, edited Brooke, Tucker and Crawford, Jack Randall, New Haven, Yale University Press, 1947.

Sharansky, Natan, *The Case for Democracy*, New York, Public Affairs, 2004, 2006.

Sharot, Tali, "The Science of Optimism," *Time*, June 4, 2011.

Short, Edward, "Saint From Hippo," *The Weekly Standard*, May 3, 2010.

Simmons, Geoffrey, *What Darwin Didn't Know*, Eugene, OR, Harvest House, 2004.

Singer, Peter, *Animal Liberation*, 1975, New York, Harper Collins, 2002.

———, *Practical Ethics*, Cambridge, Cambridge University Press, 1979.

Skinner, B. F., *Beyond Freedom and Dignity*, 1971, Indianapolis, Hackett, 2002.

Sleeper, Raymond, *A Lexicon of Marxist-Leninist Semantics*, Washington, D.C., Western Goals, 1983.

Smith, Huston, *The Religions of Man*, New York, Harper and Row, 1958.

Solzhenitsyn, Aleksandr, *The Gulag Archipelago*, New York, Harper and Row, 1973.

Spidle, Simeon, "The Belief in Immortality," *Journal of Religious Psychology*, edited Hall, G. Stanley and Chamberlain, Alexander, Worcester, MA, Louis N. Wilson, 1912.

Spufford, Francis, *Unapologetic: Why, Despite Everything, Christianity Can Still Make Surprising Emotional Sense*, New York, Harper Collins, 2012.

Stenger, Victor, "The Face of Chaos," *Free Enquiry*, Vol. 13, Winter 1992–1993, http://www.colorado.edu/philosophy/vstenger/Cosmo/face.txt

———, *God, the Failed Hypothesis*, Amherst, NY, Prometheus, 2007.

Stott, John R. W., *The Cross of Christ*, Downers Grove, IL, InterVarsity, 1986.

Strobel, Lee, *The Case for a Creator*, Grand Rapids, Zondervan, 2004.

———, *The Case for Faith*, Grand Rapids, Zondervan, 2000.

Tattersall, Ian, "How We Came to be Human," *Scientific American*, Dec. 2001, Vol. 285, No. 6.

Taylor, Richard, *Ethics, Faith and Reason*, Upper Saddle River, NJ, Prentiss-Hall, 1985.

The Telegraph, "Darwin Proved Right on Origin of Life on Earth," *The Telegraph*; http://www.telegraph.co.uk/earth/earthnews/9079603/Darwin-proved-right-on-origin-of-life-on-Earth.html

Templeton, John, *The Humble Approach: Scientists Discover God*, New York, Continuum, 1995.

Ten Boom, Corrie, *The Hiding Place*, 1974, Old Tappan, NJ, Chosen, 2006.

Tennyson, Alfred Lord, "In Memoriam," 1850, *In Memoriam, Maud and Other Poems*, London, J. M. Dent, 1974.

Tertulian, *Apology*, 197 AD, translated Glover, T.A., New York, G.P. Putnam's Sons, 1931.

Thomsen, Dietrick, "The Quantum Universe: A Zero Point Fluctuation?" *Science News*, Vol. 128, August 3, 1985, http://www.thefreelibrary.com/The+quantum+universe%3A+a+zero-point+fluctuation%3F-a03884546

Time, "The Hero of the Code," *Time*, July 14, 1961, http://content.time.com/time/magazine/article/0,9171,27780-1,00.html

Tolkien, J. R. R., *The Letters of J. R. R. Tolkien*, edited Carpenter, Humphrey, Boston, Houghton Mifflin, 2000.

———, *The Return of the King*, 1955, *The Lord of the Rings*, Boston, Houghton Mifflin, 2004.

Tolstoy, Leo, "Three Methods of Reform," *Pamphlets*, London, Free Age, 1900.

Townes, Charles, *Making Waves*, Woodbury, NY, American Institute of Physics, 1995.
Trueblood, Elton, *Philosophy of Religion*, New York, Harper and Row, 1957.
Turek, Frank, "The Cosmological Argument," *The Apologetics Study Bible for Students*, edited McDowell, Sean, Nashville, Holman Bible, 2009.
Twain, Mark, *The Adventures of Tom Sawyer*, 1876, New York, Barnes and Noble, 2001.
Vanauken, Sheldon, *A Severe Mercy*, New York, Harper Collins, 1977, 1980.
———, "God's Will," *The Intellectuals Speak Out about God*, edited Varghese, Roy, Dallas, Lewis and Stanley, 1984
Varghese, Roy Abraham, *The Wonder of the World*, Fountain Hills, AZ, Tyr, 2003.
Von Braun, Wernher, "My Faith, A Space-age Scientist Tells Why He Must Believe in God," *American Weekly*, February 10, 1963, http://crev.info/?scientists=wernher-von-braun
de Waal, Frans, *Good Natured: The Origins of Right and Wrong in Humans and other Animals*, Cambridge, MA, Harvard University Press, 1996.
Wald, George, "Life and Mind in the Universe," *Cosmos, Bios, Theos*, edited Margenau, Henry and Vargese, Roy, Chicago, Open Court, 1992.
———, "The Origin of Life," *Scientific American*, Vol. 191, No. 2, August, 1954.
Watson, James and Crick, Francis, "Genetic Implications of the Structure of Deoxyribonucleic Acid," *Nature*, Vol.171, http://www.nature.com/nature/dna50/watsoncrick2.pdf
Weinberg, Steven, *Facing Up: Science and its Cultural Adversaries*, Cambridge, MA, Harvard University Press, 2001.
Wells, H.G., *A Mind at the End of its Tether*, New York, P. G. Didier, 1946.
———, *A Short History of the World*, New York, Macmillan, 1922.
White, Robert, "Tough Questions about Black Islam," *Who Made God?* Grand Rapids, Zondervan, 2003.
Whitehead, Alfred North, *The Function of Reason*, 1929, Boston, Beacon, 1958.
Whitesides, George, "Revolutions in Chemistry," *Chemical and Engineering News*, March 26, 2007, http://cen.acs.org/articles/85/i13/Revolutions-Chemistry.html
Wickramasinghe, Chandra, "Science and the Divine Origin of Life," *The Intellectuals Speak Out about God*, edited Varghese, Roy, Dallas, Lewis and Stanley, 1984.
Wilford, John Noble, "Sizing Up the Cosmos: An Astronomer's Quest," *New York Times*, March 12, 1991, http://www.nytimes.com/1991/03/12/science/sizing-up-the-cosmos-an-astronomer-s-quest.html?src=pm&pagewanted=3
Wilkin, Robert Louis, "Gregory VII and the Politics of Spirit," *The Second One Thousand Years*, edited Neuhaus, Richard John, Grand Rapids, Eerdmans, 2001.
Willard, Dallas, *A Place for Truth*, Downers Grove, IL, InterVarsity, 2010.
Wilson, Douglas, *Lincoln Before Washington: New Perspectives on the Illinois Years*, Champaign, University of Illinois Press, 1998.
Wilson, E. O., *Consilience: The Unity of Knowledge*, New York, Knopf, 1999.
———, "Intelligent Evolution," *Harvard Magazine*, November, 2005, http://harvardmagazine.com/2005/11/intelligent-evolution.html
Woods, W. David and O'Brien, Frank, "Apollo Flight Journal," http://history.nasa.gov/ap08fj/18day5_green.htm
Wright, N.T., *Simply Christian*, London, SPCK, 2011.
Zacharias, Ravi, *Can Man Live Without God?* Nashville, Thomas Nelson, 1994.
———, "The Church's Role in Apologetics and the Development of the Mind," *Beyond Opinion*, edited Zacharias, Ravi, Nashville, Thomas Nelson, 2007.

———, *The End of Reason*, Grand Rapids, Zondervan, 2008.
———, "Existential Challenges of Evil and Suffering," *Beyond Opinion*, edited Zacharias, Ravi, Nashville, Thomas Nelson, 2007.
———, *Jesus Among Other Gods*, Nashville, Thomas Nelson, 2000.
———, *The Lotus and the Cross*, Colorado Springs, Multnomah, 2001.
Zacharias, Ravi and Vitale, Vince, *Why Suffering?* New York, Hatchette, 2014.
Zeigler, Leslie, "Christianity or Feminism," *Unapologetic Apologetics*, edited Dembski, William and Richards, J.W., Downers Grove, IL, InterVarsity, 2001.

Name and Subject Index

The Abolition of Man, 44, 190
Aborigines, 44
Abraham, 12
Adam, 23, 38, 42, 64, 67, 85, 86, 94, 148
Aesop, 64
"After-birth Abortion: Why Should the Baby Live?" 191
Agka, Mehmet Ali, 183
Alexander III, 183
Allen, Woody, 84, 163
"All You Need is Love," 98
"Amazing Grace," 185
Amino acids, 120–22, 125, 130, 153, 209
Anders, William, 145
Animal Farm, 59–60
Anthropic principle, 151–56
Apollo 8, 145
Aquinas, Thomas, 33, 42, 76, 101, 105
Aristotle, 4, 9, 24, 30, 72, 105, 193–94
Asimov, Isaac, 138
Augustine, 33, 76, 101, 113–14, 146, 163, 165, 169, 178
Avicenna, 31

Babylonians, 44, 84
Bach, Richard, 162
Bacon, Francis, 149
Bada, Jeffrey, 120–21, 126, 209
Barash, David, 38
Barna, George, 158
Barrow, John, 108
Barton, Ralph, 80

Basil the Great, 166, 184
Baudelaire, Charles, 170
The Beatles, 98
Becket, Samuel, 87
van Beethoven, Ludwig, 73, 97, 100–101, 144, 186
Behe, Michael, 213
Belloc, Hilaire, 183
Bernstein, Leonard, 100
Berra, Yogi, 35
Beyond Freedom and Dignity, 96
Big bang theory, 106–11, 112, 116, 124, 125, 152, 154, 206, 208
Biochemical Predestination, 125
Blake, William, 57
The Blind Watchmaker, 122, 133, 134, 136–37, 147
Bloy, Leon, 193
von Braun, Wernher, 150
Brierly, Justin, 48
Brooks, Rodney, 99
The Brothers Karamazov, 51
"Bruce Almighty," 167
Bryan, William Jennings, 189
Bryson, Bill, 109
Buck, Carrie, 189
Buck v. Bell, 189–90
Buddha, Gautama, 18, 75, 159, 160
Buddhism (Buddhist), 11, 80, 87, 160

Cage, John, 32
Cain and Abel, 65
Carrey, Jim, 167

237

Chance and Necessity, 115–16, 124, 136
Chesterton, G. K., 6, 17, 27, 35, 36, 53, 57, 65, 102, 103, 109, 115, 127, 129, 130, 179, 182, 198
Chomsky, Noam, 27, 139, 140
A Christmas Carol, 49
Cicero, 130
"City Slickers," 91
Civil rights movement, 53, 185
"Cocoon," 85
Collins, Francis, 4, 25, 34, 38, 40, 51, 110, 126, 135, 152, 166, 183, 207
Colson, Charles, 6, 11, 29, 165, 181
Confucius (Confucians), 44, 58, 62
"Contact," 143
Copernicus, Nicolaus, 33, 148
Courtois, Stephane, 186
Covey, Stephen, 200
Craig, William Lane, 54, 94, 95, 96, 111
"The Creation of Adam," 94, 148
Crick, Francis, 20, 115, 119, 122, 127, 151
Crystal, Billy, 91

The Dalai Lama. 87
Dangerfield, Rodney, 200
Dante Alighieri, 186
Darrow, Clarence, 41, 92
Darwin, Charles, 22, 26, 46, 47, 94, 98, 106, 116, 117, 118, 122, 130, 131, 133, 136, 139, 149, 158, 188, 208, 210, 211, 212, 214
Darwinism (Darwinist, Darwinian), 21, 102–3, 116–18, 131–32, 133, 134, 135–36, 139, 150, 155, 188–90, 198, 199, 207
David, King of Israel, 146
Davidman, Joy, 51, 62, 73–74, 99, 175
Davies, Paul, 108, 112, 145, 155, 206
Dawkins, Richard, 19, 48, 49, 87, 122, 123, 125, 133, 134, 136, 140, 147, 151, 186, 214
Declaration of Independence, 8, 97
Dembski, William, 171
Denton, Michael, 94, 117–18, 137, 153, 154, 156
Descartes, Rene, 25

The Descent of Man, 46, 139, 188–89
Determinism, 38–41, 44
Dewey, John, 60
Dickens, Charles, 39, 49
"Dignity is a Useless Concept," 96–97
Dinur, Yehiel, 61
Disney, Walt, 85
The Divine Comedy, 186
DNA, 7, 37, 41, 98, 117, 118, 119–23, 125, 126, 130, 131, 135, 137, 138, 142, 144, 153, 209–10
Dobzhansky, Theodosius, 103, 207
Donne, John, 18
Dostoevsky, Fyodor, 51
Doyle, Arthur Conan, 24–25
Dred Scott case, 53
Dyson, Freeman, 151

Eccles, John, 20, 208
Eddington, Arthur, 107, 110
Egypt (Egyptian), 23, 44, 85, 86, 173, 178
The Egyptian Book of the Dead, 85
Eichmann, Adolf, 61
Einstein, Albert, 24, 31, 100, 106, 107, 108, 114, 143, 145, 148, 149–50, 158, 182, 205, 215
Elliott, Jim, 196
Engels, Frederick, 87
Ephram the Syrian, 146
The Epic of Gilgamesh, 84
Eve, 23, 64, 67
Ezekiel, 193

The fall, 63–70, 77, 86, 87, 90, 149, 160, 165, 170–72, 175, 178, 187, 195, 196, 200, 201, 202
Faraday, Michael, 148
Fay, Michael, 96
The Federalist Papers, 64
"The Fiddler on the Roof," 15
Field Museum of Natural History, 85
Finney, Charles, 185
"Five Sonnets," 163
Foster, Jodie, 143
The Four Noble Truths, 80, 159
Francis of Assisi, 100
Franklin, Benjamin, 49, 73

Freeman, Morgan, 167
Freud, Sigmund, 73, 84, 85, 86, 202
Fuentes, Carlos, 183

Galileo Galilei, 33, 148
Gates, Bill, 137
Geisler, Norman, 29, 52, 113, 125, 142, 171
al-Ghazali, Abu Hamid, 105, 197
Ghandi, Mahatma, 45, 53, 182
Gingerich, Owen, 3, 4, 138, 151, 207
Giubilina, Alberto, 191
God of the gaps, 22, 42, 208, 214
"Goldilocks and the Three Bears," 151
Gould, Stephen Jay, 129, 131, 150, 207, 211, 212
"The Gray Monk," 57
Greeks, ancient, 44, 64, 66, 113, 185, 193
Gregory of Nazianzus, 147, 171
A Grief Observed, 169, 175–76, 204
Guth, Alan, 109

Haeckel, Ernst, 118
Haldane, J. B. S., 120
"Hamlet," 3, 13, 37, 142
Handel, George Frideric, 186
"Hannah and Her Sisters," 163
Harold, Franklin, 116–17
Harris, Sam, 19–20
Hawking, Stephen, 37, 48, 69, 103, 107, 110, 111, 145
Heidegger, Martin, 92, 104
Heisenberg, Werner, 148
Hemingway, Ernest, 92
Herod, King of Judah, 181
Heschel, Abraham, 198
Higgins, Jack, 74
Hindu (Hinduism), 11, 18, 44, 45, 159, 180
Hitchens, Christopher, 186
Hitler, Adolph, 40, 41, 61, 66, 84, 160, 186, 187–88
Hocutt, Max, 50
Holmes, Oliver Wendell, 189–90
Holmes, Sherlock, 24–25
Holocaust, 41, 54, 58, 61, 187–88
Homo sapiens, 7, 158, 129, 138, 142

How the Mind Works, 19
Hoyle, Fred, 119, 121, 123, 155
Hubble, Edwin, 106
Human Genome Project, 4, 39, 137, 207
The Humanist Manifesto II, 87
Hume, David, 159, 170
Huxley, Aldous, 73
Huxley, Julian, 129, 198

Ibsen, Henric, 92
"I Can't Get No Satisfaction," 72
I Don't Have Enough Faith to be an Atheist, 29, 30, 45, 52, 113, 125, 171
Ignatius of Antioch, 181
"I Heard the Bells on Christmas Day," 69
"Indiana Jones and the Last Crusade," 34
Islam (Muslim), 12, 182–83, 184
"Is That All There Is?" 72, 80
"I Still Haven't Found What I'm Looking For," 72

Jagger, Mick, 72, 75
James the Apostle, 2
James, William, 103
Jastrow, Robert, 102, 106, 107, 108, 112, 113, 155, 206
Jefferson, Thomas, 8–9, 30, 45, 52, 53, 55, 97, 203
Jesus, 2, 14, 30, 61, 81, 88, 161, 174, 176, 177, 178, 180, 181, 182, 183, 184, 194, 196, 201–2, 203
Job, 88, 158, 163, 168, 175
John the Apostle, 161
John Paul II, 72, 96, 132, 162, 183
Jones, Jim, 179–80
Jordan, Michael, 97
Joseph, 173, 178
Judaism (Jewish), 12, 60, 61, 62, 158, 177, 181, 188
Judeo-Christian, 68, 70, 98, 185, 186, 191, 196
Julian of Norwich, 173
Jung, Carl, 61

Kalam argument, 104–5, 109

Kant, Immanuel, 27, 55, 59
Kaufmann, Walter, 91
Keller, Timothy, 50, 51–52, 162, 167
Kenny, Anthony, 109, 140
Kenyon, Dean, 125
Kepler, Johannes, 148, 149
Khrushchev, Nikita, 44
Kierkegaard, Soren, 200
King, Martin Luther, Jr., 43, 44, 45, 53, 55, 182, 185
Kinlaw, Dennis, 6, 64, 77
de Kooning, Willem, 93
Kreeft, Peter, 6, 16, 17, 36, 40, 58–59, 66, 68–69, 79, 86, 91, 93, 95, 170, 177, 180, 198, 201
Kushner, Harold, 157, 162

The Last Battle, 76, 89–90
"The Last Judgment," 95
"The Last Supper," 186
The Last Word, 199
Law of non-contradiction, 31, 180, 181
Lazarus, 161
Lee, Peggy, 72, 80
Leibniz, Gottfried, 103
de Leon, Ponce, 85
Leopold, Nathan, 41
"Letter from a Birmingham Jail," 45
Letters to Malcolm, 89
Lewis, C. S., 2, 3, 6, 7, 13, 14, 17, 25, 28, 36, 42, 44, 47, 54–55, 59, 66–67, 67–68, 73, 75, 76–77, 81, 88, 89, 101, 138, 160, 163, 164, 167, 168, 169, 171, 172, 173, 175–76, 180, 190, 193, 203, 204
Lewis, Harry, 190–91
Lewontin, Richard, 133
Lincoln, Abraham, 52, 53, 55
Little, Paul, 5
Locke, John, 134
Loeb, Richard, 41
Longfellow, Henry Wadsworth, 69, 83
Lucas, George, 11
Luther, Martin, 14, 63, 168

"Macbeth," 92–93
MacDonald, George, 63, 77, 173
Macklin, Ruth, 96–97
Madison, James, 64
Maimonides, Moses, 105
Mao Zedong, 59, 186
Margenau, Henry, 146
Martin, Walter, 174
Marx, Karl, 59, 61, 87, 141
Maxwell, James Clerk, 148, 149
Mayr, Ernst, 48
McDowell, Josh, 104
McGrath, Alister, 5, 15, 177
Mein Kampf, 187
Menuhin, Yehudi, 100
"The Merchant of Venice," 62
"Messiah," 186
Michelangelo, 94, 95, 97, 100, 101, 144, 148, 173, 186
"A Mighty Fortress is Our God," 168
Miller, Stanley, 120
Milton, John, 63, 186
Minerva, Francesca, 191
"Miracle on 34th Street," 2
Mohammed, 183
Monch, Edvard, 93
Monod, Jacques, 115–16, 121, 123, 124, 125, 136, 209
Moral relativism, 50–54, 55, 217–18
Moreland, J. P., 54
Moses, 12, 23, 203
Mott, Nevill, 22
Mozart, Wolfgang Amadeus, 183
Muggeridge, Malcolm, 64
Multi-culturalism, 53
Mussolini, Benito, 188

Nagle, Thomas, 27, 117, 138, 199
National Academy of Sciences, 116
National Institutes of Health, 4
Native Americans, 44
Natural law, 45–46, 52, 54–55
Natural selection, 46, 47–48, 68, 86, 98, 100, 101, 102–3, 116, 131–32, 133, 134, 135, 136–37, 139, 140, 160, 209, 212–14, 216, 217
Nazis, 41, 45, 54, 60, 153, 163, 166, 177, 186, 187–88, 191

Newton, Isaac, 14, 29, 33, 144, 145, 148
Newton, John, 185
Nietzsche, Friedrich, 30, 97, 182, 184, 188
Nirvana, 13, 18, 87
Nuremberg trials, 45

Obama, Barack, 39, 61–62
"Ode to Joy," 186
O'Hara, Maureen, 2
O'Keefe, James, 155
Old Norse, 44
On the Origin of Species, 47–48, 105, 117, 122
Oparin, A. I., 120
Oracle of Delphi, 14
Orwell, George, 59
Out of the Silent Planet, 169
Ovid, 65

Page, Donald, 155, 215
Palance, Jack, 91
Paley, William, 147
Paradise Lost, 63, 186
Pascal, Blaise, 16, 42, 63, 64, 75–76, 79, 96, 197–98
Pascal's wager, 197–98
Pasteur, Louis, 118, 124, 128, 208
Paul the Apostle, 55, 65, 81, 146, 174, 182, 196, 201
Pearcey, Nancy, 11, 165, 181
Penfield, Wilder, 20
Penzias, Arno, 106, 111
Perry, Oliver Hazard, 57
Peter the Apostle, 201
Picasso, Pablo, 93
"The Pieta," 186
Pilate, Pontius, 30, 181
Pinker, Stephen, 19, 97, 100
Pinocchio, 115
Pius XII, 132
Planck, Max, 148, 152
Plantinga, Alvin, 4, 139
Plato, 88, 105, 202
Platt, David, 196
Poe, Harry Lee, 98, 170, 200
Pogo, 57
Polkinghorne, John, 152, 154, 216

Pollock, Jackson, 93
Ponce de Leon, 85
Popeye, 16, 23
Popper, Karl, 123
Prager, Dennis, 185
Prince Caspian, 67
The Problem of Pain, 36, 164, 167, 168, 171, 172, 173, 175
Prothero, Stephen, 80
"A Psalm of Life," 83

al-Rahman, Abd, 71
Ramakrishna, 159
Rees, Martin, 154
Relative truth, 29–30
Revelation, divine, 2–3, 174
Rhodes, Ronald, 160
Richter, Sandra, 85–86
Rockefeller, John D., 73
Romans, ancient, 44, 185
Roosevelt, Theodore, 60
Rousseau, Jean-Jacques, 51
Ruse, Michael, 46, 49
Russell, Bertrand, 86, 92, 109

de Sade, Marquis, 44, 51
Sagan, Carl, 11, 104
Sandage, Allan, 110, 141
Sartre, Jean Paul, 8, 34, 92
Sayers, Dorothy, 176–77
Schaeffer, Francis, 6, 19, 41, 42, 161, 181, 190, 191, 203
Scopes trial, 189
"The Scream," 93
Searle, John, 28
Second law of thermodynamics, 86, 112–13, 127, 145, 214
The Selfish Gene, 49, 123
Seligman, Martin, 200
SETI Institute, 143
The 7 Habits of Highly Effective People, 200
Sexual revolution, 53
Shakespeare, William, 3, 13, 37, 62, 73, 92–93, 142, 205
Shankara, 18, 32
Sharansky, Natan, 98
"The Sign of Four," 24

The Silver Chair, 173
Simmons, Geoffrey, 26
Singer, Peter, 191
Sistine Chapel, 94, 95, 186
Skilling, Jeffrey, 49, 51
Skinner, B. F., 37, 96
Smith, Gypsy, 182
Smoot, George, 107
Socrates, 9, 14, 15, 144
Solon, 157
Solzhenitsyn, Aleksandr, 67, 203
The soul, 13, 18, 20, 56, 66, 83, 88, 92, 97, 132, 167, 184, 194, 196, 197, 200–201
Spufford, Francis, 62
Stalin, Joseph, 186, 188
"Star Trek," 40
"Star Wars," 11–12, 159
Stenger, Victor, 109, 146
Stott, John R.W., 176
"The Stupidity of Dignity," 96
"Sweet Beulah Land," 77

Tacelli, Ronald, 17, 66
A Tale of Two Cities, 39
Tao, 58
Tattersall, Ian, 129, 140
Taylor, Richard, 47
Templeton, John, 21
Ten Boom, Corrie, 177
Tennyson, Alfred Lord, 47
Teresa, Mother, 45, 66, 84, 201
"The Third Man," 172–73
Tipler, Frank, 108
Titian, 93, 100
Tolkien, J. R. R., 65, 174–75
Tolstoy, Leo, 62
Tom Sawyer, 43, 84
Townes, Charles, 150–51, 207
Toynbee, Arnold, 104
Truman, Harry, 36
Turek, Frank, 29, 52, 108, 113, 125, 171
Twain, Mark, 21, 43, 57, 64

U2, 72
Urban II, 182
Urey, Harold, 120

Vanauken, Sheldon, 166, 199
Varghese, Roy Abraham, 18, 31, 33, 38, 145, 148
Ventura, Jesse, 87
"The Venus de Milo," 66
da Vinci, Leonardo, 173, 186
Voltaire, Francois-Marie, 144, 197
The Voyage of the Dawn Treader, 73

de Waal, Frans, 46
Wald, George, 13, 118–19, 128, 137–38, 210
Wallace, Mike, 61
Washington, George, 3
Watson, James, 119, 122
"The Weight of Glory," 66–67, 77, 81
Weinberg, Steven, 145, 186
Welles, Orson, 172–73
Wells, H. G., 58
Wetherill, George, 153
When Bad Things Happen to Good People, 157, 162
Whitehead, Alfred North, 21
Whitesides, George, 119
Wickramasinghe, Chandra, 121, 123–24, 127
Wilberforce, William, 185
Will, George, 44
Williams, Ted, 85
Wilson, E. O., 37, 46, 116
Wilson, Robert, 106
Woods, Tiger, 80
World War I, 58
World War II, 45, 54, 58, 88, 177, 187–88, 189
Wright, N. T., 44, 78

Yew, Lee Kwan, 96

Zacharias, Ravi, 6, 32, 93, 99, 184
Zeigler, Leslie, 198

Scripture Index

Genesis

1:1	114, 132, 138
1:27	95
1:31	67
2:7	13
6:5	61
50:20	178

Exodus

3:11–12, 13	23
20:13, 15, 16	50–51
34:6	203

Job

1:12	168
2:6	168
3:11, 13, 25–26	158
14:1–2	157
38:4	163

Psalms

8:4–5	8, 66
11:2	149
19:1	146

Isaiah

64:4	88, 89

Jeremiah

6:13	61

Ecclesiastes

1:14	93
3:11	88
8:15	93

Ezekiel

33:10	193
33:11	203

Matthew

5:4	176
5:48	79, 201
11:19	14
11:28	176
15:19	61
16:24	81
16:25	203

John

10:10	81
13:35	182
14:1–3	88, 174
15:11	81
16:22	81
17:21	182
18:38	30

Romans

1:20	146
2:15	54
7:15, 18	65
8:18	174
8:28	177

I Corinthians

2:9	88
11:1	201
12:12–27	182

Philippians

2:2	81
2:5	196
4:4	81
4:11	81

Hebrews

2:6–7	8
12:10–11	172
12:14	203

I Peter

2:21	201
3:15	1

Revelation

21:4	174

www.ingramcontent.com/pod-product-compliance
Lightning Source LLC
Chambersburg PA
CBHW062014220426
43662CB00010B/1331